The Agony of the Republic

Destruction des arbres de la liberté.

The destruction of the liberty trees, Boulevard des Italiens. Paris circa 1850.
(H. Roger-Viollet, Paris)

The Agony of the Republic

The Repression of the Left in Revolutionary France
1848–1851

John M. Merriman

New Haven and London   Yale University Press   1978

Published with assistance from
the Louis Stern Memorial Fund

Designed by John O.C. McCrillis
and set in Times Roman type by
Asco Trade Typesetting Ltd., Hong Kong.
Printed in the United States of America by
The Murray Printing Co., Westford, Massachusetts.

Published in Great Britain, Europe, Africa, and
Asia (except Japan) by Yale University Press,
Ltd., London. Distributed in Latin America by
Kaiman & Polon, Inc., New York City; in
Australia and New Zealand by Book & Film
Services, Artarmon, N.S.W., Australia; and in
Japan by Harper & Row, Publishers, Tokyo Office.

Library of Congress Cataloging in Publication Data

Merriman, John M
    The agony of the Republic.

    Bibliography: p.
    Includes index.
    1. France—Politics and government—1848–
1852. 2. Radicalism—France—History.
I. Title.
DC272.5.M42   320.9'44'07   77–10434
ISBN 0–300–02151–8

For my mother

Oh! quand viendra la belle!
Voilà des mille et des cent ans
Que Jean Guétré t'appelle,
République des Paysans!

Mais ce beau feu s'écoule en cendre;
Le diable en passant l'a soufflé.
Le crédit n'a fait que descendre
Et l'ouvrage est ensorcelé.
La souffrance a fait prendre en grippe
La jeune Révolution,
Comme le vieux sorcier Philippe;
Et nous nommons Napoléon.

. . . .

C'est dans deux ans à peine,
Que le coq gaulois chantera;
Tendez l'oreille vers la plaine;
Entendez-vous ce qu'il dira?
Il dit aux enfants de la terre
Qui sont courbés sous leur fardeau:
Voici la fin de la misère,
Mangeurs de pain noir, buveurs d'eau.

Des monts sacrés où la lumière
Forge ses éclairs et ses feux,
Viens, en déployant la bannière,
Dix-huit-cinquante-deux!

Pierre Dupont
"Le Chant des paysans"
1850

Contents

Plates

Maps

Acknowledgments

Yale University facilitated this study with several grants; particularly welcome was a Morse Fellowship, which allowed me to finish writing. In Paris, I enjoyed the hospitality of Mr. and Mrs. Daniel Taylor, Jean-Claude Petilon, Joelle Desparmet, Ed Rohrbach, Richard Van Ham, and Jeanne Innes Kaqleurer. Parts of chapter 1 first appeared as "Social Conflict in France: The Limoges Revolution of April 27, 1848," in *Societas: A Review of Social History*, (Winter 1974), and sections of chapters 6 and 7 were previously published as "Radicalization and Repression: A Study of the Demobilization of the 'Démoc-socs' during the Second French Republic," in *Revolution and Reaction: 1848 and the Second French Republic*, edited by R. D. Price (London: Croom Helm, 1975); these portions are reprinted with the publishers' permission. The maps of the Nord, the Ariège, Finistère, Creuse, and Yonne were furnished through the courtesy of the Sterling Memorial Library Map Collection at Yale University.

In writing this book, I have benefited from the encouragement of a number of friends, including Roger Geiger, Tim Clifford, Ronald Aminzade, Michael Hanagan, Louise Tilly, Jonathan Spence, Henry A. Turner, David Bien, John Bowditch, Elizabeth Muenger, R. R. Palmer, Christopher Johnson, Robert Schwartz, Clark Dougan, and Peter McPhee. Three *quarante-huitards*, in particular, shared their knowledge of the period: Ted W. Margadant, who kindly allowed me to read and quote from his excellent study of the insurrection of 1851; Peter Amann, whose careful reading of the manuscript saved me from some errors and who suggested part of the title; and Roger Price. Susanna Barrows, Patricia Otto Klaus, and David Bushnell are three friends to whom I am especially grateful. Finally, at Yale, my thanks to Calhoun College, which has provided a stimulating place to live and work; Loueva Pflueger, for arranging for the

xiv ACKNOWLEDGMENTS

manuscript to be typed; Edward Tripp of Yale University Press, who helped provide a good home for the book, and Marya Holcombe and Joanne Ainsworth for their editorial advice. I am most indebted to Charles Tilly, Peter Gay, and Robert Bezucha. Bob Bezucha taught the first graduate course I took at the University of Michigan. That seems like a long time ago, and we have been down many roads since. His comments on the original draft provided the basis for some necessary reorganization. Peter Gay, colleague and friend, gave generously of his time; because of his sensible and good-humored suggestions the text has had the benefit of his unmatched sense of style. Finally, it has been my good fortune to have had Charles Tilly as a mentor. Reading *The Vendée* as a second-year graduate student turned me toward the study of social change and has now led to this book. An inspiring scholar and teacher, an imaginative social scientist, and a genial humanist and friend, Charles Tilly has greatly influenced my work and I am certainly not alone. To him and to the others, my thanks and *amitiés*.

Paris
March 25, 1977

Introduction

This book seeks to explain how Louis Napoleon Bonaparte, elected as president of the Second French Republic for a term of four years in 1848, achieved absolute power in 1851. The new republic had widespread popular support from ordinary people previously excluded from political life. How did it fail? What happened to the revolutionary coalition of radical bourgeois and their allies, the workers, who did most of the fighting in the *journées* of February 1848? The February revolution, by removing the blocks to mass collective political action, initiated a period of tremendous political mobilization and seemed to be ushering in a new era of political freedom and social harmony. Yet Louis Napoleon won an overwhelming victory in his plebiscites following the coup d'état of December 2, 1851. France became an empire. The great hopes and enthusiasm of the spring of 1848 were either forgotten or suspect. The "lyric illusion" had passed.

Two general explanations both assume that France was, in some way, not ready to be a republic, particularly a "social republic." The first and most traditional explanation is that the French retreated into the social and political conservatism characteristic of the monopoly that elites held on political life before the 1848 revolution. According to this view, when the revolutionary coalition which seized power in February began to break apart, reactionaries and moderates coalesced to "preserve" France from social revolution. In the ensuing bloody struggle in the streets of the workers' districts in Paris in June, the "forces of order" crushed the workers, who had been the revolutionary shock troops in February. Thereafter, the argument goes, Frenchmen retreated to conservatism, abandoning the "advanced and exaggerated" ideas of 1848 and finding safety in Bonapartism after their nightmarish glimpse of the social apocalypse. The

Map 1. The Departments of France

Departments presented as regional studies of the repression

Map 2. The démoc-socs in the legislative election of May 13, 1849

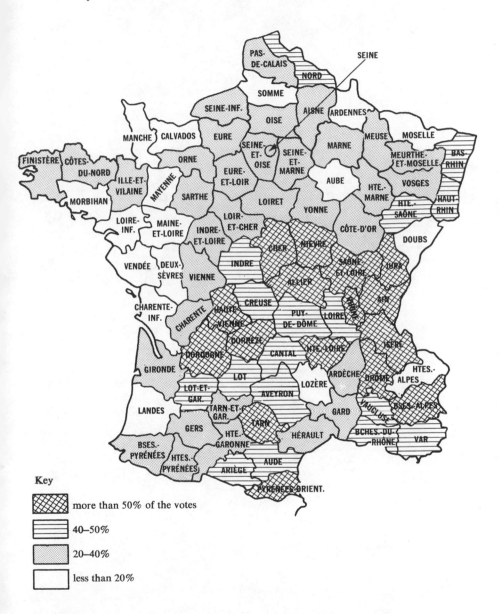

Key

more than 50% of the votes

40–50%

20–40%

less than 20%

Map 3. Departments put under the state of siege after the coup d'état of December 2, 1851

Departments under siege

coup d'état of December 2 gave Frenchmen what they had
wanted all along, an authoritarian leader who claimed to represent national glory, social consensus, and relative economic
prosperity.

A second general explanation, associated with orthodox
Marxist interpretations, was that the "time was not ripe" for the
social revolution. France's proletarians were too few and not yet
masters of their own consciences, and the country's social structure was still traditional. "The great mass of the French nation,"
wrote Marx, "is formed by simple addition of homologous
magnitudes, much as potatoes in a sack form a sack of potatoes."[1]

Of course, neither of these interpretations, Tudesquian and
Marxian, can be completely dismissed. It is undeniable that the
notables were able to rally their forces to effect a comeback after
the February revolution and to reestablish political deference in
much of France. Furthermore, the structure of French industry
was still quite traditional, with production by artisans in the
small workshops of the faubourg St. Antoine in Paris much more
characteristic than the few real factories of the capital's northern
suburbs; and rural industry was still an important part of the
French economy. French workers were neither conscious nor
organized enough to carry through a social revolution. But
neither interpretation, nor both combined, offers a satisfactory
account of the agony of the Second Republic.

We must seek an alternative explanation for the ascent of
Louis Napoleon to absolute power, because his path, as it turns
out, was not an easy one. The success of the far left in the May
1849 elections and in the partial elections of the following year
are troublesome for most standard interpretations. The extreme
left had important support in regions of the Midi and Center,
with strongholds in the East, Paris, and in other large cities. Two
years later, the coup sparked the largest national insurrection in
nineteenth-century France. The remaining fragments of the
revolutionary coalition, mostly peasants and artisans with some
radical bourgeois and proletarians, rose in defense of the democratic and social republic, the left's vision. This action hardly

supports the conventional view of a France that simply reverted to "traditional conservatism."

The Second Republic cannot be explained without emphasizing the repression which intervened to check the "great political mobilization of 1848,"[2] the first mass political experience since the French Revolution of 1789–99. The political repression, evident in the first months following the February revolution, did more than just clear the path for Louis Napoleon's ascent to power; it was essential to his success. His administration, particularly after the so-called Ministry of October 31 (1849), systematized and routinely implemented the repression of the extreme left. It broke the links of the radical apparatus, the formal and informal network of political organization and commitment fostered by the montagnards, or *démoc-socs*, who were the most organized and threatening challengers to the "men of order" who accepted Bonapartism in order to protect their economic, social, and political hegemony.

While the repression also struck at the monarchist opposition, its principal object was to destroy the montagnards. They were so named because of their radical namesakes, who had sat together in what happened to be the most elevated part of the National Assembly during the French Revolution of 1789–99. They often called themselves démoc-socs, for democratic-socialists, or socialists. The police called them, among other names, montagnards, communists, socialists, demagogues, men of disorder, and anarchists. It would be inappropriate to think of them in terms of a modern political party. They were a revolutionary coalition of leftists of various political opinions who advanced a remarkably coherent and consistent social program based on the belief that the democratic republic should become "social" by moving to resolve the "social question." The social question encompassed more than just the relatively miserable condition of the laboring classes, urban and rural. The February revolution dramatically posed the question, which had developed during the July Monarchy, of the place of workers in relationship to the ownership of the means of production and in France's national political life. The revolution of February provided the

extreme left with the means to mobilize mass political support
among those previously outside of the political process, promising
the freedoms of assembly, the press, association, universal manhood suffrage, and a relative democratization of municipal
politics. What, in Ted Margadant's words, "originated in 1848
as an urban ideology of social reform . . . a genuinely popular
government which would serve the interests of the poor, not the
rich—also became rural."[3]

The démoc-socs wanted a government which would be "social"
in the sense that it would be responsible to the laboring poor.
They were democrats who believed that universal manhood
suffrage was the foundation upon which the republic of social
justice would be built. More than this, they were social reformers
who demanded that construction of a better world start immediately. They appealed to the laboring poor by offering the "right
to work" and by encouraging associations which would lead to
the workers' control of production. In rural areas they cham-
pioned the abolition of the hated indirect taxes on drink and salt,
free court costs, educational progress, positive steps to stimulate
agriculture and create credit, and a war on usury. In addition,
they had the optimism of the utopians, believing that man was
essentially good and that he could change his world by changing
his political and economic institutions. The means by which they
reached the ordinary people—press, propaganda, associations,
electoral organizations—may strike us as relatively "modern";
at the least they are instantly recognizable as forms of collective
action and social organization more characteristic of our century
than the eighteenth. The démoc-socs were very much men of
their time, however, still imbued with principles and hopes
borrowed from the utopian socialists of the thirties and forties
and characteristic of a society which was still very traditional.

The coup d'état was not one single event, but the culmination
of a long series of blows against the montagnards. Between the
two most memorable events of the repression, the June Days and
the coup, there were thousands of incidents, and their combined
effect was to destroy the socialist organization in most areas
where it was seeking a foothold or had already become en-

trenched. The repression demobilized the major components of the democratic-socialist opposition which stood between the would-be imperial eagle and the empire. That it failed to prevent and in fact helped cause the insurrection that followed was a testimony to the durability of the montagnard organization and the popular appeal of its vision of the democratic and social republic. The Eighteenth Brumaire of Louis Napoleon Bonaparte destroyed the last links of the radical apparatus, both the visible signs of political organization and the remnants which, driven underground by the repression, formed secret societies and spearheaded the resistance to the coup d'état.

Radicalization, repression, and insurrection in 1851 was the history of the Second Republic. Of the three, we know considerably more about the first and third than about the second. Several important regional studies, notably Maurice Agulhon's brilliant *La République au village*, Philippe Vigier's exhaustive study of the Alpine region, Leo Loubère's analysis of the Lower Languedoc, and Christianne Marcilhacy's work on the Loiret, investigate the social and economic bases of political radicalization.[4] Ted W. Margadant's study of the insurrection of 1851 provides a provocative analysis suggesting a relationship between protourbanization, market structure, montagnard commitment, the secret societies, and insurrection.[5]

But despite what Peter Amann called "the changing outlines of 1848" in an important bibliographic essay more than ten years ago, the repression has never been adequately studied.[6] General accounts of the Second Republic have underplayed its importance or, at best, only sketched its outlines. Yet some historians have pointed the way, beginning with Karl Marx's remarkably accurate *The Eighteenth Brumaire of Louis Napoleon Bonaparte* (1852), which contains his observations of the repression from afar. In an excellent article written more than one hundred years later, Howard C. Payne described the administrative centralization of political policing which prepared the way for the coup.[7] Marx and Payne suggest that the bureaucracy provided Louis Napoleon with a great resource. Although prefects and magistrates might vary in efficiency, commitment, and even political opinion, the bureaucracy was far from neutral and generally obediently served Louis Napoleon and his henchmen. Other studies describe the repression as part of the histories of specific regions. Margadant's study of the insurrectionary areas of 1851 relates how the repression drove the montagnards underground in the seventeen departments in which there was major armed resistance to the coup. Several other key studies consider aspects of the repression. Agulhon's work on the Var is crucial because he clearly shows that the repression skimmed off the top of the montagnard leadership, eliminating many bourgeois radicals (democratic patrons). This forcibly opened up leadership positions to a great many ordinary people, which was one of the more important changes that occurred during the Second Republic. Other relevant works include Vigier's study of the five departments of the Alpine region; J. Dagnan's essential but largely forgotten study of the Gers, perhaps the best regional account of the repression; and Alain Corbin's recent *thèse* and my more modest contribution on the Limousin.[8] In addition, a few solid studies of the period may be found in the old and dusty *La Révolution de 1848* journal or uncovered among the rather undistinguished group of centenary works.[9]

While it would be simpler to stick to one or two departments or a specific region—and that was my original plan—the repression was a response to an almost nationwide political mobilization and is worthy of study as such. In this book I have attempted, to write a social history of the repression, to bring it alive and to avoid a purely administrative or institutional history of the republic which shoves the main characters, the ordinary people, from the stage. Nevertheless, the repression must be viewed at least partially through the eyes of the bureaucracy, because judicial, administrative, and military reporting provide a major documentary source. As Richard Cobb cautions us all, however, one must consider the tendency of officials (and historians) to exaggerate and to find social movements where there were none. This book must also, to some extent, be a history of the nascent "institutions" of political organization—the press, propaganda organs, voluntary associations, National Guard units, and even communal administrative structure—which brought ordinary people together and diffused popular ideology during the Second Republic. But I am primarily concerned with the impact of the repression upon people whose lives were touched for the first time by mass political mobilization and its subsequent repression. Cobb's relish for the brief appearances of ordinary (and often bizarre) people offers inspiration, despite his warning that there might not be such a thing as a "social movement."[10] My argument is that the common people, the laboring poor, participated in a fundamental consensus about the significance of the revolution and that the montagnards were a historically significant social movement because of the popular following they attracted in the drama of the revolutionary situation.

The works of Charles Tilly and Maurice Agulhon have most influenced my approach to the revolution of 1848 and the Second French Republic. Both investigate the mechanics of revolution and mass politicization but retain a feeling for the life of the period when they show the influence of large-scale economic and social change on the laboring poor. Tilly's studies of social change and collective action suggest the significance of the revolution of 1848 in the "rebellious century."[11] In essays with James Rule and Lynn Lees, Tilly explores the process by which a revolution fought over issues of relatively little concern or interest to most Frenchmen could bring the country into a period of intense mass political activity, organization, and social conflict. Ordinary people, who were outside of the political process and whose horizons and conceptions of politics were largely restricted to their villages and marketing areas, were involved. Many communities underwent a substantial "collective transformation of their perceptions of their world" during this period. Tilly's model of revolution can account for the expansion of social conflict and mass political organization after the revolution of February 1848.[12] That revolution created a power vacuum which allowed groups of ordinary people to contend for political power by giving them the means (freedom of the press, universal suffrage, and freedom of assembly and association) to do so. The political revolution of February became the social revolution of June and afterward.

Agulhon's *La République au village*, a meticulous and incisive study of the social and economic factors underlying the "descent of politics towards the masses" in the Var and the department's subsequent radicalization, is certainly the most important single study of the Second Republic.[13] Agulhon describes how average people in the Var became politically radicalized—politics ceased to be the exclusive privilege of the elite. He further demonstrates the role of "democratic patronage" by the radical bourgeois in the Var and the popularization of political leadership which resulted when the repression destroyed many of the bourgeois radicals and undermined the commitment of others. Popular leisure associations, the *chambrées* in particular, offered organizational possibilities and helped create entirely "red" communities which came to perceive their economic and social antagonism toward local notables or bosses in political terms. Agulhon's analysis of how the "red" republic came to the village offers numerous suggestions for the study of other regions or for generalizing about the experience of the nation during the Second Republic.

Four cautions must be made with regard to this study. First, I will not attempt to tell explicitly the story of the countermobilization of conservatives after the February revolution or of the evolution of a Bonapartist government staffed by civil servants who served loyally although they were not necessarily Bonapartist. The counterrevolution is not problematic. The revolution was over for most of the bourgeois faction who joined the coalition which overthrew Louis Philippe. They had gotten what they wanted; the workers had not. We will, in chapter 1, observe the rapid coalescence of bourgeois opinion, ably described by Marx and symbolized by the parade of the flashy *bonnets à poil* in Paris on March 16, 1848, marking the end of the bourgeois "fraternity" with ordinary people. The arrival of the conservative National Guard units from rural areas to help mop up in the wake of the June Days repression, the dismissal of Carnot as minister of public instruction in July, and the return of Guizot the next year are well-known indications of the rise of reaction. André-Jean Tudesq's study of the notables is essential here.[14]

Second, I am more interested in the repression and how it operated than in evaluating the precise nature of montagnard strength and popular appeal; pursuing the latter line of study would take this book far beyond manageable size. Ted Margadant's forthcoming study of the insurrection of 1851 covers this aspect clearly and intelligently, and Vigier's study of the Alpine region is in many ways an important contribution. We argue here that the extreme left had, by the spring of 1849, a relatively coherent and cohesive message, despite regional differences, the impact of the repression upon the montagnards' tactics, and a major split between militants and moderates over strategy in 1851. This message caught fire in the provinces. We shall have frequent occasion to observe the most salient aspects of this "message" in describing the means of collective action the montagnards had at their disposal. The freedoms of assembly, universal suffrage, and association and the democratization of municipal politics both provided the means by which the montagnards reached ordinary people and constituted an essential part of their vision of the democratic and social republic. At the same time, because we will study the repression "from the bottom up," we are most interested in its impact on ordinary people, rather than in "social control," the actions repressive regimes have to take to stifle popular collective action and oppress citizens.

Third, I have often sacrificed chronology in the interests of coherence. Between the June Days of 1848 and the coup d'état of December 2, 1851, two memorable and famous events, there were thousands of little events. Taken together, they were the repression. This book is the history of these "little events." The four principal chapters consider the repression as a general phenomenon and divide it into its basic mechanics and objects. The chronological treatment in chapter 1 and in the final three chapters should, with the chronology presented at the end of this introduction, assist the reader in keeping his or her bearings. To treat the repression in a strictly chronological fashion would be to lose its central themes and those of the republic in an avalanche of dates and names.

Fourth, I will beg the question with reference to the extent to which the Second Republic shaped the politics of France once the interlude of the empire ended at Sedan in 1870. Many regional studies (Agulhon's and Corbin's most recently) see the formation of the revolutionary coalitions of the Second Republic as portents of the politics of the Third Republic. Although each region studied in the tradition of the French thèse emerges with a unique political geography, a general process, revolutionary and then repressive, was taking place in France. Class coalitions and political organization are more important than regional characteristics in explaining the emergence of the montagnard organization. Particular economic and social configurations influenced montagnard success and even determined the popular view of the democratic and social republic, but Tilly's notion of an organizational or political process model seems more applicable to what was occurring in France as a whole. Such an approach explains the significance of the Second Republic and the arrival of the laboring poor as organized contenders for political power.

This study of the repression begins with a description of the effect of the revolution of February upon the people of Limoges and Rouen. The formation of a revolutionary coalition and subsequent countermobilization by the majority of the bourgeoisie paralleled events in Paris. While the events in Limoges and Rouen were not typical of the reception of the revolution in provincial France, these two episodes illustrate the revolutionary process taking place, to varying degrees and with different timing, in the country as a whole: the impact of the revolution of February and the entrance of the laboring poor into the political fray. Chapter 1, which introduces the means of collective action made possible by the revolution, leads us into the study of the repression of these chief agencies or institutions which had contributed to the development of the montagnard organization. The revolution removed the most important blocks which had prevented ordinary people from joining together for political purposes. Political dissidents were henceforth armed with the freedoms of press, association, and assembly. Chapter 2 describes the repression of the written word which carried the montagnard message to both those who could read and those who could not. Chapter 3 discusses the repression of voluntary associations. Encouraging and maintaining montagnard commitment, these associations included the ephemeral clubs, analyzed by Peter Amann for Paris;[15] such leisure associations as chambrées, popular societies, and circles (*cercles*); mutual aid societies; and producers' and consumers' cooperatives. Chapter 4 examines the impact of "social control" within the montagnard-dominated community, as the government moved to repress the remaining means of collective action open to ordinary people (demonstrations, banquets, forms of festivity and sedition). Chapter 5 carries this discussion further, treating the purge of radicals in positions of authority (mayors, deputy mayors, and schoolteachers) and the continuing institutional demobilization of the extreme left, the elimination of universal suffrage and of "disloyal" National Guard units.

The remaining chapters offer case studies of the repression; here the discussion again becomes chronological. Chapter 6 is concerned with the repression in cities, where special conditions offered montagnards the possibility of creating organizational bases with which to dominate politically an entire region. While earlier chapters will already have discussed several important cities, chapter 6 takes an in-depth look at the repression in Limoges and the mainly urban department of the Nord. Here montagnard organizational strength rested upon an alliance, real or potential, between the elite of bourgeois radicals and the mass of workers. Chapter 7 takes up the question of the repression in essentially rural regions, the arrondissements of Boussac and Bourganeuf in the Creuse, the Ariège, and the Finistère. Popular local radicals, allied with some communal officials, made political issues out of local economic and social problems and tensions. In the Creuse the seasonal migrants linked the rural world to France's urban centers. In the Ariège the decades of violent protest against the loss of forest rights added a special dimension to the montagnards' hopes and the repression's objectives. The

Map 4. Number of people appearing before the Mixed Commissions, accused
of involvement in the resistance to the coup d'état of December 2, 1851

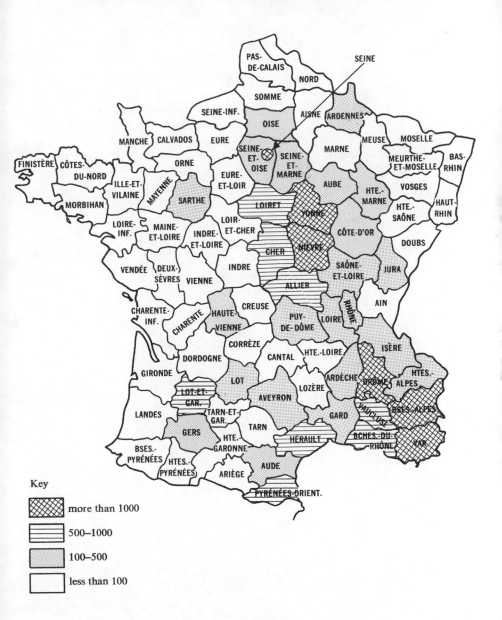

Key

more than 1000

500–1000

100–500

less than 100

Finistère is an example of the repression in an obedient and apathetic department without a revolutionary coalition and without a strong démoc-soc organization challenging the status quo.

The final chapter traces the evolution of revolution, radicalization, repression, and insurrection in one of the seventeen departments in which there was major armed resistance to the coup, the Yonne. The Yonne represents one of the departments in which the repression failed to break the links in the network of the extreme left. The coup d'état finished the task. Finally, an epilogue offers some remarks about the significance of the repression and the experience of the republic, a look at some typical activists, and reflections on the significance of the period.

Chronology

1846–47	Severe agricultural crisis
1847	Revitalization of the reform movement
1848	
January 14	Planned reformist banquet in Paris is forbidden.
February 21	Banquet called off.
February 22	First opposition to the regime in the streets of Paris.
February 23	National Guard defects to the opposition; Louis Philippe dismisses his ministers; troops fire on the crowd on the boulevard des Capucines.
February 24	Revolution in Paris. Louis Philippe flees with his family and a provisional government is formed.
February 25	The provisional government proclaims the "right to work."
February 26	Decree abolishes the death penalty for political crimes.
February 28	Popular support for a Ministry of Work; the Luxembourg Commission is established to study the organization of work.
February 29	Provisional government announces it will end the salt tax and the municipal customs tax.
March 2	*Marchandage* (subcontracting of labor) de-

clared illegal and the work day is set at ten hours in Paris and eleven in provincial France.

March 4   The provisional government declares the freedoms of press and assembly; slavery abolished.

March 7   The Paris Bourse open for business.

March 8   The National Guard declared open to all adult males.

March 14   The elite companies of the Guard are dissolved.

March 16   Demonstration of the elite of the old National Guard, the bonnets à poil. The forty-five centimes tax is levied.

March 17   Popular republican demonstrations.

March 31   A reform of the drink tax announced.

March and April   Popular disturbances in provincial France, principally attempts by peasants to reclaim rights in the forests, attacks by workers on railroads, and popular protests against taxes. The Club of Clubs of Paris sends out delegates to provincial France in the hope of assuring the election of ardent republicans.

April 23   Election of the Constitutional Assembly; moderates and conservatives victorious.

April 27   Affaire de Limoges; workers disarm the National Guard by force; a new provisional administration is established in that city.

April 27–28   Bloody repression of a workers' insurrection in Rouen.

May 4   The republic is proclaimed officially.

May 9–10	Executive Commission is elected by the Assembly.
May 15	A crowd invades the National Assembly after a demonstration in favor of the Poles.
May 20	Assembly debates on the national workshops, in operation since the first days of the republic.
June 5–10	Agitation among the Paris workers; some arrests are made.
June 21	The national workshops are ordered closed; the drink tax is reestablished.
June 23–26	The June Days; civil war in Paris.
June 26	Insurrection crushed.
June 28	Cavaignac becomes the president of the Council of Ministers and organizes a new ministry.
July 5	Carnot replaced as minister of public instruction.
July 28	Decree on clubs.
August 9–11	Decrees on the press.
September 17	Partial elections; Louis Napoleon Bonaparte becomes representative of the people.
November 21	Constitution proclaimed.
December 10	Louis Napoleon Bonaparte elected president.
December 27	The salt tax is reestablished.
1849	
January 29	National Assembly approves the Rateau

	proposal, putting an end to its own author-ity, with new elections to take place.
March	Trial of those implicated in the journée of May 15.
April 30	First attack by French troops in Rome, in the defense of the pope against the republicans there.
May 13	Election of representatives; montagnards gain strength.
June 13	Popular demonstrations in Paris against the Roman expedition; Ledru-Rollin involved.
June 15	Insurrection in Lyon; Paris and Lyon regions placed under the state of siege.
June 19	New law banning clubs.
July 3	Rome falls to French troops.
July 27	Another press law passed.
October	Trial of those implicated in the journée of June 13.
October 31	New ministry; minister of justice calls for monthly political reports from his procureurs.
1850	
January 11	"Petite loi" on primary instruction.
March 10	Partial elections for the Assembly, including some to replace representatives implicated in the demonstration of June 13, 1849; eleven montagnards victorious.
March 15	Falloux Law on education passed.
April 28	Eugène Sue elected representative from Paris.

May	Commission meets to discuss revision of the electoral law; petitions of protest circulate.
May 31	New electoral law eliminates about one-third of those previously eligible to vote; those excluded are mostly what Thiers called "the vile multitude."
June 8	Another press law passed.
July 16	Another club law passed.
August 26	Louis Philippe dies in England.
September 20	Count of Chambord's proclamation prevents any fusion between Orleanists and legitimists.
October 24	So-called Plot of Lyon alleged network of conspiracy and insurrection in the Midi, uncovered.

1851

January 3	General Changarnier dismissed as commander of the Paris military division.
January 24	New ministry appointed.
March and April	Petitions circulating in favor of revising the constitution to allow Louis Napoleon to become elected president for another term; more petitions against the electoral law are signed.
April 10	Another ministry, this one more acceptable to Louis Napoleon.
July 19	National Assembly votes against any constitutional revision.
October	Ardèche, Cher, and Nièvre placed under the state of siege.

October 4	Louis Napoleon declares himself in favor of returning to universal manhood suffrage.
November 13	Move to abrogate the electoral law of May 31 defeated.
November 17	National Assembly votes against the Questeurs proposition, which would have given it the right to call out troops to defend itself.
December 2	The coup d'état; National Assembly dissolved and many representatives arrested.
December 3–4	Resistance in Paris.
December 5–10	Resistance in provincial France.
December 21	Plebiscite.
1852	
February, March, and April	Departmental mixed commissions continue the repression.
March 28	State of siege lifted.
November 21	Second plebiscite.
December 2	France becomes an empire.

1

The Expansion of the Revolution: Social Conflict, Collective Action, and Violence in Limoges and Rouen

The political revolution in Paris in February 1848 initiated a period of mass political involvement in France, although its implications have been obscured by the emphasis placed on the June Days in the capital in the historiography of the Second Republic. By April 27, 1848, social division and threatened violence, similar to that which racked Paris in the months following the February journées, occurred in Limoges and Rouen. These events reflected two of the most salient aspects of the experience of the republic. First, the social question and the optimism that changes in France's political structure would have a salutary impact in the economic and social realms emerged in popular consciousness. Second, this new awareness increased social conflict in France, bringing about a mobilization and radicalization of the laboring poor in both urban and rural areas.

Although the June Days and the other urban insurrections of the first year of the republic neither typified what Agulhon has called the "Republican apprenticeship" nor ended violent social conflict and political mobilization during the Second Republic, they do illustrate the mechanics of the revolutionary experience. These memorable journées exemplify the process which Charles Tilly and Lynn Lees see as

> the tremendous widening of political organization, involvement, and conflict *after* the revolutionary seizure of power
> ... behind these public scenes lay a newly mobilized popula-

tion responding to a changed political climate. For the first time in decades the government permitted men to write, to assemble, and most important of all, to organize with complete freedom. The political life that Orleanists had tried so hard to limit to the *juste milieu* now extended to the entire population.[1]

The February revolution broke down the legal and social bulwarks which had restricted the development of mass political participation and organization. The subsequent proliferation and development of the means of collective action encouraged the emergence of political commitment in ordinary people who previously had been outside the political process. This facilitated the development of a relatively sophisticated left-wing or montagnard political organization which spread from cities like Paris, Lyon, Montpellier, Colmar, Reims, Auxerre, and Toulouse and engulfed wide areas of the country, particularly the Center and Midi.

The expansion and contraction of the political institutions in this period both aided and reflected the organized political response of Frenchmen to a revolutionary situation which seemed, in a brief moment of incredible optimism, to offer a political solution to the social question. The events leading to the June Days in Paris point to a process common throughout France: ordinary people were being drawn into the revolution. A detailed examination of events in Limoges and Rouen after the February revolution in Paris will enable us to better grasp the impact of the revolution on collective action and, ultimately, to understand the goals of the repression.

Limoges and Rouen had similar histories in the first months of the republic, but travelers in mid-nineteenth century France would not have confused the two cities. A former *ville parlementaire* and an important port of considerable charm only 139 kilometers from Paris, Rouen must have been much the more pleasant place to live. Limoges is almost 500 kilometers south of Paris, on the edge of the Massif Central as it tilts toward the coastal plain. Despite Turgot's attempt to improve the bumpy road to the capital so that Limoges porcelain would not crack during the long journey, the trip to Paris was not easy until the completion of the railroad during the first years of the Second Empire. Rouen was renowned for the martyrdom of St. Joan and for its magnificent churches and cathedral which inspired Flaubert and, later, Maupassant and Monet. Limoges's Cathedral of St. Étienne represented a considerably more modest effort, and few people outside of the region had heard of the city's patron saint Martial, martyred in Roman Lemovicum. The Limousin's largest city, it was the birthplace of generals (Jourdan and Bugeaud) and later became such a dreary place of exile for them that it inspired its own verb, *limoger*, meaning to cashier, fire, or dismiss. Before and after the events of 1848, there was little reason to discuss the two cities together, though one might have noted that they had roughly similar social structures: prosperous bourgeoisie, a small group of dissenting middle class radicals' known for their interest in "advanced ideas," and, in addition to the artisan community, a growing class of industrial proletarians.

Two months after the February revolution, the workers of Limoges took arms, disarmed the bourgeois National Guard, seized power, and a full two months before the June Days in Paris established a radical provisional government.

This little known but significant journée marked the victory of the local revolutionary coalition of a radical bourgeois elite and workers that had first formed during the July Monarchy. A group of young socialist lawyers provided the most vocal opposition in Limoges to the regime "so lacking in principle that it could only be named by the month of its founding."[2] The prefect of Haute Vienne, Limoges's department, had frequent reason to add to the dossiers of the two most influential bourgeois republican-socialists, Théodore Bac, articulate court defender of the opposition, and Marcel Dussoubs-Gaston, another lawyer and political offender who was under constant police surveillance.[3]

With the arrival of the utopian socialist Pierre Leroux in the Limousin in 1844, socialist influence expanded. Pilgrimages to Leroux's printing shop in Boussac in the Creuse and gatherings of socialists in Limoges convinced the prefect in 1847 that the "communist" ideas of the coterie of utopian socialists were also profoundly influencing the workers.[4]

Limoges, by 1848 one of France's most rapidly growing cities, with a population of 38,000, reflected the geography of class segregation which characterized cities undergoing large-scale industrialization.[5] The prefect noted in 1830 that if the National Guard were organized by quarter as required by law, companies of "aristocrats" and companies of "proletarians" would have been created.[6] The *masse ouvrière* included approximately 4,600 porcelain workers, including 1,200 women and children working in eighteen factories and in about the same number of smaller decoration workshops, at least 2,600 textile workers, 2,300 workers in leather, 500 in the building trades, 150 producing weights and measures, 150 hatmakers, and a wide range of artisans who generally were faced with a declining standard of living.[7]

Periodic unemployment compounded the problem of low wages for workers in the porcelain factories, since, as a luxury industry, porcelain manufacture was exceptionally vulnerable to commercial crises. The origins of working-class organization in Limoges were to be found among the porcelain workers, who ranged from the elite decorators, or *artistes en porcelaine*, to the turners and molders who formed the porcelain, to the unskilled laborers. The workers reacted to wage reductions in 1833 and 1837 with unusually long and successful strikes. By 1848 seven mutual-aid societies offered some protection to the skilled workers, although it was often only meager assistance during illness or unemployment and burial expenses. The workers' low standard of living contrasted with that of a prosperous bourgeoisie dominated by the porcelain *patrons* and identified with the Orleanists.[8]

The economic crisis of 1847 laid bare social tensions in Limoges. Throughout the country the winter of 1846–47 was disastrous. In Limoges the price of bread rose to a high of sixty-seven centimes per kilo, compared with forty-three the previous September.[9] As unemployment approached 15 percent the municipal council voted a subsidy of 10,000 francs to provide temporary employment in public workshops.[10] At the same time, the council provided four times that amount to welcome royally the Duc de Nemours, an expensive gesture which the laboring poor resented.[11]

During this same year the bourgeois National Guard became a symbol of class conflict in Limoges. Workers had long been excluded from this civilian militia, which was theoretically a city's second line of defense. The first redistribution of guns since 1831 included only four citizens whose occupations were listed as "worker" (*ouvrier*).[12] In April 1847, the officers petitioned and received permission to make the uniform obligatory for all guardsmen. A second petition in June requested that all non-uniformed guardsmen be dropped from the rolls, which eliminated virtually all workers from even symbolic membership in the Guard. This second petition described the Limoges bourgeoisie as "the elite of the inhabitants . . . honest people . . . good citizens" who gathered together to protect "their institutions" against "the inferior classes," tactlessly compared with the 1,100 convicts in prison in the city.[13] The petition caused an uproar in Limoges; it outraged the workers and the nucleus of radical political opposition. While expected disturbances in the summer never materialized, the intensity of the bitterness between the classes ultimately led to the Affaire de Limoges.

The news of the revolution in Paris in February 1848 initiated a period of uncertainty in Limoges, during which the workers took advantage of the power vacuum to press for participation in the presumed benefits of the republic. Despite the indifference of most workers to the issue of narrow electoral reform, news of the barricades in Paris brought them into the streets to parade and sing the "Marseillaise."[14] A provisional committee of administration consisting of three moderate republicans and the radical lawyers Bac and Dussoubs-Gaston declared the republic in Limoges before the official proclamation arrived from Paris.[15]

The workers hoped that the revolution would become, in the contemporary parlance, "social," and that "the people," so often at first seemingly victorious and then betrayed, would profit from the advent of the republic. This hope was echoed in the meetings of the Société populaire, Limoges's club, which was formed on February 26 and presided over by the porcelain worker Bulot. The predominantly working-class club met three times each week in the only building large enough to hold its nearly six thousand members, the Salle de manège. The club reflected the politics of two vehemently republican newspapers created in the first days after the revolution, *Le Peuple*, edited by Denis Dussoubs, and the political cartoonist Alfred Durin's *Le Carillon républicain*.[16]

Despite the arrival of the Paris-appointed commissioner for Haute Vienne, the provisional committee of administration retained the allegiance of the workers. The "forces of order" were neutralized as the *ad hoc* committee refused to recognize the authority of the general commanding the small garrison in Limoges. The general remained in the barracks with his troops, and the commissioner of police abandoned his post.[17] The provisional administration solidified its authority by dismissing the unpopular procureur général (state prosecuting attorney) and replacing Orleanist officials in the department. Workers forced the committee to release thirty-seven peasants from the Cher, imprisoned in Limoges for their participation in disturbances over grain during the hard times of the previous winter.[18] Several subsequent announcements and proclamations of the committee were cosigned by "eight delegates of the workers," further indicating the push for representation.[19]

The timing of social conflict in revolutionary Limoges is explained by the impact of the revolution of February. Working-class political involvement after February focused on issues which emerged from the evolution of the "social question" during the July Monarchy. (The social question implied that the republican government would protect the workers from economic crises and aid in the search for an organizational solution by supporting the establishment of producers' cooperatives.) The first of these three related controversies was the arming of the workers and their active participation in the National Guard. The second was the "right to work," which was essential for the resolution of the social question. The third was working-class representation in the Constitutional Assembly to be elected in April. These demands, along with the workers' mobilization, provoked middle-class resistance and intensified social polarization along relatively clear class lines.

The Limoges National Guard remained the subject of volatile social controversy as it had been in 1847. The sweeping reorganization of the Guard after the revolution resulted in the popular election of new left-leaning officers. But the elite Guard of the July Monarchy still controlled the available weapons. Only a few of the 138 guns distributed at the prefecture after the revolution had gone to workers.[20] A technical challenge to the election prevented official recognition of the new officers.[21] Bulot, president of the Société populaire, traveled to Paris to request weapons for the unarmed faction. He returned to Limoges with only the promise of 3,000 guns. Matters worsened when the commissioner appointed the still officially recognized and armed Orleanist National Guard to maintain order during the election. The establishment of armed Orleanist posts at all important points in the city inspired rumors that the Guard would take arms against "the people."[22]

In Limoges, the revolution was followed by a severe economic crisis, which contributed to the urgency of the second major issue, the "right to work." Within a few days of the revolution in Paris all credit stopped and most factories closed their doors.[23] The municipal council, as it had done in the winter of 1846–47, financed public workshops to employ as many workers as possible. By April, 3,700 workers were enrolled; each worker earned 1.25 francs per day.[24] Bulot pleaded in Paris for assistance for the workers of his city. The porcelain workers only accepted the workshops as a temporary measure until the commercial crisis subsided. They asked the government's assistance in finding a systematic and permanent solution to their economic vulnerability. At least three plans for producers' cooperatives within the porcelain industry indicated the determination of the porcelain workers to circumvent "the brutal and oppressive law which guides the porcelain industrialists."[25] The provisional administration and the Société populaire appointed commissioners to study the organization of work in Limoges. One of the projects was the Experimental Manufacture of Associated Workers of Limoges, a producers' cooperative which anticipated government financial aid. The provisional administration's more moderate commission suggested that the industry could be organized into labor and capital cooperatives with the help of a loan of 700,000 francs to be borrowed from the leading citizens of Limoges at 5 percent interest.[26] The leading citizens, however, were not in the least interested; they already viewed the municipal workshops with alarm. The municipal council was hard pressed to find the funds to keep the workshops open, yet, like its Paris counterpart, feared to close them. Rising unemployment, the workers' demands for assistance, and the proposals to reorganize the porcelain industry heightened class tensions as the elections approached.

The National Guard controversy and the economic crisis intensified the importance of the national elections. The Constitutional Assembly in Paris would create the political institutions of the new republic. But Limoges was divided concerning the very nature of the new regime. The majority of the middle class, distraught at the news of the revolution or alarmed by its apparently radical turn, organized against the political challenge of the lower classes. The middle class saw "communism" and "anarchism" reflected in the faces of unruly workers straggling to and from the municipal workshops, in the frequent and often tumultuous meetings and parades of the Société populaire, and in the occasional jostling of a bourgeois citizen by workers in a café. Bourgeois order and political and social institutions seemed to be under assault. The socialist antecedents of the radical leaders and the arrival and rumored candidacy of the utopian socialist Pierre Leroux reinforced bourgeois suspicions that the republic would only be a larger version of the disorganized and expensive municipal workshops.[27] Conservatives and moderates formed a rival political club inappropriately named the Club des travailleurs and, while supporting the Orleanist paper *L'Ordre*, briefly published another newspaper, *La Fraternité*, which the workers publicly burned in April. The Société populaire and *Le Peuple* offered Théodore Bac, Dussoubs-Gaston, two other socialist lawyers, Frichon and a former disciple of Cabet's, François Villegoureix, and Ancel, a porcelain worker, as candidates for the National Assembly. Their program seemed simple: the end of the social, political, and economic privilege characteristic of the Orleanist regime, and the evolution toward a social republic. They specifically demanded the adoption of a progressive tax, limitation of official salaries, the end of taxation on such goods of "primary necessity" as salt, and the implementation of the "right to work." Capital and labor were to be organized to end what Villegoureix called, in his campaign statement, the "unpredictable direction of unchecked competition." To most of the Limoges bourgeoisie, these radical candidates challenged order, religion, family, and property, and to defend these values the bourgeoisie supported a conservative slate of Orleanists, legitimists, and conservative republicans.[28]

The periodic reports of the representative of the Paris political clubs in Limoges reveal the preelection tension.[29] Louis Marie Genty, bookbinder and Jacobin club representative to the Paris Club of Clubs, arrived as a delegate to the Limousin in early April to assist the "good republicans" to prepare for the election by bringing the "socialist philosophy" to Limoges. He discovered, as he reported to the president of the Club of Clubs, Citizen Longepied, that Limoges was divided into two classes, the bourgeoisie and the workers "who are very advanced in socialism, wanting to cease being what they have been, the cause of the industrialists' fortune without advantage to themselves . . . I am on a volcano." At his instigation, the Société populaire ceremoniously adhered to the "Declaration of the Rights of Man of Citizen Robespierre." Genty, the Parisian revolutionary, rose to a position of influence in the Limoges club and helped regularize contacts with other clubs in Haute Vienne. On April 24, he predicted that if four or five of the "good republicans" did not win election, "there will be shooting because the working classes of this region are very radical."[30]

On election day, Limoges appeared split ideologically and physically into two camps. The bourgeois National Guard had established posts at key points in the city. The Société populaire also mobilized, meeting early in the morning at the Field of July to organize delegations to meet the peasants arriving to vote.[31] Members of the Société soon swarmed through the streets singing the "Marseillaise," "Chant du départ," and "Ça ira, ça ira, les aristocrates, on les pendra (we will hang them)!"[32] At the city gates and the voting stations, they hoped to counter prevailing conservative influence in the countryside by urging the peasants to vote for the candidates of the workers. Thus began the Affaire de Limoges, culminating on April 27 with the destruction of a part of the electoral ballots, the forced disarmament of the National Guard by workers, and the establishment of a new and more radical provisional committee of administration, which included proletarians.

Peasants arriving to vote on April 23 encountered groups of between fifteen and one hundred fifty club members. About one hundred workers harassed peasants arriving at one customs barrier. Workers stopped a column of about four hundred peasants, telling them, "In the name of the law, let us see your ballots." Other country-people were informed that they had not chosen "the good candidates" and were tricked into accepting ballots listing only the radical slate of candidates. These pressures were duplicated at the voting stations. The workers returned home after the balloting to await the results of the republic's first election.

On April 26, the tabulation of votes began in the Salle de manège, which was also the meeting place of the Société. Members added to the confusion by singing, and a worker allegedly threatened that the votes would be burned if they were not favorable to the "good republicans." Another said, "we want the five candidates of the Société populaire . . . we will have them; anyway, the worker is everything." Yet only one minor scuffle had taken place by the time the counting was stopped, suspended until the following morning, the twenty-seventh, when the results were expected to be known.[33]

That night, in a long and noisy session interrupted by a march through Limoges, the Société resolved that arms should be distributed to the workers and that the municipal council ought to be dissolved. All members were again asked to meet early the following morning and to proceed to the Salle de manège to await the election results.[34] A delegation of 150 members, led by Genty, notified the government commissioner at the prefecture of these decisions. A smaller group threatened the acting commanded of the National Guard in his house, demanding that he order the Guard disarmed the following day.[35]

Very early on April 27, the workers gathered at the Field of July on the outskirts of the city. The director of the municipal workshops, an active member of the Société, suspended work for the day. Messengers left for the work areas on the roads outside of town to call back workers who were already at work.[36] Workers from the poor river district of Naveix arrived armed with the lances they used to move logs down the Vienne River to provide fuel in the procelain factories. Three thousand people crowded around the Salle, a good number already armed. The three hundred citizens who had squeezed into the hall were the first to know that Limoges's radical vote had not been seconded by the rest of Haute Vienne. Despite the workers' efforts, only Bac and Frichon were elected from the radical list. Amid an uproar in the Salle, the crowd destroyed the only remaining ballots.[37]

Outside, the angry and frustrated workers turned against the Orleanist National Guard posts. Part of the crowd surged toward the munitions building outside the city to seize what weapons they could find. Two workers went to capture the National Guard's two cannons, and found them turned toward the Field of July where many workers were again gathering. This story spread rapidly, both infuriating and panicking the workers. Genty urged the replacement of the mayor and commissioner by two of the defeated radical candidates. Emissaries were sent to neighboring communes to sound the tocsin. The crowd at the Field of July moved across town to join the others at the munitions building.

At five major *places* on the way, national guardsmen were disarmed during confrontations with the workers. Some guardsmen
left their posts under the protection of radical leaders. Théodore
Bac sent two notes to the commissioner, the first asking that the
small garrison of troops be sent from the city and that the complete disarmament of the National Guard be ordered. The second
warned that if these measures were not taken, there would be
civil war in Limoges.

The crowd moving toward the munitions building broke into
the shops of three gunsmiths and took hundreds of rifles. Outside
the building, they constructed barricades to deny access to any
troops that might arrive from the barracks. The commander of
the National Guard post there was forced to turn over his command to a cabinetmaker from the crowd and a provisional
administrative committee dissolved the National Guard. The
Société populaire now effectively controlled Limoges. Workers
singing the "Marseillaise" followed the commander of the troops
to the barracks from the prefecture where he had failed to con-
vince the commissioner to send the small garrison into action. The
crowd called for the troops in the barracks to join them. At the
town hall, the last remaining National Guard post fired shots
into the air over the crowd of thousands, and then was disarmed
by the workers.[38]

That night, a new administrative committee moved into the
prefecture. Its membership reflected the impact of the revolution
in Limoges. While the commissioner accepted a position in hopes
of helping to maintain order, the moderates were eliminated and
replaced by four of the workers' candidates in the legislative
elections and four workers.[39] This committee dissolved the
municipal council, thus achieving the immediate goals of the
Société populaire, and ordered all arms deposited at the town hall
the following day.[40]

The next day, the twenty-eighth, there were two related disturbances. In the first, national guardsmen bringing their weapons
to the town hall were taunted, intimidated, and disarmed by
workers. In the second, a crowd of twelve hundred threatened a
miller with death and forced him to sell his grain at what the

crowd considered the "just price." Bac's intervention saved the miller, who left town, returning only under the protection of troops several weeks later.[41] Stores and factories closed. By proclamation of the provisional committee, all persons and property were placed under the protection of "the people." Directives to all subcommissioners and mayors called for total support and reports on disloyal officials. The purge of functionaries, begun in early March, was to continue until the revolution had faithful representatives at every administrative and judicial position.[42] Many bourgeois would later refer to this period as the "terror" in Limoges. The new procureur général wrote the minister of justice on April 30: "Limoges is still in the power of the workers; their posts [referring to an unarmed "mobile guard" organized by Bulot] occupy . . . even the courthouse from where I am writing you. The terror continues to reign in the town."[43]

The Société populaire's control of Limoges soon ended, as the commissioner hurried to the capital to report to Ledru-Rollin. On April 21, the general commissioner for the departments of Allier, Cher, Creuse, and Haute Vienne arrived, refused to recognize the authority of the existing provisional administration, and appointed a new commissioner for the department.[44] Three thousand troops surrounded Limoges, quartering in nearby towns. Despite a petition of middle-class citizens calling for the immediate occupation of the city, the bulk of the troops did not enter Limoges until May 16 and 17, in order to avoid a "butchery as in Rouen."[45] Had they moved into the city at the end of April, a small-scale June Days might have occurred. Unlike Paris, in Limoges the repression of the insurgents began in the courts, not in the streets.[46]

In Rouen, also on April 27, a significantly similar scenario had bloodier consequences. Rouen (population 88,000) and its industrial suburbs included a concentration of textile workers. The transformation from cottage industry to factory-based production altered the textile industry in the Seine Inférieure, making Rouen and Elbeuf, a small wool-producing town twelve miles down the Seine, decidedly industrial in character.[47] Like Limoges, the *patronat* dominated the Rouen bourgeoisie, and the National Guard symbolized its hegemony and its devotion to the government of July.

The bourgeois republicans closely watched the development of the reform movement in Paris and distributed a petition supporting reform which fifty-four persons, including thirteen municipal councilmen, signed. They also sent a delegation to the fateful banquet scheduled for Paris on February 22. The prefect prevented a similar gathering in Rouen. With the news of the Paris revolution, Frédéric Deschamps, a young "old republican" (Républicain de la veille"), virtually installed himself as "director of the department charged with organizing the department and the municipality of Rouen." Ledru-Rollin formalized his authority by naming him commissioner. Durand, as Rouen's new revolutionary deputy mayor, assisted Deschamps. Representatives from the new municipal administration in Elbeuf arrived to help coordinate local government.[48]

The new administration faced the militancy of the workers, who were still suffering from the effects of the economic crisis of 1846–47; in December, many workers could still only find three days employment per week. The revolution, because it decreased the demand for textiles, only contributed to this underemployment. After hearing the news of the revolution, workers burned the railway bridge to Havre. Their action was the first attack on the Paris-Rouen railway line by transport workers who felt their livelihood threatened by the railroad or who resented English engineers and workers.[49]

Workers took their grievances into the streets. Almost three thousand workers participated in attacks against textile factories. Local workers also blamed the English for their misery; in Sotteville they attacked factories owned by Englishmen. General Castellane, commander of the Rouen military division, dispatched troops to protect a linen factory employing English workers who had been imported to run some new machines. A crowd of angry workers forced one factory-owner to walk barefoot from Malaunay to Maromme; arrests followed and workers from the valley of Cailly tried to free the prisoners. Castellane, fearing that his soldiers would be forcibly disarmed, withdrew them. The National Guard, establishing regular posts and patrolling from the moment of the first news from Paris, constituted the only regular armed force remaining in the city. Its members had helplessly watched the workers triumphantly surge through the streets after the revolution.[50]

The economic situation seemed bleak; even the purchase of bread and salt slowed noticeably. Commissioner Deschamps, attempting to maintain order, confronted the municipal council and, after being formally introduced, announced the council's dissolution, creating another whose members included a few workers. The council opened municipal workshops as a stopgap measure, paying from sixty-five to seventy-five centimes per day.[51]

The bourgeois National Guard of four hundred members and a squadron of artillery and cavalry opposed "the new order of things." The commander of the departmental gendarmerie noted that "the prosperous people and the merchants and the National Guard are coming out against the Republic." Guardsmen had been heard to shout "Long live the king!" during the first days of the republic. The workers particularly resented the wealthiest battalion, which was from the faubourg Cauchoise (called the "côte d'or" or gold coast). The Guard, in turn, forced to defend the railway lines against the workers, hated Deschamps, whose leftist political opinions had made him an outsider during the July Monarchy and who now seemed to be betraying his class out of "ambition or envy."[52] The workers poured into the municipal workshops, eight thousand enrolling by March 28, fourteen thousand by the middle of April, and perhaps sixteen thousand by the time of the elections. The municipal council could contribute only 10,000 francs for the workshops; the remainder was to come from public subscription.[53] The council's subsidy enraged the bourgeoisie, who saw the workshops as little more than regular gathering places for indolent workers. Every day before work, "popular tribunes formed and amateur Parisians or others—they say even members of the provisional authority or of the Municipal Council" showed up to electioneer or to organize patriotic singing. Despite the dismissal of a few workers and some honest efforts to prevent workers from outside of the city from enrolling, it seemed to conservatives that the workshops were serving as supplementary clubs at seventy-five centimes per session.[54]

Deschamps, like his colleague in Limoges, ordered guns from Paris in order to incorporate the workers into the National Guard. Although the moderate newspaper *L'Ami du peuple* favored the workers' joining the Guard, assuring them that it is "not your enemy . . . it is with contact with people that one begins to understand them, and that prejudices disappear,"[55] a great social gulf separated workers from the Orleanist National Guard. To the members of the radical Club St. André, the National Guard remained the "enemy of the workers." Brigades of workers guarded the newly planted liberty tree, fearing that guardsmen would tear down this symbol of the rooting of the republic.[56]

By the end of March, confrontations between workers and guardsmen became serious. A proclamation by Deschamps failed to calm the "considerable agitation" against the Guard. On March 28, two thousand workers stormed the prison in Rouen to free those arrested during the month, including the itinerant coppersmith who had allegedly started the fire which destroyed the railway bridge after the revolution. In nearby Lillebonne, Castellane's troops, having returned to Rouen, and supported by the Guard, fired during a clash with workers who were attempting to plant a liberty tree. Six were killed and twenty-two hurt.[57]

In the frantic optimism of the first months of the republic, the elections seemed to offer the Rouen workers some hope that just men, elected representatives of the people, could solve the problems of the laboring poor. As in Limoges, the crucial issues of the National Guard and the economic crisis heightened the drama of an entire generation's first mass political experience. A radical electoral committee, the Comité central républicain, opposed the conservative Amis de l'ordre et liberté. Rouen's Club St. André and the conservative Société central des travailleurs, the electoral organizations, and the press thus bitterly divided on two quite different lists of candidates. The difference was symbolized by Sénard, conservative leader of the old dynastic opposition and new procureur général, and Deschamps, who represented the revolution's radical potential.[58] However, the election passed without serious incident despite the social cleavage, although the workers were disappointed by the outcome as the conservative slate emerged victorious.[59]

What became known as the "butchery of Rouen" began on April 27 at about three o'clock in the afternoon with a confrontation at the town hall between the workers and the National Guard, who feared the destruction of the ballots. A crowd entered the galleries of the building and Guard tried to evict them. Outside, in the courtyard, a group of children between twelve and fifteen years of age, led by a drummer and carrying a flag, began to "parade in front of the officials in a way calculated to brush against them." The crowd, predominantly working class, applauded. When the little troop returned, several of the unnamed officials (almost certainly guardsmen) blocked their path and grabbed their flag. The workers shouted at the guardsmen, who fixed bayonets. Several scuffles broke out as some soldiers arrived on the scene. The inevitable shot followed, from somewhere, perhaps the result of the accidental discharge of a gun stacked in the *hôtel de ville*. Two guardsmen then fired pistols at the workers, killing one. The crowd panicked and fled in confusion. As the National Guard reorganized and moved through the streets, they were pelted with rocks which the women had gathered. The dragoons charged, driving the crowd back into the narrow side streets. As news of the confrontation spread ("they have killed our brother!"), the workers built barricades. Other guardsmen arrived at the hôtel de ville; a few were surrounded while returning to their posts after eating (on mange quand même) and disarmed. Two or three shots were fired from houses. More barricades were constructed, with such enthusiasm, efficiency, and solid construction that this was later taken as evidence of a plot originating in Paris, where, after all, the best barricades had always been built. By nightfall, there were thirty-six barricades;

only three had been taken by troops and national guardsmen as night fell. Sénard, elected representative, reassumed his position as procureur général, with every intention of crushing the "insurrection."[60]

During the night, workers loaded guns and prepared piles of rocks to hurl at the troops and guardsmen who were moving cannons to positions across from the major barricades. One exchange of gunfire took place as guardsmen fired into the darkness. The next morning, the first seven corpses were found. At dawn, the troops and guardsmen issued the three legal warnings before moving against the barricades. One by one they fell, until there only remained the enormous obstruction at the faubourg St. Sever, which was manned by seven hundred textile workers from Sotteville and St. Quevilly. Twelve cannon blasts battered down the last defense. The cavalry chased down fleeing insurgents, killing three, including one innocent farmer from the hinterland who arrived to sell his produce. The insurrection ended at noon on the twenty-eighth, with thirty-nine dead, all of them, excluding the farmer, insurgents, and countless wounded, who had been dragged back to the safety of the workers' quarter. Five hundred arrests followed and eighty-one people were brought to trial; virtually all were workers, particularly spinners and day laborers. Deputy mayor Durand was the most important exception (others included a mathematics professor and a former schoolteacher), and, because of his influence with the workers, the courts dealt with him harshly.[61]

The violence in Rouen had direct repercussions in near by Elbeuf, where one magistrate later neatly summed up the social structure as consisting of a working class which was

> very numerous, confronted by *chefs d'industrie* who are very rich or appear to be; between these two parts of the population, the line of demarcation is clearer than in towns which are not purely industrial. In Elbeuf there are men working by the day and the men who make them work.[62]

The Elbeuf workers' bellicosity was well-known. Another official observed that "these tendencies toward insurrection have their

origin in the suffering of the worker."[63] After the revolution, the
workers attacked the factory of the most unpopular and powerful
boss, Victor Grandin, member of the dynastic opposition during
the July Monarchy and a conservative candidate in the April
elections. His buildings were stoned after he posted a controversial notice setting the hours of work. The workers' club supported the election of Bertrand Espouy, a follower of Étienne
Cabet. But Grandin emerged victorious, and on the morning of
April 28, the news of the Rouen insurrection sparked violence
in Elbeuf.[64]

The Elbeuf National Guard assembled at the courtyard of the
town hall was assailed with stones thrown by an angry crowd of
hecklers. A shot was fired, allegedly at the guardsmen. Workers
scattered to regroup. The alarm was sounded in the surrounding
"industrial villages," including Lalonde, where the mayor led
his townspeople to aid the workers. In sharp contrast, the "agricultural villages" came to the aid of the National Guard. The
people of St. Aubin lifted their bridge across the Seine and
stopped the fleeing mayor of Lalonde. Seven barricades were constructed in Elbeuf. Several members of the municipal council
approached them to listen to the demands of the workers, who
were mostly spinners. They wanted Grandin, an Orleanist, to
resign from his day-old position as republican representative, and
his replacement by one of the workers' candidates. They also
demanded the disarmament of the National Guard, arguing,
"We are one hundred poor against one rich; we have obeyed our
bosses for too long—it is our turn to be the bosses today."[65]

The next day, Saturday, the twenty-ninth, workers and guardsmen exchanged fire at a barricade near Grandin's house, killing
one worker and injuring several others. The arrival of troops
from Rouen and the news of the defeat of that insurrection easily
dispersed the workers of Elbeuf. The barricades came down. In
Paris, Auguste Blanqui issued his famous proclamation: "The
counterrevolution has just bathed in the blood of the people.
Mete out immediate justice to the assassins!"[66] The Rouen
affair became a major issue in the Constitutional Assembly and
in the Paris clubs. A bitter caricature of the event was mistakenly

attributed to Daumier by his friend and admirer Charles Baudelaire, and thus described:

> Since the February revolution I have seen only a single
> caricature whose savagery reminded me of those days of
> fine political frenzy . . . Daumier's print came shortly after
> the terrible massacres at Rouen. In the foreground, on a
> stretcher, is a corpse, riddled with bullets; behind it are
> assembled all the town bigwigs, in uniform, well crimped,
> well buckled, well turned out, their moustaches *en croc*, and
> bursting with arrogance; and also present, necessarily, some
> bourgeois dandies who are off to mount guard or to take a
> hand in quelling in riot with a bunch of violets in the but-
> tonhole of their tunics—in other words, the ideal image of
> the *garde bourgeoise*, as the most famous of our demagogues
> once called it. On his knees before the stretcher, wrapped in
> a judge's robe with his mouth open to show his double row
> of saw-edged teeth like a shark, F.C. is slowly passing his
> claws over the corpse's flesh and blissfully scratching it—Ah!
> That Norman! he says, He's only shamming dead so as to
> avoid answering to Justice.[67]

Revolutionary enthusiasm by itself could not account for the
affaires of Rouen and Limoges. The revolution brought more
than hope to ordinary Frenchmen; it brought the means of
collective action which permitted the political mobilization
evidenced most dramatically in the June Days, and characteristic
of the montagnard movement which developed during the
Second Republic. The most incisive accounts of the first four
months of the republic have stressed the role of the popular
press—hundreds of papers appearing within a matter of weeks—
political clubs, and workers' associations. These were the means
by which ordinary people, hitherto outside of the political process, entered the political and social struggle initiated by the
February revolution.[68]

If the Paris clubs, as Peter Amann convincingly argues, ultimately failed to obtain their ostensible goals, they nevertheless
provided an organizational framework, however loose, by which

Parisian workers entered the political fray. Amann has rightly stressed their role of familiarizing ordinary people with the ideological phraseology—"democratic and social republic," "right to work," and so on—of revolutionary politics.[69] The clubs of Rouen and Limoges, particularly those in the latter city, played a decisive role in providing workers with a means of collective action. Clubs and the formal and informal electoral organizations which at first paralleled and then succeeded them provided a consciousness of political alternatives which permitted Frenchmen to view universal manhood suffrage as an opportunity to influence their own futures. At the same time, other nonpolitical associations, particularly in the Midi, came to assume some of the same functions, and they performed them more efficiently, because their members had the habit of working together, joined by ties of occupation or leisure. Many of these organizations, formal and informal, long outlived the clubs and provided a means and frame of reference for mass political involvement.

Workers' associations were more important than the Paris clubs in drawing workmen into the life and death struggle of June.[70] In Limoges, more than in Rouen, workers' associations helped shape the workers' response to the revolutionary situation by encouraging them to think of their collective interests and by strongly influencing their perception of the "social republic." The porcelain workers tried to organize associations which they hoped would evolve into producers' cooperatives; ultimately, they believed, the laboring poor would form a community of political *and* social equals. Louis Napoleon neither forgot nor forgave the links between the Paris workers' associations, working-class militancy, and the barricades.

The first months of the republic were also the halcyon days of the political press, now freed from the fetters of Orleanist censorship. The editorial offices of *Le National* and *La Réforme* were organizational (if not conspiratorial) centers for the most damaging opposition to the Orleanists. In Limoges and Rouen new papers provided leadership and achieved radical electoral consensus based upon the rapidly emerging ideological vision of the democratic and social republic, by selecting candidates and printing their statements of candidacy (*professions de foi*) while attacking the bourgeoisie and their Guard. Familiar candidates and socioeconomic issues, however vaguely defined in the spring of 1848, reached virtually every corner of France during the republic thanks to the press of the extreme left. The freedoms of press and of association were the hard-earned spoils for those who wanted to defend the republic and carry forward the Revolution.[71]

Another major change was the shift in the balance of power within each community. As Orleanist prefects slipped away, many justices of the peace and mayors found themselves rudely notified of their replacement by letters on official stationary in which "Cour royale" had been scratched out in favor of "Cour d'appel." Town halls changed hand in half of the French communes during 1848. Schoolteachers were asked their political opinions and were requested to suggest candidates for the April elections. In some places (Limoges, for example) a marked popularization of leadership roles already seemed possible, auguring the decline in "democratic patronage" later in the republic.[72] The political influence of men like Théodore Bac and Frédéric Deschamps, although they were hardly *enfants du peuple*, was still a new phenomenon; they were much too far to the left to have had any "respectable" following during the *monarchie censitaire*. They profited from the chance given them by the revolution. The year 1848 gave thousands of "new men" influence in political debates, in the National Assembly and in relatively insignificant town halls.

Was deference dead? Ordinary townspeople pressed close to watch the planting of the liberty tree, while local notables looked sullenly on from the rear or were conspicuously absent. The "Marseillaise" was sung where it could be remembered. The republican conspirators of the July Monarchy became heroes. The notable became, in principle, just another citizen. One enthusiastic mayor in Haute Vienne dated his letter of adhesion to the republic "3 mars, an I."[73] Popular communal demonstrations of attachment to the republic and its symbols were legal, encouraged, and, for civil servants, advisable.

But if the means of collective action open to Frenchmen were greatly enhanced by the surprising events of February, the means of repression open to the "men of order," back in the administrative saddle again by the beginning of 1849, already existed and had been frequently tested during two earlier regimes. As the shaky revolutionary coalition which drove Louis Philippe from power began to disintegrate, because its members had in common only the fact of political opposition, the repression began in Paris—its shadow quite visible as the clubs were repressed and the National Guard pompously demonstrated its strength.[74] Marx correctly points to the rapid coalescence of the bourgeoisie as one of the most striking and significant aspects of the period immediately following the February revolution.[75] The bourgeois National Guard of Limoges nervously eyed *les blouses bleues* as they oiled their rifles, while that of Rouen shouted "Long live the king!" after the republic was declared. The men of order, led by Sénard, who gained a reputation that later won him the post of minister of justice, were out in force early, and their armed presence precipitated the just-discussed journées in Limoges and Rouen. Certainly no one could have been more class conscious after the February revolution than the bourgeoisie.

By April, in the third month of the republic, the lines had been drawn between the forces of revolution and reaction. Moderate republicans stepped aside and disappeared from politics, or they became either much more conservative or more radical. Most legitimists, at least until 1851, were perplexed. Few Orleanists mourned Louis Philippe. By 1849, montagnards and the men of order, many of the latter already embracing the Bonapartist symbol, faced each other. Repressive legislation added to the arsenal of the men of order and their faithful henchmen in positions of administrative and judicial responsibility. The revolution expanded after February, after the June Days, and after the May 1849 elections, as the means of collective action offered common people hope and organization. The repression was the process by which the revolution contracted; its outlines may also be seen in the first months of the republic in Paris, Limoges and Rouen. The republican experience was radicalization and repression, and, in eighteen departments, insurrection after the coup d'état. The next four chapters will consider the repression of the means of collective action by which the extreme left had been able to build an organizational network of remarkable strength, efficiency, and durability.

2

The Targets: The Press and Political Propaganda

When it temporarily brought about the end of the tight censorship which characterized the July Monarchy, the February revolution offered perhaps its greatest single gift to the extreme left. The revolution of 1848 initiated a period during which the periodical press and the irregular forms of political propaganda—brochures, pamphlets, almanacs, and printed songs—played a determining role in the first mass exposure to political questions in nineteenth-century France. Socialist newspapers and propaganda probably provided the first regular reading for the laboring poor. Alfred Terrain, a "property-owner, but hardly well off" and a wheelwright by trade from Saints-en-Puisaye (Yonne) indicated as much when interrogated by authorities after the coup d'état; he stood accused of forcing someone to ring the tocsin and of belonging to a secret society in the Yonne:

> RESPONSE: If I participated in politics, it was when I read the newspaper. I subscribed, only one month ago, to *L'Union républicaine*. This paper and others are the cause of all of this. Certainly, if I had not read them, I never would have done what I did.

> QUESTION: What other journals did you read?

> RESPONSE: Biard the grocer subscribed to *La Feuille du village* and I read it when I went to buy some merchandise at his place. I also read a copy of *Bien-être universel* which Gibelin the sabot-maker received.

The dissemination of montagnard propaganda and the vigorous

repression which countered it were crucial parts of the experience
of the Second Republic, as national political questions entered
the café, the workshops, and the marketplace. A typical official
complaint described the workers of a porcelain factory in Vierzon
in the Cher listening to the public reading of "socialist writings"
in a shop adorned with portraits of Barbès and Blanqui.[1]

The first months of the republic were to be remembered as the
heyday of the free political press. New papers inundated Paris. At
least 171 papers appeared in the capital between the revolution
and the middle of June.[2] New provincial journals joined the
political fray, supporting candidates and printing their statements. Some were begun solely to engineer electoral campaigns.
The titles of the most radical were indicative of their politics: *Le
Prolétaire, Le Peuple, Le Travailleur, La Voix du peuple, L'Ami
du peuple, Salut du peuple*, and so on. Montagnard papers eventually appeared in at least fifty-six departments during the Second
Republic;[3] their offices provided centers of action for political
organization and mobilization.

The format of political papers during the republic remained
quite consistent: a minimum of four pages, usually six or eight,
with one or two lead editorials; a column of international news;
brief dispatches from London, Vienna, Berlin, Madrid, or New
York that were usually culled from the larger Parisian papers; a
chronicle of local events, accidents, deaths, military promotions,
unusual and usual occurrences; and an even more random
column of "diverse facts" garnered from the region. Smaller
provincial papers frequently reprinted editorials from the most
influential papers of their political persuasion, particularly *Le
Siècle* in Paris, but also *La Voix du peuple* of Marseille, *La Civilisation* of Toulouse, *Le National de l'Ouest* of Nantes, and *Le
Messager du Nord* of Lille. Some papers in cities relatively near
the capital, such as *L'Ami du peuple* of Montargis and *L'Union
républicaine* of Auxerre, ran a column of "Parisian correspondence." Most provincial papers included information on fairs,
market prices, and the weather. Advertisements for cure-all
tonics and real estate foreshadowed the mass press of the later
nineteenth century.

The most popular feature of any mid-nineteenth-century newspaper was the *feuilleton*, usually a serial, which appeared at the bottom of the first page. An attractive serial could ensure regular subscriptions and readers. The montagnard press coopted the serial to preach its political message. Those of *L'Ami du peuple* were typical: "How the Poor End up," in the first issues of the paper in January 1850, described the plight of the laboring poor; "A *Chouan* Exploit" recalled reactionaries of another revolutionary era; "The vigils of Master Jean—a political manual for workers, peasants, and the poor" was an example of the rather condescending wisdom preached to the poor by bourgeois ideologues.[4] These subjects and themes contrasted sharply with the serials of the July Monarchy, many of which kept the Bonapartist myth alive by regaling the faithful with the imperial exploits of Napoleonic marshals and mistresses. Other feuilletons were not really serials but entertaining essays or the songs of Pierre Dupont or Alfred Durin. *Le Messager du Nord* bowed out on December 3, 1851 with a letter from Félix Pyat to Lamartine, prepared for publication before the coup d'état, as its serial.

Despite the domination of Parisian events and politics, the provincial papers had considerable local content. Regional journals, addressing themselves to specific constituencies, reflected the local dimensions of national social, economic, and political problems. For example, *L'Union Républicaine* of Auxerre harped on the drink tax, a lively issue in the surrounding cantons, particularly Chablis. The Lyon démoc-soc newspapers and *L'Association rémoise* discussed "the right to work" and working conditions in the textile industries dominating their respective regions. In the larger cities, particularly Lille, Nantes, Colmar, Nancy, Marseille, and Toulouse, the editorial offices served as organizational centers for electoral campaigns for the Assembly, the departmental general councils, the arrondissement councils, or even the municipal councils. The danger lay, for the men of order and their administrators, not only in the ideas diffused by the journals but in the organizational centers provided by their offices.[5]

Because the montagnard press reached ordinary people, suggesting an attractive alternative to the social, economic, and political domination of France's traditional notables, the government moved to repress it. Circulation figures provide only a starting point for any estimate of how many people were reached by the montagnard newspapers during the Second Republic. Excluding the large Paris papers, which could have thousands of subscribers, most montagnard papers had between 300 and 1,100 regular subscribers, as the following sample figures for September 1850 indicate:

> *Le Peuple* (Marseille), 2,000
> *Le National de l'Ouest*, 1,000
> *Le Messager du Nord*, 1,000
> *Le Progrès du Pas-de-Calais*, 850
> *Le Républicain cochois*, 850
> *Le Démocrate de Vaucluse*, 600
> *Le Démocrate de Saône-et-Loire*, 400[6]

All printed more copies than these figures show, however. They sold the excess copies or distributed them at no charge. *L'Éclaireur républicain* in the Puy-de-Dôme, for example, had between 700 and 800 subscribers, but it printed an average of 1,100 copies.[7]

Numbers of subscribers or copies printed also vastly underestimate the number of readers reached by montagnard newspapers, and this fact only strengthened the resolution of officials to deal harshly with the radical press, which seemed to them to be promoting socialism through legal means. *La Constitution de 1848* (begun in May 1849) had few subscribers but, like the others, "was profusely distributed in the surrounding towns."[8] The cost of a subscription, however small, was beyond the means of the laboring poor. While single copies of *L'Ami du peuple* of Montargis and *La Feuille du village* seem relatively inexpensive at ten centimes, yearly subscriptions ranged from ten to twenty francs, a week's pay for most workers.

Furthermore, not all regular "readers" could actually read. Outside of eastern and northeastern France, there were few departments in which more than half of the people could read and write, as shown by the Inquiry into Industry and Agriculture of 1848. In the Limousin, the cantonal estimates ran from a caustic "none" for Châteauneuf (Haute Vienne) to 50 percent for Eymoutiers (Haute Vienne). In the countryside, between 5 and 20 percent of the people could read: in Rochechouart, 20 percent, Ambazac, 10 percent, and Nexon, 5 percent (all Haute Vienne), and about 10 percent in Bort, Egletons, and Argentat (Corrèze). The rate of literacy was approximately twice as high in the towns, about 60 percent in Limoges, 30 percent in Brive, and 25 to 30 percent in Tulle (compared to 5 percent for the remainder of the canton of Tulle). Literacy rates were invariably lower for women than for men, varied according to occupation, and were complicated by separate listings for people who could read, but not write. More exact figures from the military conscription list for the class of 1847 for the Corrèze, which show that less than a fourth (703 of 3,165) could read and write, also demonstrate that the region was considerably more illiterate than France as a whole.[9] In the canton of Montargis (Loiret), one-half of all males and one-third of the females could read and write; in most cantons of the departments of Vosges and Yonne well over 50 percent of the population could read and write.[10]

Through cafés and popular societies, circles, and chambrées, newspapers reached far more people than the number of subscribers. Of *Le Démocrate du Var's* 124 known subscribers, 28 were cafés, and 22 were societies and chambrées which had between thirty and one hundred members.[11]

The démoc-soc press and political brochures and pamphlets reached the technically illiterate as well. Police entering cafés found that papers were read "in a loud voice" to others. The literate artisan, radical bourgeois, and fearless schoolteacher helped bridge the gap between the illiterate and politics, and of course oral propaganda, including speeches, songs, stories, and conversations, was an essential part of the process. After the coup d'état, the procureur général of Colmar, in whose district the percentage of literacy was quite high, wrote of the montagnard press:

One found [the montagnard press] everywhere, in the cot-
tages, in the workshops. There were even some factory-
owners blind enough to subscribe for their workers. [The
press] was almost a superstition in the countryside.[12]

Maurice Agulhon's study of *Le Démocrate du Var* demonstrates
how the montagnard press reached many times more people
than the subscription figures would indicate, and influenced
the common people collectively. *Le Démocrate* was "widely
known" in a *bourg* of 1,800 people. Although only eight to ten
copies reached the town; each edition was publicly read out loud.
A gendarmerie report from Trets (Bouches-du-Rhône) noted
the impact in a chambrée: "This [public] reading overexcites and
inflames the members of this society, almost all illiterate, as well
as the workers from outside the region who are working on
departmental route number six, and who are admitted [to the
club]."[13]

The repression of the radical press began when seals were
placed on the presses of eleven papers in Paris on June 25, 1848.
Through the first months of the republic, the newly freed press
had, in the eyes of those who became the men of order, shown
itself doubly dangerous by providing a means of regular expression of leftist social and political sentiments and by furnishing an
organizational base for political agitation, often paralleling the
efforts of the clubs. *Le National* and *La Réforme* had been instrumental in the coalescence of the ultimately successful opposition to Louis Philippe's last ministry. An atmosphere of political
excitement and organizational furor had characterized the offices
of Paris's multiplying political tabloids before the elections and
before the June Days. So in August, the "caution" laws that had
been in effect during the July Monarchy, according to which
newspapers were required to pay large sums of money against
possible future political offenses, were reinstituted; and editors
were once again menaced by arrest for some of the political
offenses tabled by the revolution. The *journée manquée* of June
13, 1849, served as a pretext for a series of new press laws which
made any attack upon the president a crime, raised the caution

money for many papers, revived an 1835 law requiring all political papers to print government decrees and notices, and forbade the printing of "erroneous or inaccurate facts likely to disturb the peace."[14] By 1850, even stronger press laws armed the procureurs and prefects.

The repression was vigorous. There were 335 court cases involving 185 republican newspapers in 77 cities and towns between December 12, 1848, and the end of December 1850; 240 of these involved provincial papers.[15] Multiple prosecutions brought the same editors and managing directors (*gérants*) before the court time and time again. Virtually every montagnard paper in France suffered prosecution for political "crimes." With money in short supply and capital difficult to raise under ordinary circumstances, the high stakes of political trials—fines and court costs, to say nothing of the prospect of prison—made the cost of publication often unbearable. By virtue of the caution law, the responsible (in a legal, financial, and, from the government's point of view, moral sense) managers had to deposit their "caution" before publishing. The required sums, in July 1850, ranged from 1,800 to 6,000 francs in provincial France, depending on the importance and size of the city involved. The large Parisian dailies paid the staggering sum of 24,000 francs. Only the small apolitical announcement papers escaped the caution law.[16] Despite this, a portion of the montagnard press survived, remarkable testimony to the endurance and dedication of a generation of bourgeois publishers and writers. Withstanding numerous legal attacks and overcoming severe obstacles, these survivors permitted the démoc-socs to plan bravely their strategy for the 1852 elections.

This war between the repressors using political prosecution as a means of censorship and the montagnards involved a labyrinth of legal obstacles that limited what could be safely printed without being considered legally subversive, seditious, or inflammatory. Certain political offenses were most likely to bring the confiscation of an edition and legal persecution. Editors and managers were legally liable if their papers contained anything which could be construed as urging people to break a law (by not paying taxes, for example) or to disrupt the "public peace" in some way. Likewise, papers were forbidden to urge "one group of citizens to hate another group of citizens" or "to attack the government and its authority and the institutions of the republic" or to defend any act officially declared to be criminal, such as by implying that the death of General Bréa during the June Days was justified.[17]

The "social economy" was not to be discussed, and the government could not be attacked. When the *République du peuple/ Volksrepublik* of Colmar editorialized that "the land belongs to everyone" or discussed the "right to work," its editors were charged with supporting "communist ideas" (*idées partageux*) which would, legally, be "urging one group of citizens against another." The *Courrier républicain* of Dijon faced prosecution after lapsing into revolutionary rhetoric: "1830 ... 1848 ... Perhaps a third will be necessary, and soon." "Inciting civil war" became a fairly common charge after the June Days. References to 1793 or to Robespierre could either fall under the legal statutes forbidding "inciting hatred" or be considered a public "apology for acts previously declared to be criminal."[18]

"Slandering" (*méprise*) the government emerged as a common charge as montagnard papers defended the republic, for example, following the law of May 31, 1850, which ended universal suffrage. There were many examples of such slander. *La Constituante démocrate* printed "As the government has apparently decided to persist in its liberticidal ways ... " *Le Peuple* (Marseille) criticized the administration's policy toward exiled revolutionaries in "Kossuth chased from France." *Le Messager du Nord* hinted in December 1849 that the anniversary of the Eighteenth Brumaire of Napoleon was cause for reflection among republicans. When *La Civilisation* of Toulouse attacked the government for "selling out the nation's honor" by sending troops to Rome, the manager and editor were hauled into court on three charges, "inciting to hatred and slandering the government of the republic, and the crime of apologizing for acts deemed crimes or offenses by the law." All charges applied to reprinting anything previously declared illegal, a stipulation which deterred provincial journals from systematically reprinting editorials received from the larger Paris papers. The seizure of *Le Montagnard* in Montpellier after it reproduced an extract from *La Voix du peuple* concerning the drink tax, a major issue in the wine regions of the Hérault, is a case in point.[19]

Certain technical restrictions also assisted prefects and procureurs. A copy of each edition had to be deposited at the prefecture before it was circulated, and after July 1850 every article was to be signed or initialed. All changes in a paper's legal status had to be reported immediately—variations in the number of issues per week (they decreased with the financial pinch), new editors or directors (often replacing the victims of successful prosecutions), or changes in the residency of the managing director.[20]

Procureurs could prosecute practically at will, but convictions were another matter. Juries, drawn from the ranks of ordinary citizens, returned verdicts of "not guilty" time and time again in cases where editorials and articles seemed to the authorities outrageous and illegal. The procureur général of Riom, lamenting the acquittal of *L'Ami du peuple* in that city, explained that the jury members were of the same political persuasion as the accused. Worse, such "outrageous acquittals" tended to focus public attention on the issues involved in the trial. French courtrooms became forums for debate on the press laws, the "right to work," the "democratic and social republic," and the repression. Defense lawyers, a closely knit group whose training had been gained in representing the political opposition during the July Monarchy, eagerly made fools of their less polished and often less experienced adversaries who argued the government's unpopular cases against well-known local figures. Townspeople gawked as Théodore Bac, J. Faure, and Madier de Montjau arrived to defend local montagnard leaders.

Crowds jammed courtrooms to watch their lawyers publicly raise fundamental questions about the regime and the repression, putting the government on the defensive. When the managing editor of *Le Bien public* stood trial in the cour d'assises of Dijon, the prefect of Haute Marne complained that the court personnel was inadequate to overcome the slick defense and oratory of Madier de Montjau, who traveled through the country taking similar cases. In that particular trial, in which it seemed as though the republic itself stood accused, the "courtroom was transformed into a club" and Madier won the support of the jury, whose foreman was a simple gardener. When the verdict of "not guilty" was announced, Madier left the courtroom to be feted at a banquet before leaving town to take on his next case.[21]

Often press trials had the opposite impact to that intended, "stirring up passions" and bringing the social question further into public view, particularly as the summaries of the trials were reprinted in the local press, often the same montagnard papers whose editors were on trial. Procureurs généraux urged the minister of justice to upgrade the personnel in the district courts. The authorities sought to exhaust the démoc-socs through multiple prosecutions. *Le Progrès du Pas-de-Calais* faced a jury twenty-eight or twenty-nine times between the June Days and February 1850, despite the prosecution's relative certainty that the montagnard leader Frédéric DeGeorge would always manage to "get to the jury" and avoid conviction.[22] In Toulouse, where the procureur complained that "the press is never convicted," *La Constituante démocrate*'s editors were acquitted on charges of "exciting people to hatred," even though the paper had been so carried away with the rhetoric of the barricades that it had announced early in 1849 that it was time "for the people to load their rifles and arm themselves." Several months later a similar "direct provocation to revolt" resulted in another astonishing acquittal in a trial in which the defense attorney persisted in calling the president of the court "citizen president."[23] By the end of 1850, such acquittals forced a more realistic assessment of the merits of each prosecution, based upon the presumed political inclinations of the jury, the probable damage from presenting a démoc-soc spectacle for public consumption, and the extent to which the government would lose face by allowing a particularly outrageous accusation or assertion to stand unchallenged. Prefects and procureurs would gladly have eliminated jury trials by the end of 1850, but they persevered by necessity.[24] Where convictions could be obtained, large fines and jail sentences drove many montagnard papers from business.

The cases of *Le National de l'Ouest* of Nantes and *Le Travailleur* of Nancy typify the ferocity with which prosecutors attacked their political nemeses. Victor Mangin, the most successful montagnard organizer in the traditionally conservative west, first appeared in court during the Second Republic to charge the editor of the legitimist *Le Courrier de Nantes* with slander, accusing him of instigating trouble in Nantes during the June Days. Henceforth, Mangin came to the court as the accused, facing prosecution four times in 1849 for offenses including "inciting civil war," "inciting hatred," and "apologizing for criminal acts" (attacking the government for executing General Bréa's killer). Twice acquitted (once on appeal), but twice convicted, he faced sixteen months in prison and a fine of 3,500 francs. Théodore Bac successfully defended Mangin on the most serious charge, inciting civil war; the minister of justice found this acquittal particularly "regrettable." Appeals kept Mangin out of jail and *Le National de l'Ouest* continued, edited by his two sons, while he signed the political articles. The politics of *Le National de l'Ouest* did not change. Mangin just barely escaped prosecution for publishing a song, "Le Christ socialiste," in which the representatives of order at the press trials became Pontius Pilate, nailing Christ, the montagnard, to the cross. When Mangin published two letters from junior officers protesting political repression within the army, the military division commander feared publicity of the incident and the eventuality of acquittal. The procureur let pass an editorial which stated that the people would take to the barricades to defend against any violation of the constitution. Mangin's vehement protests against the withdrawal of universal suffrage led the minister of justice to mark his case "urgent." In June 1850, Mangin received yet another jail sentence, and *Le National de l'Ouest* was suspended for one month. In July, the suspension became permanent and the paper's last edition was July 23, 1850. A crowd of 1,200 protested an ex-post facto conviction in October. By that time, Mangin was in prison; *Le National de l'Ouest*'s subscribers henceforth received *Le National* from Paris.[25]

When a jury failed to convict *Le Travailleur* of Nancy in

September, 1850 for publishing an uncomplimentary article about the prince-president, the prefect of the Meurthe alleged that the verdict was due to the influence of a socialist lawyer who had enjoyed the hospitality of some of the jurors. Three successive prosecutions in November brought just one conviction. "Guilty" in December, *Le Travailleur* switched managing directors. In February 1851, the paper changed both its management and its name, becoming *Le Travail* in the hope of avoiding prosecution. New charges brought Jules Favre to Nancy to win acquittal; cries of "Long live the Republic!" echoed in the courtroom, and *Le Travail* survived until the coup d'état.[26]

Prefects and procureurs had indirect means of combatting the press, including pressure on the owners of cafés where the montagnard papers were read, harassment of hawkers and peddlers ("Police agents ferret out the people who distribute our paper," complained Amédée Jacques of *La Liberté de pensée*[27]), creation of alternative "official" Bonapartist papers, such as *Le Conciliateur* established in Guéret in 1851, and persecution of printers. At least fifty-one printers faced political prosecution in France between 1849 and the summer of 1851; once again the stakes were high. Printer's licenses (*brevets*) were costly, and they were difficult to obtain. Printers responsible for brochures, socialist engravings or lithographs, songs, or petitions against the electoral law of May 31, 1850, were subject to harassment.[28] A Carcassonne printer was fined the enormous sum of 5,000 francs for failing to sign or initial—as required by law—500 copies of the petition against the electoral law. The prefect's actual target was *La Fraternité*, the Aude's montagnard paper, and, reeling under the fine, the printer severed his relationship with that newspaper. None of his competitors would risk having the paper as a client, and *La Fraternité* disappeared.[29] When the prefect of the Doubs discouraged local printers from publishing *Le Peuple de l'Est*, its prospective editors investigated the possibilities in the Haute Saône, where one printer had received a hitherto unused license in the wide-open spring of 1848. Officials there had suspected his politics, but could not withdraw his license because he was not printing anything. Closely watched, he was soon noted to be "in flight." *Le Peuple de l'Est* failed for lack of printing presses. The word spread of the dangers of accepting montagnard business.[30]

Facing persistent official opposition and financial ruin, montagnards sometimes turned to one of the "pernicious" symbols of the revolution itself, association, to keep the free press alive. At the end of 1849, seven papers were organized as joint-stock partnerships: *Le Jura* (Besançon), *Le Peuple* (Dijon), *Le Républicain démocrate* (Metz), *L'Oeil du peuple* (Niort), *Le Démocrate du Var* (Toulon), and *La Réformateur du Lot* (Agen). When, in June 1850, *Le Républicain des Ardennes* of Metz proposed legal reconstitution as a joint-stock partnership (announcing, "Universal suffrage has been stolen from socialism; the press must be saved for the benefit of socialism") of 15,000 shareholders, the procureur in that city scrutinized the laws governing association to see if they applied to newspapers. And in Colmar, where the radical press thrived in both French and German, Charles Schmidt, editor of *Volksrepublik* and an insurgent of June in Paris, began a "list of subscribers to assure the continuation of democratic propaganda in the Haut Rhin" in July 1849.[31]

How could this loophole in the law be closed? The law specified that the shareholders elect the director of a joint-stock partnership, but the director of *Le Républicain des Ardennes* had been elected only by a board of four, making the paper's administration technically illegal. But what if all the shareholders should gather to elect the director, which seemed theoretically possible? The minister of justice instructed his subordinates to consider such a gathering a club or a meeting which could compromise the public peace. Furthermore, how could several thousand people all actually know each other? If they did manage to get together, the society would necessarily be "anonymous" and not a partnership and the statutes filed at the prefecture would be neither "lawful" nor "serious." Such official logic justified the suspension of *Le Démocrate de la Loire* (St. Étienne) which sold shares at five francs apiece. A meeting of potential shareholders in Nîmes was also thwarted. These legal obstacles limited attempts to maintain the montagnard press through the formation of associations.[32]

The state of siege gradually facilitated the repression of the press by eliminating certain legal complications. The case of Lyon provides a good illustration. France's second city had a tradition of working-class militancy, and *L'Écho de la fabrique* in 1831 was probably the first working-class newspaper in the world.[33] After the revolution, *La Représentative du peuple, Le Peuple,* and a number of other papers celebrated the lifting of press restrictions: the first was suspended in August. *Le Censeur, La Démocratie, L'Espoir,* and *Le Républicain* orchestrated protest against martial law established after the insurrection of June 1849. *Le Peuple souverain* faced jury trial for asserting that two classes existed, reactionaries and proletarians, and that France would be "democratic and socialist or perish in its own debris," an interesting expression of the 1834 motto of the silkworkers, "Live free or die fighting." But a jury, drawn largely from the Croix Rousse, acquitted the editors, and thereafter martial law proved to be more effective, eliminating jury trial. *Le Peuple,* suspended, was succeeded by a "literary" paper, *L'Escope,* a "journal fabuleux," which boldly announced in its first edition that it would break the silence imposed on the socialist press. Prosecutions and suspensions rapidly followed. *Le Censeur* stopped publication in June 1849, after three court cases. The Conseil de Guerre handed down sentences of two years and two months to the directors of *Le Républicain de Lyon,* who accused General Bugeaud of "dreaming of the destruction of Lyon and the massacre of its inhabitants . . . [and] wanting to march on Paris after having ravaged Lyon and return[ed] the monarchy on the heap of cadavers and ruins."[34]

In April 1850, the Lyon socialists organized a "bargain" newspaper, to discuss "the social question" and—the paper was undoubtedly linked to Lyon's three consumers' cooperatives—to assist the workers in the exercise of political rights. This "vast association to create socialism," according to the prefect, intended to begin publication when 12,500 one-franc shares had been sold in the workshops of the Croix Rousse and La Guillotière. General Castellane thwarted this effort. Finally, with *L'Écho de la fabrique* suspended in 1850 for publishing the "very worst doctrines of the organization of work," *La Tribune lyon-*

naise stepped forward, declaring itself a monthly in order to avoid paying caution money. Despite the fact that it dubbed itself a "review of social economy, of industry, literature, science and the arts," *La Tribune's* discussion of the social economy necessarily involved political considerations and the newspaper was banned.[35]

The repression, although not completed until the coup, took a heavy toll of the press of the extreme left. *L'Égalité* of Auch was confiscated five times within a three-month period and bowed out with huge black letters which proclaimed, "Long live the freedom of the press, which kills tyrants." *Le Peuple* (Nevers) succumbed after five trials in five months. Over forty montagnard papers were forced out of publication in provincial France.[36] When the editor of *Le Travail* (Dijon) "tried everything" to raise publication money after being fined 3,000 francs, the procureur général ordered his immediate imprisonment for six months, closing the paper in August 1850. With *La Tribune de Jura* finished and *Le Peuple de l'Est* stillborn for lack of a printer, the magistrate's colleague in Besançon could report that "there no longer exists a single demagogic journal in the three departments of this region and the most perfect tranquillity reigns everywhere." Some papers changed their names (*L'Événement* to *L'Avènement*, *Le Franc-parleur de 1850* to *Le Franc-parleur de la Meuse*, etc.) and submitted new declarations to clean their slates.[37] Some organizational continuity could be maintained, because the editors and directors of defunct papers tried again, but not without disruptions of publication and enormous expense. Editors tempered their rhetoric and became more veiled in their attacks on the administration. Occasional blank spots appearing in columns indicated to readers that something had been censored or prudently withdrawn. Only a very few papers managed to escape conviction. Symbolically, two directors of *Le Siècle*, two of *La Presse*, two editors of *L'Événement*, and two journalist sons of Victor Hugo were among the political prisoners in the Concièrgerie in 1851.[38]

And yet some important montagnard papers survived, such as *L'Ami du peuple* of Auch, which somehow withstood eight confiscations and eleven prosecutions in three years. Despite some failures, a number of montagnard papers (*Le Démocrate de Loir-et-Cher*, for one) were begun in 1851, anticipating the elections of 1852 and what they hoped would be a return to the freedom of the press characteristic of the spring of 1848. "The work of social demoralization continues . . . the press feeds and nourishes the hate of the lower class for everyone above them," reported one procureur. The number of papers closed after the coup, though not all were démoc-soc, evidenced the durability of the montagnard press (*Le Républicain de la Moselle*, *Le Républicain alsacien*, *Volksrepublik*, *Le Travailleur de l'Allier et de la Creuse*, *La Constitution de l'Allier*, etc.).[39]

As the coup approached and was rumored, feared, and expected, *La Tribune de la Gironde* continued to protest the destruction of the institutions of the republic, despite a 20,000-franc fine. Four articles from the constitution (1, 4, 25, and 110) appeared at the top of each edition, despite the efforts of the procureur of Bordeaux to prevent this seemingly perfect protest. The extension of the state of siege to all of France with the coup d'état of December 2, 1851, resolved the situation. Over seventy journals were suspended, including *La Tribune*, *Le Démocrate de Vaucluse*, and *Le Messager du Nord*, and the other montagnard papers could never again find legal loopholes through which to attack authoritarian government. The free political press was finished off with one inevitable thrust.[40] The year 1852 marked the return of almost all press legislation passed since the beginning of the restoration, eliminating jury trial for political offenses, raising the stamp tax, granting prefects the power to suspend newspapers without authorization from Paris and, most significantly, banning any discussion of the "political or social economy."[41]

Seemingly "incessant, mysterious, and almost unseizable" political pamphlets, brochures, almanacs, engravings, printed songs, and even Montagnard "catechisms" constituted at least half of the problem posed by written démoc-soc propaganda, particularly in the countryside.[42] "Here as in Paris," complained the procureur in Aix before the May 1849 elections, "we are inundated with [Pierre] Joigneaux and the anarchic writings."[43] Montagnard propaganda flooded the countryside, moving along normal routes of communication and transportation, disseminated by hawkers and peddlers, political activists, and ordinary people. Astonishing numbers of political brochures turned up in every corner of France. Three thousand copies of one "call to revolt" were confiscated in Strasbourg.[44] One of Eugène Sue's brochures sold perhaps a million copies. A twenty-one-page brochure, Malardier's *The Gospel and the Republic or the Social Mission of Schoolteachers*, another best-seller, informed readers and listeners that whereas the struggle of 1789 was between the people and the coalition of nobility and clergy, "today the struggle is between the bourgeoisie and the people." The songs of Baudelaire's friend Pierre Dupont added a political dimension to village and group songfests. Approximately 60,000 copies of some brochures circulated in the Dordogne; other pamphlets with only local appeal, such as *Reflections of a Good Villager from Picardie to his Fellow Citizens*, had a much more limited printing.[45]

Montagnard propaganda in provincial France was directed toward the laboring poor, particularly the peasants. Sue's *La Républicaine des campagnes*, which appeared in four editions after the revolution, began with political basics, explaining the republic, elections, and the "right to work" before moving subtly into a discussion of montagnard ideology and specific reforms with popular appeal, including the progressive tax, the abolition of the salt tax, free education, agricultural schools, a schoolteacher in every commune, and others. A printed version of Félix Pyat's toast at a banquet commemorating the revolution one year earlier was widely distributed in rural areas:

> To the men of the soil, these true sons of the earth, to the most numerous, the poorest, the most patient of our fellow citizens . . . It is, indeed, the peasant who cultivates the earth, who fertilizes it with his sweat; he nourishes the people, he produces bread and wine . . . and defends the earth. Oh! He who saved the country should be called peasant!

> As for their seigneurs and masters, as for those who call
> others 'peasants,' they are correct. They are not worthy to
> be called peasant. They do not merit it; they do not have
> the right to the name. They are not peasants, to the contrary,
> these people are, as Homer once said, the useless burden of
> the earth.[46]

Joigneaux, a representative of the Côte d'or, was the master
propandist in the countryside. An early Blanquist and Babou-
vist who had been jailed in 1839 for participation in a secret
society (Homme libre), he became a populist during the Second
Republic.[47] One of his speeches, given in April 1849, had *narod-
niki* overtones, stressing as it did the natural organization of the
village unit as an "association" benefiting all of its members.
For Joigneaux, the democratic and social republic would be the
extension of the best of what he believed the peasants already had,
natural association and harmony, based upon an essential de
facto equality. Unlike Cabet and other utopians who believed the
community of equals would be reached through an organized
retreat or withdrawal from corrupt bourgeois society and unequal
economic and social relationships, Joigneaux, like the later
Russian populists, thought he had discovered it in the village.

Joigneaux's newspaper, *La Feuille du village*, was the most
influential propaganda organ in rural France, the subject of
countless official complaints and reports in seemingly every
canton. First appearing on October 25, 1849, *La Feuille*'s origins
reflected the impact of the repression on the peddling of political
pamphlets and brochures:

> Because we no longer can have hawkers and peddlers in the
> service of our ideas, we will make use of the postal system to
> reach people's homes. The goal which the political brochure
> cannot attain, the newspaper perhaps will. For this reason
> we founded *La Feuille du village*.

With the ambitious goal of "enlightening the inhabitants of the
countryside on their true interests, to make them understand the
cause of their misery . . . and to blaze the trail which should lead
them straight to the great day of deliverance," the content of *La*

Feuille's editorials typified the irregular political pamphlets and brochures that sought to awaken Jacques Bonhomme. They were concerned with pasturage rights, the drink and salt taxes, the plight of rural schoolteachers, and the promise of universal suffrage. The serials or feuilletons, for the most part written by a locksmith, preached in a particularly didactic, almost condescending fashion: "The Popular Devotions," "The Priest and the Farmer," "Still the Salt Tax?" and "Biographies of Obscure Men." With an eye toward improving living conditions in the countryside, *La Feuille* included various "how to" articles, news of agriculture, and notices of fairs and markets.

In August 1850, Joigneaux and his paper went on trial. After a conviction brought a jail sentence of six months and 2,000 francs in fines, the administration raised the caution money from 12,000 francs to 20,000. *La Feuille* ceased publication, and, although it returned shortly thereafter with offices in Paris and Troyes, it survived only until February 1851.[48]

With the assistance of Mathieu de la Drôme, Agricol Perdiguier, and four other montagnard representatives, Joigneaux undertook a new project. The result was one of the most successful political almanacs of the republican period. *Le Almanach du village pour 1852* adopted the format of the "official" departmental almanac, which listed market days, feast days, the times of the rising and setting of the sun, and so on. Relatively inexpensive at fifty centimes, the *Almanach du village* offered brief didactic dialogues, usually written by Mathieu de la Drôme. These "conversations" harped on indirect taxes, the affection of montagnard representatives for peasants, and the approaching elections. Several brief examples are worth citing. "The Story of Jacques Bonhomme called Père-aux-Guêtres, or the Republicans under the Republic" included this passage: "Do you now understand your role, the extent of your power? You hold the destinies of the world poised on the electoral urn of 1852. . . . Reread together the advice of Père Mathieu, of Joigneaux, and your other friends. Keep away from police spies, they are everywhere." "Two Farmers" contained an attack on usury and indirect taxes, which kept the peasant in misery: M. Simon, "The tax is the safeguard of society, and is beneficial even in excess! Big taxes keep the peace!" M. Pascal: "But they wipe everyone out!" M. Simon: "Your doctrines are subversive, M. Pascal. It is not good to stir up everyone and aggravate the evil passions. I want peace. I am of the great party of order." Agricol Perdiguier urged peasants not "to brawl" but to unify: "Use your leisure time to study . . . to propagate the new idea. Be the friends, apostles, defenders of the Republic." Joigneaux warned against disease from smoke in industrial towns and discussed ways to care for vegetables and to can fruit ("Oh, yes, M. Mathieu, it is a good thing to know how to preserve pears and winter apples, it is a good thing to know also how to pack fruit when one wants to send it far by railroad! My boy, it's as easy as pie. You prepare a chest with a hinge. . . . ").[49]

November 1849 marked the beginning of more systematic surveillance of such irregular propaganda, which was subject to the same laws as the periodic press.[50] Once again, prosecutors had plenty of laws on which to base their cases; their problem was to catch the propagandists. Much of the written propaganda originated in the capital, and the dissolution of Solidarité républicaine and the Comité pour la propagande démocratique et sociale in 1850 ended two of the most productive sources. From its tiny office on the rue Montmartre, the Solidarité républicaine had enrolled affiliates in many towns.[51] In 1851 the secret press of the Comité de résistance, linked to Greppo and Faure, was finally discovered on the rue Madame after sending its "Tenth Bulletin" into the provinces.[52]

However, most propaganda was not so systematically organized and could not be traced to a single origin. Officials therefore used other means of pressure, including many of the same methods used to silence the periodic press. In this effort, too, the government withdrew printers' licenses. A Le Mans printer was driven from business by a fine of 2,000 francs in March 1850 because of "the numerous socialist writings coming off his presses" which turned up in small villages in the Sarthe. The procureur had reported that if this printer's license were to be withdrawn, "the political arsenal of the socialist party of Le Mans [would fall]."[53] A man from Thiers was fined for printing Pyat's much-traveled *To the Peasants*, which was read by and to Auvergnat peasants, and an application for a printer's license in the Ain was rejected because the prefect did not want another printer in such a "perverted" department.[54]

The authors of pamphlets, songs, and brochures, like newspaper editors, could be prosecuted if what they wrote was deemed politically or socially inflammatory. Prosecutors could bring to trial any material smacking of radical politics. Typical examples include Frédéric DeGeorge's *The Crux of the Situation*, which suggested a tax on the rich (thereby contributing to class "envy") and a brochure distributed in the Haute Saône which asked, "Why do we have the Republic and misery?"[55] Pamphlets like *Democratic ABC*, *The Pope before Christ*, Greppo's *Social Catechism*, and Proudhon's *What Is Property?* were classic examples of material considered capable of "inciting one group of citizens against another." The brochure *Violation of the Constitution* represented an obvious attack on the government of Louis Napoleon. The song "Le Lyonnais" could be declared "an apology for criminal acts," that is, the insurrections of 1831, 1834, and 1849. Engravings of Greppo, Barbès, Blanqui, and other insurrectionaries were banned because they glorified condemned criminals. Thus a "History of the Revolution of 1848" denied the authority of the present government; the popular engraving "Jesus the Montagnard" represented an attack upon religion.[56]

The following newspapers, almanacs, brochures, pamphlets, songs, and engravings were banned under the "state of siege" in the departments of the Lyon region between November 1849 (when the repression seems to have become more systematized) and March 1850. They illustrate several main themes of socialist propaganda circulating in the cities and countryside, most interestingly the continued influence of the utopian socialists, the strong heritage of the Revolution of 1789–99, and the identification of the montagnards with the suffering Christ.[57]

Date Banned	Item Banned
November 1849	*L'Almanach d'un paysan* (Joigneaux)
December 1849	*L'Almanach des cultivateurs et des vignerons* *L'Histoire de la révolution de 1848* *L'Histoire de la convention par le même* *L'Almanach du nouveau monde de Louis Blanc* *L'Almanach phalansterien* *L'Almanach napoléonien* *L'Almanach du peuple* *L'Almanach l'ami du peuple* *Jésus le montagnard* (engraving) *L'Almanach démoc-soc*
January 1850	*L'Almanach des réformateurs* *Le Républicain démocratique* *L'Évangile du peuple* *L'Almanach des associations ouvrières*
February 1850	*Histoire des montagnards* *La Propagande* *Le Populaire* (Cabet) *La République* *Le Démocrate pacifique* *La Terreur blanche* *La Bible des idées nouvelles* *Le Pape devant le Christ* *Galerie des républicains socialistes* *Prêtres et socialistes* *Les Revenantes*
March 1850	"La Lyonnaise" (song) *Le Pape au XIXe siècle* (Mazzini) *Le Prolétaire* *Qu'est-ce que la propriété* (Proudhon) *Le Berger de Kravan* (Eugène Sue) *Jésus Christ devant les conseils de guerre*

Plus d'octrois, plus de droits réunis
Deux Jours de condamnation à mort
(Barbès)

Uncovering secret presses and prosecuting printers was not enough for the authorities, however. Neither printers nor authors regularly distributed propaganda in provincial France; booksellers were increasingly reluctant to handle illegal propaganda.[58] Because propaganda traveled with people on the move, its repression involved monitoring the movements of the common people. Hawkers and peddlers of all kinds frequented the roads of France; they worked the markets and fairs in large towns, bourgs, and hamlets. Some did well enough, but most did not, and their various indiscretions had been manifest during the hard times of 1827–32, 1840–41, and 1846–47. In June 1849, in response to complaints from prefects that peddlers seemed to be "employed in the service of the bad doctrines . . . throwing disorder into people's minds," tougher regulations were enforced.[59] Subsequently, tradesmen were required to have prefectural authorization and notes of good conduct from each town visited. The prefect of Haute Garonne revoked all authorizations for hawking and peddling and examined each one separately. Results were immediate, and by February 1850, the peddling of propaganda had "disappeared" from the Seine Inférieure. The incarceration in Abbeville of three peddlers who had carried petitions against the electoral law had produced "an excellent result."[60]

With the number of people peddling socialist propaganda rapidly diminishing, how did propaganda continue to move in the provinces? At least part of the answer lies in France's relatively high degree of geographic mobility.[61] Radical literature moved with the normal flow of traffic of ordinary people, for example, the artisans whose work took them along fairly regular routes.[62] Seasonal migrants returning from Paris carried the latest brochures and pamphlets.[63] Itinerant musicians moved from market to fair, perpetuating the oral tradition of song and entertainment in the patois. Thus the prefect of the Aude notified his colleague in Toulouse that Guillaume Ambay, a wandering singer and agent of the "socialist" party, arrived in Narbonne, where he spent one month in jail because he had clandestinely distributed "anarchist" songs while wearing a Phrygian cap. The same prefect of Toulouse advised the departmental gendarmerie in July 1851, that "the numerous roads of the department are traveled by a mob of strangers who, under the pretext of selling books or songs, stop in the small towns and contact the enemies of the government and spread democratic and social propaganda."[64] Copies of "Au Dru-Rollin," in Breton were distributed by a cooper from the Finistère; in the Lot a small "plot" that involved the passing around of songs in patois by a schoolteacher and the post office manager was foiled.[65]

Gendarmes watched the usual trade routes, surveying the comings and goings of vagabonds "who sometimes render services to the secret societies," traveling musicians and artisans, and peddlers. One such musician was arrested in the Haute Pyrénées while distributing leaflets and songs with his eight-year-old daughter; police suspected that these "seditious" materials had been obtained in La Guillotière, outside of Lyon, where his sister lived. A "merchant of songs" in Toulouse first sold, then sang seditious songs to a gathering of fifty; when a policeman intervened and attempted to arrest the man, he was "mistreated" by an angry crowd which grew to three hundred. A vagabond carrying "anarchist" letters was stopped in Châlons-sur-Saône, on the main route from Paris to the Midi. Traveling with his domestic, wealthy man who was a montagnard *papa gâteau* (sugar daddy), used his funds to spread propaganda. Rural postmen occasionally helped in the brazen distribution of propaganda through the mails.[66] These examples are merely illustrative; they reflect the fact that democratic socialist propaganda, particularly in 1850 and 1851, was spread by very ordinary people.

The propaganda network in Haute Garonne is particularly well documented. During the summer of 1851, the prefect of Haute Garonne discovered that "from the capital of the department, anarchist propaganda radiates toward its extremities, taking advantage of the naiveté of the masses."[67] *L'Émancipation* reached sympathetic "subversive" soft-drink sellers in the small bourgs free of charge, and in Barbazan, the mayor joined a group who read the paper. Cafés in Muret and Latrap became veritable reading rooms. The police commissioner of Toulouse believed that a central committee of thirty "advanced" members of the workers' associations sent out emissaries who disseminated the Toulouse propaganda and press. He provided a list of about forty-five names "to add to the red collection." Artisans were prominent in this network, especially tailors (seven) and shoemakers (nine), who frequented other workshops and even the Toulouse garrison. At least eighty soldiers were accused of "receiving their moral nourishment from brochures and journals."[68]

Although some of the propaganda originated in Toulouse, the police commissioner believed that much of it had arrived from Paris, courtesy of a former police employee, a joiner, and a tailor who had recently visited the capital. Their local contacts included the former director of the shoemakers' association, a saddler named Big Jules, a hatmaker trying to unite the *compagnonnages*, and the secretary of an association of "philanthropic travelers." Other "democrats" who traveled for *L'Émancipation* included a former master shoemaker who, having lost his clientele in Carcassonne because of his politics, became the go-between for socialists in the two cities; a leather merchant who knew Toulouse and its suburbs well; a grocer who traveled to the small villages near Toulouse; the joiner Castilbou, who combined business trips and propaganda; a waiter at the Grand Café of Toulouse, whose job permitted numerous contacts; a printer familiar with the Montauban region; and another Toulouse man with influence in his native village, Carbonne. The authorities alleged that the former prefect, a professor, and a group of lawyers coordinated the seditious acts and intrigue of these more ordinary citizens.[69]

The information provided by the alert commissioner of police, who made the rounds of Toulouse's cafés each day, enabled the prefect to build a collective biography of the chief propagandists in his department. Shoemakers, tailors, and hatmakers seemed the most active; other categories of artisans and workers involved included saddlers, locksmiths, blacksmiths, mechanics, masons, printers, wig makers, tapestry-workers, painters, assorted tradesmen, innkeepers, and café-owners. Toulouse's bourgeois radicals, the sponsors of L'Émancipation, originally provided much of the organization; residents of lesser status did the leg work.[70]

As in the case of the press, the repression of these channels of propaganda was relatively successful. But a certain proportion remained "mysterious and almost unseizable."[71] Searches and seizures had limits. During the summer of 1851, it seemed to officials that more propaganda was circulating than at any time since 1849,[72] and montagnard papers, brochures, pamphlets, and printed songs continued to offer the democratic-socialist alternative until the coup d'état.

3

The Targets: Voluntary Associations

The February revolution, which widened participation in the political process by permitting freedom of the press, also stimulated a proliferation of popular associations by offering freedom of assembly and, by logical extension, freedom of association. Universal suffrage was another political fruit of the democratic republic. At the same time, the "right to work," an 1848 watchword, clearly included the "right to associate" in an economic sense as the extension of the right of popular political assembly; the freedoms of assembly and association were linked in the minds of most republicans as they would be in the minds of the repressors. A placard on the barricade at the porte St. Marceau on June 23, 1848, defined the "democratic and social republic" as "democratic in that all citizens are electors . . . social in that all citizens are permitted to form associations for work."[1] The republic of political justice was only the first step toward a republic of social and economic justice. Workers and their bourgeois allies believed that associations were a peaceful way to transform society and ultimately to resolve the social question—the spirit of the utopians lingered.

But while the revolution spawned great popular faith in the political and economic benefits of association, no guarantee existed that the right to associate freely could be preserved. Associations of ordinary people challenged traditional patterns of hierarchy and deference, and they thoroughly frightened most of the middle class. The "disorder" of popular revolt in 1848 in towns like Limoges and Rouen remained etched in the minds of the men of order just as a generation of bourgeois in Tours, Bordeaux, and Amiens lived in the shadow of the Commune of

51

Paris and its "incendiaries." As Blanqui asserted, "None of the citizens who lived in Paris [in 1848] will ever forget the long processions of workers, who carried sinister placards and seemed pledged to a perpetual strike." [2] The repression was the revenge of a threatened elite and marked a victory of the policy that had characterized the July Monarchy. This containment of popular organization is the theme of this chapter.

The apparently spontaneous turn towards voluntary associations after the revolution of February, as part of the vision of the democratic and social republic and as part of the means of obtaining it, had historical precedent. I. Tchernoff, one of the most perceptive of the early historians of 1848, suggested that the experience of the republicans from 1830 until 1851 had "the purpose and result of conditioning individuals to unify their efforts, to form associations with the most varied goals and objectives." [3] During the 1840s, faith in association was the central theme of the social program of most republicans. Workers hoped that producers' cooperatives would ultimately allow them to gain control of their own trades. [4] The July Monarchy blocked the development of political and economic associations; its law on associations (1834), a catalyst for the insurrection of the Lyon silk workers (*canuts*), reflected the underlying conviction of the social and political elite that most kinds of associations were fundamentally unwholesome. [5] Although the individualistic and familial orientation of the French bourgeoisie in the nineteenth century has been exaggerated, most economic associations, such as the *sociétés anonymes*, which grouped together people unknown to each other, did provoke considerable conservative resistance. Economic associations among workers seemed utopian and dangerous; strikers legally could be guilty of a crime of *coalition*, of organizing. While employers had sometimes even encouraged mutuality because it removed from management all responsibility for the workers' welfare, coalitions or unions whose purpose was to agitate for higher wages or better working conditions were not to be tolerated. Like most of their middle-class constituents, the government viewed workers' associations as little more than the organized extension of seditious gatherings.

Although temporary political associations, such as clubs and electoral organizations, and working-class groupings, such as popular societies and economic associations, were not at all the same thing, the repression did not differentiate between them in its treatment. The Ministry of Justice filed together all documents pertaining to such associations, and they are still grouped together in the National Archives today.[6] Popular organizations were the real targets, and victims, of the repression. The June Days identified the ephemeral Paris clubs and other kinds of popular organization, particularly workers' associations, with social upheaval. The repression of popularly constituted voluntary associations, then, began with the repression of the clubs, and this in turn influenced and hastened the repression of both the freedom of assembly and of association. As Peter Amann demonstrates, the repression of the clubs, "the most conspicuous and most characteristic of ... political institutions ... through which the newly mobilized worked," was probably superfluous. Their accomplishments paled in comparison to their grand goals: they sought to confront the wavering provisional government on behalf of committed republicans, to educate citizens in their civic duties and obligations, and at the same time to work for the election of strong republicans in the April elections.[7] The clubs failed and ultimately disappeared because they "offered no credible answers to the most pressing problems of the day." For the most part, they were a mixed bag of lower and middle class members (although their leaders were largely bourgeois). The clubs, in short, united people who had relatively little in common. Drawing ordinary citizens into the political process, the clubs were visible and noisy, and they received most of the blame for the June Days, although workers' associations were certainly more important in mobilizing the insurgents.[8] The Club of Clubs, an ineffectual grouping of representatives from the Paris clubs, sent delegates to the provinces to influence the departmental elections; there they met with considerable and publicized resistance, because they appeared as intruders from unruly Paris who sought to interfere with local elite politics.[9] Although

they were not legally constituted as associations and were actually
regular public political gatherings, the clubs became the first
associations to feel the impact of the repression. This discouraged
many bourgeois who might not necessarily have been driven into
the arms of the reaction by the June Days. All political gatherings of ordinary people were thereafter suspect, as the repression
first abridged and then eliminated the freedom of assembly. The
assault against more permanent and at least ostensibly apolitical
workers' associations was inevitable.

In the wake of the June Days, the decree of July 28 regulated
the clubs. While nominally recognizing the right of assembly,
the decree stipulated that the clubs publicize their meeting,
notify the police twenty-four hours in advance, and allow police
to be present; in addition a résumé of the meeting with a list of
members attending was required. The decree also forbade
affiliations between clubs and banned secret societies. Nonpublic meetings with nonpolitical goals were licit, but if political
matters were discussed, the authorities could consider the
gathering a "secret society" by virtue of its "false declaration"
of legal status.[10]

Some of the clubs, many "under the guise of electoral associations," reappeared as the May 1849 elections approached, four
months after the election of Louis Napoleon Bonaparte as
president.[11] In the Dijon region, the procureur général found that
"the spirit of the working classes, at least in certain arroundisse-
ments, is becoming perverted through the influence of the
clubs."[12] But it was difficult to justify banning political meetings
before the elections. The procureur in Riom caught the essence of
a central contradiction of the republic:

> How are we to consider these meetings, which we recognize
> as the exercise of the right of national sovereignty and
> maintain that their public convocation be illegal? The *goal*
> being legitimate, can the indispensable means to obtain it be
> illegal?[13]

But when Léon Faucher in the spring of 1849 proposed the law
to ban political clubs, he argued that the July decree had not

been effective, because the disruptive influence of the old clubs, some of which had formally or informally been reconstituted, had continued unabated: "[Seditious] doctrines are openly preached there, as are antisocial passions which tend to dissolve [the bonds of] society. Hate and disharmony are sown between citizens".[14] An annually renewable law banning clubs passed in June 1849 permitted advertised political meetings before elections, but amendments in 1850 eliminated the twenty-day period before elections during which political meetings could be held without official authorization. Most important, the original law stipulated that *any* meeting or gathering which "might compromise the public peace" could be prevented in the name of public order, allowing local officials considerable leeway. The minister of justice interpreted the law to forbid "clubs or public meetings in which public affairs are discussed," establishing its application over the next two years.[15]

Existing legislation also supported interference with political gatherings. The police presence remained an effective restraint on public meetings of any kind, since any speaker could be arrested. Applied to public statements or speeches, an article of the penal code which made it illegal to incite hatred among citizens proved useful. To cite but one example, an Orléans musician was prosecuted for having shouted, at an electoral meeting, "Down with the taxes, down with the aristos!"[16]

Policemen became uninvited but unavoidable guests at political gatherings, which were legal if they did not meet regularly (as clubs did, for example,) and if their purpose was preparation for the elections. Two examples, while drawn from club sessions that took place shortly before clubs were banned, illustrate the impact the police could have at any political gathering. When the Club de la salle Notre Dame met in St. Quentin (Nord) in June 1849, its president first read the minutes from the previous meeting and excerpts from *La Révolution démocratique et sociale*. The club voted to present an address to the montagnard representatives, and a short talk on the theory of socialism followed in which the speaker divided society into three classes (the necessary, the necessary and useful, and the necessary, the useful, and the pleasant). The next speaker presented a discourse on the outbreak of cholera. A Monsieur Ducré passionately attacked the Roman expedition and remarked in so doing that if the constitution were violated, it would not be by the "reds" as people once claimed, but by Louis Napoleon, "no longer our president." The police commissioner jumped to his feet and demanded that the speaker's exact words be included in the record of the meeting. The speaker vainly tried to justify his words, igniting a furious debate, followed by a more reasoned discussion on the response of the St. Quentin National Guard to any threat to the constitution. When the minister of justice read the police report on the meeting, he marked the offense "flagrant" and ordered the club closed, just days before the club law passed.[17]

A few months earlier, in February 1849, police had observed a similar meeting of the three hundred members of the Club du salon d'Idalie in Châlons. Club officials read excerpts from montagnard papers and attacked a local "so-called society of order." When a member presented a stirring account of the workers' poverty in Lille, Mulhouse, and Lyon, someone shouted from the audience, "We will avenge them!" The commissioner of police rose and demanded that the remark be entered on the legal record of the meeting. The session ended in chaos with cries of "Long live the republic!" The club was closed, reconstituted briefly under another name, and lasted until the club law of June 1849.[18]

The presence of police, the risk of legal liability for any public statement deemed inflammatory, and the club law were effective restraints on all public political meetings during the republic. At least 110 political meetings and 74 banquets were prevented from taking place between June 19, 1850, and May 5 of the following year. Minister of the Interior Faucher cited the Gironde as an example of a department he did not include in his statistics because the repression had been so successful in 1849 and the first half of 1850, when far more gatherings were attempted and prevented, indicating the club law's effectiveness. He also reported the ominous fact that the repression had been particularly efficient in departments placed under the state of siege.[19] With public political meetings considered "improvised clubs" during the duration of the republic, political organization was forced underground. The freedoms of assembly and political association were curtailed even before the law restricting universal suffrage (May 31, 1850) marked the end of any pretense of a "democratic republic."

Clubs and electoral organizations were temporary associations of ordinary people for political purposes. If, according to Peter Amann, the club movement was characteristic of "societies in transition" before mass organization took root, the rapid proliferation of ostensibly permanent and nonpolitical voluntary associations after the revolution seems typical of more modern or at least more contemporary forms of social organization in which such associations, even (and especially) those that are nominally apolitical, act as political pressure groups.[20]

Maurice Agulhon's masterful study of the Var facilitates understanding of how voluntary associations developed in nineteenth-century France, although the subject is tremendously complex and strong regional variations have a tendency to shatter the boldest generalizations. The Var chambrée, patterned after the bourgeois circle (cercle), lodge, and religious confraternity ("sociability by popular imitation") developed during the first half of the century in Provence. Here, ordinary people could go to "chat, drink, play cards ... for the humble Provençal people to join together in a chambrée was, at this time, much more than to learn to read; it was to expose themselves to what was new, to progress [mouvement], to independence."[21] Chambrées, whether their members were artisans, property-owners, poor peasants, or practitioners of diverse occupations, became centers of montagnard political activity. "All of the chambrées," wrote the procureur général of Aix in April 1849, "now only occupy themselves with the so-called socialist politics."[22] Through the combination of the ideological patronage of the radical bourgeoisie and the social and economic antagonism between communities and notables in the Var, politics in the department were transformed from a vertical arrangement (with a monarchist tendency) to a horizontal and basically egalitarian process in which popular associations were instrumental in bringing the "republic to the village."[23]

While such "sociability" was certainly not unique to the Midi (consider, for example, the "carnival societies" in the Nord), here the development and politicization of popular societies and their part in the "descent of politics towards the masses" was most marked. But before discussing popular societies, circles, and associations in the Second Republic and their repression, we should know something about the heritage of the traditional circle.

The circle, in its traditional form, was bourgeois. The Cercle de la ville, the Salon littéraire, and the Salon St. Pierre of Castelnaudary (Aude), where the elite gathered to "consume beer and coffee . . . read journals . . . and play the games of society" were typical. High fees and selective membership policies maintained their social exclusiveness, which was part of the rationale for their creation:

> The detestable clientele of cafés generally frequented by people of at best doubtful education led to the creation of these circles where one can gather, even today [1850], with most of the public officials and honorable citizens.[24]

Similar gatherings could be found in the other main towns of the Aude, such as the Cercle littéraire and the Société St. Roch in Limoux (one religious, the other philanthropic) and the Cercle philanthropique in Narbonne whose members paid fifty francs per year in dues. Many of these gatherings were quite old. The Salon Panissars of Villefranche (Aveyron) was established either in the year VIII or X (no one could remember); its 120 members paid fifteen francs per year and gathered to read and discuss books. The Cercle d'Espalion (Aveyron), founded in 1822 and officially authorized two years later, subscribed to newspapers and included twenty-five local officials; similarly constituted, a circle in nearby St. Genez met at the town hall.[25]

In 1849–51, few of these traditional circles seemed politically dangerous to the government. Their elite membership ordinarily guaranteed their conservatism, and the administration rarely dissolved them. Exceptions were those dominated by the socialist "men of envy" and those accused of "corrupting the poor people of the vicinity."[26] Like traditional circles, Masonic lodges were cited only rarely for "occupying themselves with the malevolent goal of political matters." Again, their almost exclusively middle-class membership guaranteed good behavior. By long-standing agreement between the grand orient and the minister of interior, they were immune from police surveillance, although lodges could be asked to list their members and the purposes of each meeting. Masonic lodges were dissolved only when they became the regular meeting places for local radicals, as they did in Limoges, Joigny, Moissac, Condom, Reims, and Château-Thierry.[27] But these were exceptions. Bourgeois associations rarely challenged the economic, social and political hegemony of the men of order—rather, they embodied that "order." From the administration's point of view, the danger lay in associations which grouped ordinary people for nontraditional goals.

Four kinds of associations, despite their somewhat different origins and antecedents, were often indistinguishable focuses of collective political action by ordinary Frenchmen during the Second Republic: (1) popular societies, circles, and chambrées, which developed as imitations of the traditional bourgeois circles; (2) traditional mutual-aid socieites; (3) producers' cooperatives, the most ambitious and significant workers' associations, which hoped to substitute working-class control over production for the direction of the bosses; and (4) consumers' cooperatives, which were similar to and sometimes overlapped with producers' cooperatives. Cooperative movements, such as the *associations pour la vie à bon marché* begun in Grenoble, Lille, Puy, Rouen, Clermont, Nantes, Lyon, Metz, Reims, St. Quentin, the Aisne, and the Somme, seemed to provide a starting point for the total organization of the working class.[28] It was often impossible to separate mutual-aid societies from more ambitious working-class associations because mutualism was a foundation upon which the greater dreams and organizational hopes of both were built. Likewise it makes little sense to try strictly to separate mutual-aid societies, popular societies, circles, and chambrées. Some circles and popular societies provided for mutual aid or at least had the tradition of such help (in fact, some were called *sociétés philanthropiques*); chambrées could use their funds for mutual assistance.[29]

The proliferation of popular associations was most spectacular in the Midi during the Second Republic. Although nonpolitical private associations did not require official authorization after the July decree, they did have to submit their statutes to prove that they were nonpolitical. Recreational gatherings of ordinary people which had regularly occurred for years often took names and were legally constituted, many taking an identification as cercles, a name usually reserved for exclusively bourgeois gatherings. At the same time, legitimists and some men of order countered the formation of politically radical circles and societies with their own associations. In the legitimist stronghold of the canton of Uzès (Gard), all of the circles and societies were constituted during the republic. Likewise, in Vigan, four of the five circles dated from after the revolution; only the Loge viganais, whose eighty members included local officials, dated back "a long time." In the canton of St. Hippolyte, where there were no circles or societies before February 1848, the Cercle des travailleurs (linked to several montagnard gatherings of the same name) began meeting in cafés as a mutual-aid society of 450 members "from the lower ranks of the population." Two opposing groups were formed, the Cercle démocratique with 190 members and a legitimist Association de secours mutuelles with 117 members of "all professions."[30]

Some, but not all, societies and circles were registered as mutual-aid societies. For example, of the fifteen associations in the arrondissement of Lodève (Hérault), nine were circles with ostensibly recreational functions, and six were philanthropic societies. In some areas, the fraternal associations seemed to be the least politically inspired; but in Prades (Pyrénées Orientales), the "good fathers of family" were affiliated with the societies while the "bad workers without a future" joined the Union humanitaire and the Association philanthropique.[31] Prefects compiled figures on the approximate strengths of the societies

Table 3.1   Vaucluse: Political Tendencies of Circles and Societies

Arrondissement	Socialist	Legitimist	Moderate Republican	Men of Order*
Apt	48	0	0	33
Avignon	11(1)†	8(1)	1	5
Carpentras	3(1)	1(1)	0	1
Orange	0	1	0	3
Total	62(2)	10(2)	1	42

SOURCE: AN BB³⁰ 391, report of the procureur général of Nîmes, February 3, 1851

*Men of Order includes not only active antisocialist groups but also those which were basically nonpolitical.

†Figures in parentheses are groups that had already dissolved by the end of 1850.

and circles in their department. Table 3.1 gives the findings of the prefect of the Vaucluse, where both legitimists and montagnards were strong.

Religion had a significant influence in some regions of the Midi. Some societies, such as those of the Lot-et-Garonne, were religiously inspired. The politics and constitution of popular societies reflected religious divisions—in the Gard and Vaucluse, for example, the montagnards challenged the domination of the Catholic legitimist notables. Although the relationship between religion and radicalism in the Midi warrants considerably more study, Table 3.2 provides some insight into the role of religious differences in social and political conflict in one case—the Gard. Divided between Catholics and Protestants with bitter memories of the White Terror of 1795 and 1815, the Gard also illustrates the impact of the revolution on voluntary associations.

Many popular societies and circles were dissolved by prefectural decree during the republic. Prefects in the Midi signed over two hundred such decrees, affecting chambrées in the Bouches-du-Rhône, Var, and Vaucluse.³² The Cercle démocratique of Mazamet (Tarn) provides an example of a popular association dissolved for its political activism. Founded in 1848, its members

Table 3.2   Circles and Societies in the Cantons of Aiguemortes,
Aramon, and Beaucaire, Arrondissement of Nimes
(Gard, 1850)

Canton	Commune	Circles and Societies and Their Politics	Characteristics
Aiguemortes	Aiguemortes	2 "of order," both nonpolitical	One composed of artisans, the other of the "most wealthy and honorable" people.
Aiguemortes	St. Laurent	1 of order	Five years old.
Aramon	Aramon	1 socialist	200 artisans and farmers, mutual-aid society known to legitimists as "Montagne"; dissolved after coup.
		1 legitimist	The largest, bourgeois and farmers.
		1 of order	Bourgeois only, twenty years in existence.
		1 presumed socialist	La Vraie Fraternité; 150 artisans and peasants.
Aramon	Montfrin	2 legitimist	Includes the Cercle dit du jardin of the "richest" citizens, politics forbidden.
		1 socialist	Cercle démocratique, mutual-aid society with 400 members, known as "Montagne" and closed in November 1850.

Aramon	Vallabrègues	1 socialist 1 legitimist	Cercle démocratique, dissolved in November 1850.
Aramon	Comps	1 socialist	Cercle démocratique, few members, little influence.
Beaucaire	Beaucaire	8 socialist	All mutual-aid societies whose members paid one franc per month. The most "dangerous" were the Grande Montagne and the Petite Montagne, founded in 1848–49; other 6 named for saints, "more or less democratic" with between 20 and 100 members.
		1 of order	Mixed legitimist and other "conservatives"; 120 members.
		1 legitimist	Concorde, 90–100 young legitimists involved in troubles in Beaucaire, January 1850.

SOURCE: AN BB³⁰ 391, Report of the Procureur général of Nîmes, February 3, 1851. Excludes the communes of Jonquières and Fourgues in the canton of Beaucaire.

gathered each day to read newspapers, a traditional leisure activity in the bourgeois circle. However, the newspapers were *La Réforme* and *Le Peuple*, and the circle was connected to another of the same name in Albi, although the latter was soon closed because of its efforts on behalf of the montagnards. Mazamet's population of 10,000 included almost 6,000 workers, and the circle's leaders claimed to speak "in the name of the so-called interests of the people and [to] have found a following as devoted as it is intelligent."[33] Other groups dissolved included the Cercle de la solidarité démocratique of Blois (November 1849) and a society, organized by two doctors and a school-teacher in St. Savienien (Charente Inférieure), whose goal was "reading and instruction a practical course in geometry in the image of the world." The "image of the world," however, turned out to be that of *La Feuille du village* and *La Réforme*, read publicly before the members sang political songs.[34]

This repression drove the montagnard organization under-ground. Secret oaths pledging allegiance to the "democratic and social republic" replaced association statutes registered at the prefecture. Agulhon's description of this evolution from "above board" popular organization to conspiracy in Le Luc is illustrative of a process that took place in at least seventeen departments:

> ... the associations were engaged in almost daily struggles. The era of the clubs was followed by the age of the chambrées, little private groups engaged in political discussion and the collective reading of newspapers, as the law actually forbade true clubs of the 1848 variety. Of course, when the authorities had proof that the chambrée had exceeded per-missible limits, they dissolved it, but the chambristes had only to regroup under another name, until the next time. This little war went on throughout 1850.
>
> Then, when the worsening political situation forced the democrats to act together more efficiently and discreetly, the chambrées were succeeded by secret societies.[35]

Although the repression failed to prevent the largest national insurrection in nineteenth-century France—the resistance to the coup d'état of December 2, 1851—it probably prevented an uprising of even greater proportions by severing the organizational links which maintained montagnard commitment.[36]

Another form of popular organization, the traditional mutual-aid society, also held an important place, as "the practical application of socialism," in the workers' view of the democratic and social republic.[37] The evolution of mutual-aid societies during the July Monarchy was an important stage in the development of working-class organization. There were 262 mutual-aid societies in Paris in 1846; during the Second Republic, there were 348. In Lyon there were 114; and in some of France's most industrialized departments the number ranged from 225 in the Gironde to 54 in Loire Inférieure, with Nord (over 40,000 members), Haute Garonne, Bas Rhin, Tarn, Var, Tarn-et-Garonne, and Isère, and Loire Inférieure ranking in descending order between the two extremes. But the impact of the revolution can be even more clearly seen in the rapid increase, from 1848 to 1850, of such associations in (again, in descending order of the rate of increase) the Lot-et-Garonne, Dordogne, Drôme, Loir-et-Cher, Gard, Charente Inférieure, Landes, Hérault, Pas-de-Calais, Oise, and Seine Inférieure. The procureur général of Bourges complained of the "organization of the working class into groups that multiply under the name of fraternal societies."[38]

The new mutual-aid societies tended to be more politically active than those extablished during the July Monarchy; perhaps some, like a Société fraternelle in the Haute Loire, were actually continuations of clubs begun after the revolution. Of the twenty-seven mutual-aid societies in the Gard in 1850, only ten predated the revolution. The procureur général of Montpellier divided the seven traditional societies in the arrondissement of Lodève (Hérault) from the "false" mutual-aid societies, which, although ostensibly philanthropic, actually seemed to "mask socialist politics." Among the traditional societies were those of the weavers, the textile workers, and the former soldiers of Lodève, all begun between 1828 and 1837, and three others in Clermont ("workers of the land," former soldiers, and a "society of elders" which split bitterly over Second Republic politics). Those societies that were judged to be "masking politics" included the Société des fileurs (1835) of Lodève, and another, more typical of the Second Republic, founded in June 1848, whose members could be found in either of two cafés in Lodève and who were suspected of having political connections with other socialists in the Hérault. In nearby Clermont, 150 "socialists" belonged to a philanthropic Société des cadets.[39]

Outside of the Midi, where mutual-aid societies and other popularly constituted circles and societies were sometimes indistinguishable, relatively few mutual-aid societies were dissolved except in the Saône-et-Loire and Cher. Authorized as nonpolitical and nonpublic associations, officials had to catch them *en flagrant délit*; for example, reading newspapers at their meetings or, like the Bienfaisance mutuelle of Lectoure, passing around a petition opposing the law of May 31, 1850. The Société des amis réunis of Rochefort (Charente Inférieure) was dissolved because "most of the members of the association [begun in April 1849] were known for the fanaticism of their political principles; to leave them with a means of gathering is to favor this sort of a club rather than the work of charity."[40] Other notable dissolutions took place in Paris, Caen, Tourcoing, Roubaix, and the Haute Marne (where twenty-two workers' associations had over two thousand members). In January 1851, imposition of the state of siege meant that all fraternal associations were banned in the Rhône, Ain, Drôme, Saône-et-Loire, and Jura.[41]

However, while the politics of their members could be "of the worst," mutual-aid societies were less dangerous than the more ambitious workers' associations; mutuality per se did not challenge the separation of capital and labor in nineteenth-century France. Workers' associations with wider goals felt the weight of the repression more heavily. Such societies, asserted the prefect of the Rhône, "are founded on the principle of association; their goal is to substitute the workers themselves, organized into societies, for the boss, the master, and the entrepreneur."[42] By the time of the February revolution, as already mentioned, the

Paris workers, among others, assumed that the "right to work" included the right to organize, with the active cooperation and even the support of the new government. This understanding of the "right to work" was, of course, ultimately the result of the evolution of the social question during the last twenty years. During the July Monarchy, workers came to view association as the "way to end exploitation by capitalist owners of the means of production." By 1834, members of the Society of the Rights of Man believed that "the essential duty of the republic will be to furnish the proletarians with the means of forming themselves into cooperative associations and exploiting their industry themselves."[43] This faith in association came to characterize the social vision of republicans,[44] and it was already an essential part of the workers' collective mentality by the time of the revolution and the economic crisis which ensued.[45] The July allocation of 3 million francs for industrial associations, a measure passed by the moderate republicans as "an alternative to violence," heightened the government's preoccupation with workers' associations. "The revolution of February has given birth to hopes which have not been realized," stated the new Lyon Association fraternelle de l'industrie française, "the workers [travailleurs] have looked among themselves for a solution to their problems . . . they have found it in the association."[46] The repression, administered on behalf of the men of order, was the reaction of conservatives, particularly the bourgeoisie, to the fact that the working class had become contenders for political power.

So many associations (586) requested funds from the grant that a form letter was prepared to speed up official responses. Paris, as always, profited the most, although the 76 beneficiaries represented a wide geographic distribution.[47] The division of the funds received by the Société des forges et fonderies d'Arcachon (Gironde) was typical: 10 percent for the assistance fund (which again shows the importance of the heritage of mutuality), 30 percent for reserve funds, 40 percent to be divided by the members as salaries, and 10 percent permanent reserve.[48] In Paris alone, about 300 such associations involving 120 trades and approximately 50,000 members were started during the four years of the republic.[49] Most were victims not so much of the repression as the refusal of the government to provide necessary follow-up aid, particularly during the economic crisis. Official support vanished, at least partially as a result of the faltering economy, and only a handful of requests for aid were granted in 1849. Perhaps even more important, these associations lacked the required experience, tradition, managerial skills, credit, and customers.[50]

Among the most novel and threatening workers' associations were those first established as consumers' cooperatives. They cut across trade distinctions and espoused far-reaching goals. Ultimately, the most ambitious combined mutual-aid societies, producers' cooperatives, and consumers' cooperatives. While the consumers cooperatives were not usually treated as harshly as producers' cooperatives during the republic, the most success-ful were dealt with severely because, embracing mutuality and cooperative production, they threatened to become all-encom-passing working-class organizations. Their most aggressive spokesmen hoped to associate all workers in all trades and to solve the social question by the implementation of worker control over production, consumption, and protection. The most prom-ising consumers' cooperatives were begun in Lyon, Reims, and Nantes; their experience, confident enthusiasm and organization followed by repression and failure, typified the fate of the most successful montagnard-dominated voluntary associations.

The procureur général of Lyon blamed the infatuation of its workers with the principle of association on "the theories so imprudently advocated by the Luxembourg Commission" and the "spread of the economic utopias of Louis Blanc and Proud-hon."[51] Actually, although the Lyon commission studying the organization of work, which received funds from the depart-mental general council, seemed to have influenced the workers, the most salient influence was twenty years of militancy and collective organization.[52]

Early in 1849, three associations were founded which "hoped for political miracles through the principles of association":

the Société des travailleurs unis, the Association fraternelle de l'industrie française and the smaller and less successful Association démocratique des industries réunis. Aspiring to establish the "philosophical basis of socialism" by bringing "production and consumption into harmony," society members purchased *actions* or shares at one franc, and the societies opened a total of nine "fraternal" stores in Lyon, the Croix Rousse, and La Guillotière, which sold wood, coal, bread, groceries, and household items to members at relatively low prices. The societies issued notes (*billets d'échange*) redeemable in merchandise, thus obtaining credit from their suppliers, and their shareholders bought other notes issued by the society, providing another source of funds. The members were to meet each year to elect a board of directors composed of representatives from each participating industry. Each society maintained a mutual-aid fund and paid store employees three francs a day. The first two associations maintained sizable inventories of considerable value, while their liquid funds were relatively limited. The third association, which operated a "democratic café," survived, it appears, only through loans from its founders and share holders.[53]

Local officials viewed these innovations with considerable alarm; if the social funds and capital doubled or tripled, they reasoned, "serious damage to rival industries" of the patronat would result. The Lyon associations appeared to be "nothing less than the realization of socialism," particularly as they did not make distinctions between the various trades. The Société des travailleurs unis was viewed as "putting into practice the maxims of communism which are the most hostile to property," because profits were not divided among the shareholders, but reinvested. A similar association of shoemakers and bootmakers was accused of being a "political association," because its statutes included the phrase "we are far away from the idea of an annual sharing of profits." These associations, so it was reasoned, could not be serious commercial enterprises; they had merely borrowed the organizational structure from legitimate bourgeois commercial associations.[54] With some of their members compromised by participation in the June 1849 insurrection in Lyon, these consumers' cooperatives were treated as variants of the secret societies in the Lyon region, the Carbonari, Voraces, Society of the Rights of Man, and Mutualists, and they were temporarily closed when Lyon was placed under the state of siege.[55] They did, however, return and they survived the republic.

Surprisingly little has been written concerning the most impressive and significant consumers' cooperative, the Association rémoise, which aspired to spread the principle of association throughout France, uniting workers of different occupations.[56] The association began as a consumers' cooperative with a mutual-aid fund, but it anticipated the development of permanent producers' cooperatives embracing every trade, first in Reims and then in its hinterland. Before succumbing to the repression, it exerted a marked influence in north and northeastern France, in the Marne, Ardennes, Vosges, and Moselle. Its story is worth telling, for its demise represented an important victory for the repression.

The Association rémoise was largely the inspiration of Dr. Agathon Bressy, an oculist who had been an assistant surgeon in Lyon during the 1830s. An active mutualist whose involvement in the insurrections of 1831 and 1834 had led to his exile, Bressy was one of Karl Marx's correspondents during the 1840s. He was called to the capital after the revolution as a surgeon attached to the Republican Guard when his friend Marc Caussidière became prefect of police. Implicated in the journée of May 15 and dismissed from his position, he moved with his family to Reims and assumed a position of influence in the working-class community,[57] where he already had friends among the socialists in one of the strongholds of icarianism.[58]

The industrial structure of Reims, a city with over forty-eight thousand inhabitants, changed in the 1840s as the textile industry was mechanized. Working conditions deteriorated, and wages declined. Most of Reim's three thousand spinners now worked in factories, while approximately seventy five hundred weavers worked in about thirty five hundred shops. There were also about two thousand combers. Wine and champagne production also employed roughly two thousand workers. In the hinterland, almost every village produced some wool; small factories operated in the valleys of the Suippe and Vesle, the traditional home of hand-loom weaving. The economic crisis of 1846–47 worsened the textile workers' already bleak situation.[59]

The Association rémoise, created in October 1848, espoused the ultimate goal, "based upon the principles of solidarity and mutuality," of the "emancipation of the proletariat and the exploitation of work by [the proletarians] themselves." Its Corporations réunis included twenty-one corporations of workers. (Its motto was "union makes force.") In addition to five thousand members who paid an initial fee of fifty centimes and fifteen per week, another five thousand participants belonged as family members, lived outside of Reims, or were "foreign workers." Each corporation elected a coordinating committee of five and two delegates to the central committee, which in turn elected the association's officers.[60]

The association, which was both a mutual-aid society and a consumers' cooperative, purchased coal, oil, and unspecified "colonial foodstuffs." Spokesmen claimed that cooperative purchases and a cooperative bakery (*boulangerie sociétaire*), established in November 1849, resulted in "advantages and notable savings" for the workers. Each corporation of workers was designed to be eventually transformed into a producers' cooperative, although only the weavers and tailors seem to have been able to set up production on their own—it was proudly noted that the products of these tailors were "equal in beauty and in quality" to those of the regular Reims workshops.[61]

The Société rémoise d'assistance fraternelle served as the mutual-aid branch of the association, hiring unemployed workers to do unspecified tasks. All benefits were contingent upon an applicant's acceptance into the fraternal association; according to the statutes, members of the association were to visit the "indigent" regularly and to attest to "their conduct and morality."[62]

Bressy edited the association's newspaper, *L'Association rémoise*. Louis Lecamp, an influential worker, acted as managing

director and the curator of the municipal library, and Eugène
Courmeaux contributed regularly to the paper's columns. Shares
of five hundred francs from each corporation were supposed to
support the paper, but apparently only two corporations were
able to pay, and the paper depended on its more than one
thousand subscribers.[63]

L'Association rémoise propagated the virtues of association,
encouraging all people of the Marne to associate themselves:

> The principle of association applied to us all will give us
> the means to fulfill all the strong desires for order and
> prosperity. Association makes [it possible] for men to
> understand each other, to establish links of union and
> fraternity. Once association reunites men on a neutral
> and common ground, progress will be possible and will
> bring all of the ameliorations which society so urgently
> calls for.[64]

Bressy wrote that "we do not include as workers [travailleurs]
only those [ouvriers] who receive a salary; we include industrialists, manufacturers, merchants, farmers, and intellectuals in the
great family; we urge all of the great social family to help us
[and to] have the workers of the countryside participate in the
benefits that association will spread among us."[65] Bressy thus
outlined a plan for the creation of a vast "association of agricultural workers in all communes of the republic" and urged "small
commerce" to rally around the corporations of workers, warning
them that if they failed, small businesses would quickly suffer
the same fate.[66] Editorials and serials discussed the leading
social and economic issues of the day ("we will point out the
hideous social evils which plague the people"): wages, taxes,
customs barriers, mutual aid, the "right to work," workers'
housing, and conditions within the various industries.[67]

Despite the association's initial avowal that "the politics of
the day will occupy us little" and the central committee's statutes
forbidding political activities, the association could not remain
indifferent to politics. Bressy organized a banquet before the
presidential election and headed the Central Democratic Com-

mittee for the Defense of the Constitution before the May 1849 elections. The association found its choice clear between "royalists, among whom we classify the candidates who will make a profession of faith of devotion to the family of Napoleon, moderate republicans, and republican-socialists." "What is socialism?" Bressy asked, "[but] the formula of application of social reforms, begged for by civilization and by our new political state ... socialism, for us, consists in making those who ought to pay taxes pay them, in organizing industrial and agricultural work in order that the worker [travailleur] shall not perish from hunger and misery."[68] The association supported seven leftist candidates and in the Marne bitterly opposed the candidacy of Léon Faucher, who, they alleged, was supported by the administration and the "great industrialists ... capitalists pretending that [we] will ruin their industry." *L'Association rémoise* was confiscated after printing a particularly sarcastic article on April 15, 1849 professing "profound solicitude" for "capital, [which is] oppressive, exploiting, damaging [and] controlling [our] work." The Association rémoise was considered a political organization of montagnard sympathies and means were sought to destroy it.

The involvement of some association leaders in a disturbance related to the June 1849 movement in Paris provided the procureur général with his opportunity. On the afternoon of June 12, the Central Democratic Committee for the Defense of the Constitution and the workers' corporations had delegated Bressy, Courmeaux, and some others to take a letter to the town hall protesting the Roman expedition. The delegation demanded the suspension of the subprefect, renowned for his hostility to the association, and the recognition of the "democratic and social republic" by the municipal authorities of Reims. By the next day, when the mayor agreed to meet them, news of the repression of the insurrection in Paris had come, and Bressy, although he had been responsible for calming the workers awaiting news from the capital, was arrested with seventeen others. He spent seven months in prison awaiting trial, and the police undertook several searches in the Reims region, hoping to turn up some evidence of a plot,[69] while the managing editor's son continued to publish *L'Association rémoise*. Although charged, among other things, with conspiracy and spreading false rumors, those accused were acquitted in Melun and returned to Reims in triumph to continue their work.[70]

Foiled in their attempts to dissolve the association, the authorities maneuvered indirectly. They expelled from the city a number of foreign workers who belonged to the association, dismissed Courmeaux from his position at the municipal library, and closed Bressy's Masonic lodge. The Reims industrialists formed an "association for antisocialist propaganda and for the amelioration of the condition of the laboring classes," while aiding a weaving foreman's efforts to begin a competing mutual-aid society with more traditional goals.[71]

The association changed its legal organization several times to avoid prosecution. The directing committee (conseil central) became the conseil central des corporations. After organizing an assistance committee for the families of men imprisoned in June 1849, a chambre du travail was established. It was the continuation of the corporations réunis, and its seventeen hundred members supported its efforts to "concern itself with the moral and material interests of the working class and to research ... all of the means of amelioration compatible with the resources and the laws which govern us." This chambre du travail functioned as the coordinating committee for the entire association and as a sort of *bourse du travail* for members and a place where they could study "the social economy."[72]

While the minister of agriculture opposed an immediate dissolution of the association because it had rendered services to the poor during the previous winter, the procureur général pressed for an end to it: "Their statutes clearly indicate that, above all, they have the goal of organizing and maintaining the antagonism between the working class and their bosses and [are ready] to provide for all eventualities with this in mind." The procureur général accused the association of plotting strikes and expelling workers who accepted wages below levels approved by the association. Furthermore, the association paid members

who lost work time because of civic service (on the labor arbi-
tration council, municipal council, or jury) and this, officials
reasoned, was a political act. Because the association studied
"solutions for the social economy," its economic goals "easily
coincided with political considerations." The association supported a wool-spinners' strike and provided mutual-aid funds;
moreover, its leaders were active in the elections. To the procureur
général, the Association rémoise remained ready to "serve and
propagate the success of the most hostile undertakings against
the government."[73]

Most threatening, the association had developed influence
among workers elsewhere in the Marne and in the Ardennes,
Moselle, and Vosges. Bressy, a talented propagandist, edited
an *Almanach démocratique de 1850*, which, in addition to
providing useful agricultural information, disseminated news
about the association. "Subcommittees" in several towns
propagated Bressy's program for countrypeople, which included
educational progress, credit facilities, and medical services in
addition to the usual pitch for an end to indirect taxes.[74] Association members "fraternized" with workers in the textile town
of Rethel in April 1849, and encouraged the formation of a
similar organization "to unite workers in a common interest."
An administrative council, perhaps from "outside of the working
class," organized a mutual-aid society.[75]

Likewise, in Metz, a textile and garrison town, the members of
the Association fraternelle des ouvriers fileurs were "honorable
people" in the eyes of the government officials who carefully
observed them, but the procureur there feared that that association was behind other mutual-aid societies which might one day
"win over" the people of the region. In one instance, in the
agricultural canton of Juniville, the small property-holders had
already demonstrated a "pronounced tendency to make common
cause with the mass of workers and to abandon the men devoted
to order."[76] The president of the Metz association was remembered for wearing a Phrygian cap to a December 1849 meeting,
and his society reimbursed workers for jury duty in a region
where prosecutors were unable to obtain convictions against the

press. In Sedan, not yet identified with Louis Napoleon, a workers' cooperative grocery with fourteen hundred members borrowed the statutes of the Association rémoise. Although its goal was apparently charitable and its membership was "honorable," this organization was deemed to have created a "bad spirit" among the workers, as evidenced by a strike.[77] Several "socialist inns," undoubtedly cooperative restaurants serving workers inexpensive food, were created in the vicinity. The workers of Vouziers and Attigny (Ardennes) joined similar associations. The organization in Vouziers, with an "egalitarian triangle" as part of its symbol, was inspired by a defrocked priest known for his "socialist eccentricities." In Vrigne-aux-bois, the ironmongers, dissatisfied with their salaries, began an association to produce and market iron; the procureur admitted that their success was "possible, even probable" but noted that they were led by a man "whose [political] opinions offer [us] few guarantees."[78] A number of mutual-aid societies and sociétés pour la vie à bon marché were underway in the arrondissement of Laon (Aisne). The president of the Vouziers association seemed prophetic when he told the subprefect that "when a common link unites all of the democratic elements the earthen pot will break the pot of iron."[79]

The Société rémoise d'association fraternelle, the mutual-aid branch, was dissolved in June 1850; six months later the corporations réunis and the chambre du travail followed "for submitting fradulent statutes" to the prefecture. Several of the other newer associations were also dissolved or deprived of a place to meet. Costly press convictions brought about the end of L'Association rémoise, also in June 1850. Its last issue included Bressy's confident assertion that "the democratic spirit is penetrating the masses."[80] During the first months of 1851, Louis Lecamp fled to London after being convicted of wearing a red tie with a tricolor embroidered on it. Eugène Courmeaux was sentenced to one year in jail and fined for predicting the coup d'état six months early. Bressy began a café (Le Progrès) which failed, and then, with a friend from the Ardennes, established a café-restaurant called The New World. In November 1851, he began to collect eighteen hundred francs caution money to establish another newspaper for the workers. On December 3, after posting a placard calling Louis Napoleon a traitor, Bressy spoke to a gathering of between 150 and 200 people, until the gendarmerie dispersed the crowd and the commissioner of police placed him under arrest. The mixed commission of the Marne ordered him sent to Algeria, along with his friend Lecamp, who was still listed as "in flight."[81]

Bressy's counterpart in the West was Dr. Ange Guépin, founder of the cooperative bakery of Nantes. Guépin, a noted utopian socialist theorist and propagandist during the July Monarchy, had traveled widely in search of adherents, once losing his position at the medical school in Nantes after being cited before the academic council for unspecified outrages.[82] Serving briefly as commissioner after the revolution of February, Guépin was known for his ponderous didactic tomes on the development of socialism through the ages, *Philosophie du socialisme ou étude sur les transformations dans l'humanité* (1850) and *Le Socialisme expliqué aux enfans du peuple* (1851).[83] From his study, he concluded that the creation of cooperative bakeries was the easiest and most useful way to begin the implementation of the principle of association in France.

Before the June Days, Guépin and a coalition of radical bourgeois and workers, influenced by Proudhon, had founded a mutual-aid organization, the Société fraternelle universelle, which had ties to similar organizations in Tours and Indret. It was not until February 1849, however, that the society began to function. After printing a letter in Mangin's *Le National de l'Ouest* on June 1, 1849, calling for the organization of socialist propaganda in the region, Guépin met with workers near Nantes and soon created a cooperative bakery linked to the Société fraternelle universelle, which undersold and infuriated the other bakers of Nantes. In addition, Guépin, who had also been involved in a stillborn clothing cooperative in the early 1830s in Lyon, planned a cooperative butcher shop because the butchers of Nantes "so often cheat and sell at false weights because of competition" and then a similar grocer's shop because the local

grocers "cheat everyone." By eliminating competition and
ultimately profit, Guépin hoped to peacefully achieve the "sup-
pression of all hangers-on and parasites: the town will soon
consist only of a mass of consumers, associated to produce, at
the lowest and best prices possible, food, clothing, and shelter."[84]

The administration did not share in Guépin's hopes for Nantes.
When the prospering cooperative bakery requested the mayor's
permission to build three more ovens, it was refused. The mayor,
confronted by unhappy competing bakers, was aware that
"socialists" produced the relatively inexpensive bread. Under
orders from the minister of interior, he withdrew the license of
the cooperative's master baker. After failing to prove Guépin's
involvement in the Plot of Lyon, the prefect used Guépin's
political tirade at the banquet in Nantes of the Société fraternelle
as an excuse to order searches of members' homes in several
cities during the first months of 1851. Police confiscated letters
containing political references that were sent to members, and
all of the mutual-aid organizations implicated were dissolved.[85]

The history of the repression betrays an interesting difference
in the official attitude toward clubs and popular societies, on the
one hand, and workers' associations, including those begun as
consumers cooperatives, which ultimately intended to "substitute
workers for the bosses, masters, and entrepreneurs," on the
other. Politically involved clubs, popular societies, and circles
were easier to deal with legally because their political activity
either violated their own statutes or the law banning clubs.
Workers' associations, though not properly speaking political,
were ultimately even more menacing. Such organizations as the
Association rémoise, with its mass support and revolutionary
goals, were a novel threat to the bourgeois social order. Associations troubled administrations in every department. No longer
was working-class organization to be feared only in Paris and
Lyon. The revolution acted as a catalyst for working-class
organization, and preoccupation with the social question arose
in unexpected places like Rethel, Altkirch, Mazamet, La Garde
Freinet, Niort, and Sedan. Democratic patronage by men like

Bressy and Guépin was often a factor, but the working-class presence was undeniable.

The authorities' mistrust of producers' cooperatives must be seen in the context of their categorical suspicion of popular organization.[86]

> For the party of order in 1850 popular organization is ... a veritable obsession. They did not want to distinguish between peaceful organization and conspiratorial organization, between the organization of work and that of combat; all free association is an evil, a danger which has to be smashed.[87]

Authorities saw political conspiracy and the specter of the June Days behind any meeting or gathering of ordinary citizens which had political or economic change as a goal. In contrast, ordinary people in associations were usually convinced that they were working peacefully or legitimately towards the transformation of society. As Bressy's prospectus, which was published by the newspaper Association rémoise, put it:

> We want to organize ourselves by association ... to educate ourselves and to defend our interests forgotten until this day, or misunderstood ... we will arrive peacefully at our goal; the emancipation of the proletariat, as the bourgeoisie attained its emancipation by the same path.

Jeanne Deroin, at her trial in Paris in November 1850, pleaded: "Far from wanting to lead or bring about a violent political movement, we were profoundly affected by the antagonism which exists between all classes of society ... it is our profound conviction that society can be transformed by peaceful means."[88] Association represented the harmonious means of freeing the workers from the horrors of the capitalistic social economy. Socialism, explained Dr. Guépin to the "children of the people," is the improved "social state which will succeed the present situation ... it is, for most people, the near future of humanity and the science which should lead to it; the goal and the means."[89]

Yet popular associations with such goals were accused of

conspiracy, of inciting violence, or of causing citizens "to hate each other." Bressy, Guépin, and the worker Lecamp, for preaching their perception of the social question, were branded "men of disorder," because they had pronounced the awful truth—that there was antagonism between classes. Agulhon notes the interrogation of Adrien Pons, active in the cork-workers' association of La Garde Freinet. He was told, "It appears that your association became a political instrument, the end result of which was most certainly the destruction of the harmony which until then existed between workers and bosses."[90] This represented a deft, but hardly surprising, reversal of reality. The social antagonism resulted from the existing relationship between patron and worker; the cork-workers had formed an association to harmonize society through peaceful means, by becoming their own bosses. They were succeeding quite nicely when the repression struck.

The illusion that most socialist workers were "corrupted" by misguided or evil bourgeois gradually faded away. When an indigenous working-class leadership came, during the course of the republic, to play organizational roles previously almost exclusively reserved for bourgeois ideologues, the administration moved to crush the associations as well, treating them as subversive, just as it had the earlier clubs which had been characterized by mixed social composition.

Workers' associations succeeded the clubs and noisy banquets as signs of popular organization in the Second Republic. Not only were the "new barbarians" visible in the factories of the industrial suburbs, they were forming associations with far-reaching goals which, in the words of one procureur général who was indignant over increased wage demands by workers, "introduce economic ideas which touch upon the entire order of society."[91] In addition to the clubs, electoral meetings, and popular societies, which could be written off as political and banned under post–June Days legislation, it became necessary to label workers' associations as political. Most of their leaders and members were strong and consistent republicans. The procureur général of Riom's assessment of the Association alimentaire of Puy suggests the way the repressors came to redefine "political" to serve their purposes: "It is not to be doubted that these meetings have a political character. The persons who take part in them are notorious for their advanced opinions and they hardly hide themselves while propagating their antisocial doctrines to the outside world."[92] "Antisocial" propaganda was that which preached insubordination and threatened to overturn the "entire order of society." "Anarchists" were men who did not recognize the "natural order of things"; they had what was called "mauvais esprit." Disorder was a society out of harmony, and harmony was contingent on the principle of social hierarchy. Associations challenged this conservative harmony, this "order." Therefore, "if politics consists in wanting to change the social regime, to substitute associated producers for the private patron" then the act of association was political.[93]

Such voluntary associations came to be condemned as "political," like the clubs, popular societies, and even secret societies, because they challenged fundamental notions of hierarchy, deference to social and economic superiors, and ultimately, the fundamental determination of power. Popular circles threatened the status and exclusiveness of the bourgeois circles as well as the political hegemony of the local notables.[94] Economic associations were doubly dangerous because they challenged both the economic and the social hierarchy. The successful operation of the cork-workers' association in La Garde Freinet not only threatened to contribute to the election of montagnard representatives from the Var, it threatened the patronat.[95] The inevitable result was "unwavering opposition of those in power to all attempts on the part of individuals to try to resolve, by their own efforts, the various questions touching upon the social economy."[96] Most of the bourgeoisie and French civil servants also underwent a *prise de conscience* during the Second Republic.

Ultimately, both the repressors and the repressed were consistent. Démoc-socs believed that the republic could not be separated from social progress; associations were an important part of the montagnard ideology. In this sense, they menaced the

social and economic domination of the notables, just as montagnard candidates and universal suffrage challenged traditional
politics. The repression of the popular associations was perfectly
consistent with the world view that social and economic hierarchy
was sacred and that capital was the preserve of the elite.

4

Social Control: The Repression of Ordinary People

Although Louis Napoleon's prefects and magistrates largely succeeded in cutting off the freedoms of the press and of association, the extreme left still possessed mobilizational resources. Thus the repression struck entire communities, major communal factions, and individuals capable of mobilizing collective protest, as well as the formal "institutions" of radicalization like written propaganda and voluntary associations. Social control implied, for the government and its police, the elimination of the remaining means of collective action and opportunities for people to mobilize and to express support for the socialists. In addition to such activities as banning workers' associations and confiscating editions of newspapers, the repression touched the lives of ordinary people participating in collective political action, most for the first time, by confronting them with the so-called "forces of order."

This chapter discusses one aspect of "social control," the repression of collective demonstrations with organizational significance (banquets, informal electoral meetings, political gatherings, café discussions) and those with more purely symbolic value ("seditious" demonstrations, songs, shouts, montagnard symbols such as red ties, Phrygian caps and so on); and finally, the harassment and surveillance of montagnard leaders and organizers capable of mobilizing collective dissent.

Banquets had been an established means of organizing political opposition long before they became one of the repression's targets. Even before the fateful reform banquets preceding the

February revolution,[1] these gatherings had symbolized popular participation and "fraternization." But the spring of 1849 would be remembered as the political "banquet years" of the French left during the Second Republic, beginning with the celebration of the anniversary of February 24 and culminating with the banquets prior to the legislative elections. Whereas the banquets of the July Monarchy were largely gatherings of bourgeois opposition leaders, those of the hectic preelection days of 1849 had a decidedly popular character. In Caen, three hundred "workers" toasted "social regeneration" while a crowd of twelve hundred in St. Jean-de-Losne (Côte d'or) was more than the town's entire population. Pierre Leroux sponsored a "Banquet égalitaire des rois" at the Barrière Maine in Paris and rumors of appearances by Ledru-Rollin and Félix Pyat increased the number of revelers to six hundred, "mostly workers," in Neuville St. Amand. An enthusiastic gathering in Lyon allegedly included even the operators of houses of prostitution. Sizable gatherings also took place in Manosque (Basses Alpes), Figanières (Var), Blois, Le Mans, Troyes, Château-Gontier (where a worker was stabbed by a National Guard bayonet), St. Amand, Limoges (sponsored by the "young socialists"), Douai, and Beauvais, where about eighty workers defied their employer and attended.[2]

Offering considerable more oratory than food, these occasions were hardly the *bouffes* of the *belle époque*. With relatively low admission fees (between eighty centimes and two francs) to attract the workers, few seemed to have actually served meals. Paté and wine usually sufficed. After the 1849 elections, banquets, as a form of political organization and popular fraternal festivity, were almost exclusively characteristic of the extreme left, and took place on three occasions: the republican anniversaries of February 24 and May 4, the periods before elections, and the arrival of a montagnard luminary or the return of a local son from prison. Formal toasts and speeches were planned in advance and those present drank to the "democratic and social republic," "the people of the countryside," "revolutionary France," or "the workers of the towns and of the countryside." The banquets were interrupted by shouts of "Long live Barbès!" or "Ledru-

Rollin," or "Blanqui" and accompanied by the off-key singing of the "Marseillaise", the "Chant du départ" or the "Chanson des vignerons."

The police commissioner in Colmar faithfully described a banquet in May 1849. Although the menu, if any, has been lost, we know that there were 150 participants at this gathering, including 6 or 7 national guardsmen conspicuous by their presence. Five citizens offered toasts, accompanied by short speeches. Charles Schmidt, editor of *La République du peuple*; an unnamed citizen; a tailor (who, the police noted, had written his own brief discourse); an unidentified "foreign refugee," undoubtedly German, who presented a "true communist speech" on the theory of the democratic and social republic; and another unnamed person whose talk seemed blatantly anti-Semitic, not surprising in view of the serious anti-Jewish disturbances in Alsace-Lorraine after the revolution.[3]

Until the summer of 1849, banquets were legal and guests subject to arrest only for "outrages." But after the repressive legislation passed, prefects could forbid political banquets on the grounds that they might "trouble the public peace." Thereafter, because banquets required some planning and publicity, prefects were able to prevent most of them, such as a sizable gathering in Nantes in February 1850. Others were dispersed while they were in progress, forcing the disappointed guests to break up and to gather discreetly in restaurants and cafés.[4] Occasionally the police, perhaps anticipating the opportunity to identify montagnard sympathizers, looked the other way, and a few banquets took place with the collusion of local authorities, another reason for the purge of the town halls during the republic. The mayor of Manosque presided over one gathering and the deputy mayor of another town organized a banquet at which a "gâteau aux rois" was consumed while one participant brazenly toasted, "That we will soon see every chief of state torn to pieces and drowned as well!"[5]

From all evidence the social composition of banquets continued to reflect the Agulhon's "descent of politics toward the masses." Gendarmes observed that most participants at one celebration were "dressed in workers' attire [*en blouse bleue*]." While the organizers set places at a banquet in Orléans in September 1850 for montagnard Representatives Péan and Martin, four members of the Conseil Général of the Loiret, and three editors of *La Constitution*, there were also places for three shoemakers, two contractors, two property-owners, two boarding-house keepers, two grocers, two tripe merchants, two publicans, and a lithographer. In addition, the organizers expected a grocer's helper, a drink retailer, an innkeeper, a grain merchant, a gunsmith, a café-owner, a zinc worker, a manufacturer, a tax employee, a baker, a merchant, a sabot-maker, a notary's clerk, a tailor, a jeweler, and a tinsmith.[6] A small gathering in tiny Combeaufontaine (Haute Saône) included the deputy mayor, a former bailiff, the tax collector's secretary, the town butcher, a tinsmith, a café-owner, the grocer's son, a doctor, one property-owner, a maker of harnesses and saddles ("a *very* bad citizen"), and an unknown man from a nearby village. Ultimately, the names of two very minor officials reached the desks of the ministers of interior and finance.[7]

After 1850 the banquet no longer could be used as a collective demonstration of montagnard support or a means of planning electoral organization. The government successfully thwarted most attempts to commemorate republican anniversaries in 1850 and very few were attempted in 1851, the last year of the republic. The montagnard chiefs allegedly instructed their followers to avoid all banquets and demonstrations on the May 4 anniversary of the proclamation of the republic in 1848.

The systematic closing of opportunities for public political expression was in response to a marked politicization of communal festivals and carnivals; "the political history of the Second Republic was being played on the stage of the popular theater of carnival." In 1850 there was a relatively clear break between the traditional carnival celebrations and those whose theme was "La République en danger."[8] The carnival, particularly in the Midi, was transformed into a political allegory with bizarre costumes identifying the enemies of the montagnard community, local "whites," "aristos" and officials, and Louis Napoleon himself. Popular justice, symbolized by the red Phrygian caps, letters and ties, or by the appearance of Liberty herself, was "dispensed" symbolically on that day of justice and allegory. "Seditious" songs characterized these and less theatrical carnivals. Not far from the picturesque fishing village of Collioure in the Pyrénées Orientales, the carnival featured a man as Liberty, dressed in red, wearing a Phrygian cap, and carrying a knife symbolizing justice.[9] Carnivals in the Var reflected the merging of folklore and popular revolutionary politics.[10] Bakers celebrating the feast of their corporation in Dole (Jura) dressed a child in a red cap. In Néronde, at the time of the patron saint's feast day, police discovered a case of pigeons while the townspeople were singing "Deliver us our prisoners." The name of an infamous prison holding political convicts (Mt. St. Michel, Doullens, Belle Isle, and Nouka Lua) appeared in each corner of the pigeon cage, which was decorated with a red ribbon.[11]

Indeed, "the future of the Second Republic looked different in Mardi Gras, 1850, than it had on the same day in 1849."[12] This was the theme of a "seditious demonstration" on Ash Wednesday 1850 in Mauzé in the Deux Sèvres where,

> under the pretext of burying carnival, a long procession passed two times through the bourg; a certain . . . apprentice joiner, nineteen years of age, coiffed in a red cap, wearing a white robe and a red vest around his body, his right wrist held by a chain which fell to his feet, and holding a tricolored flag, thus represented Liberty enchained.

Two carts led a crowd singing "Le Chant des vignerons" through the streets.[13] Anticipation of 1852, the year of elections and, prefects claimed, of insurrection, frequently provided a carnival theme in 1851. In Albi, six masked men buried the Republic in March. Except for one man wearing the blue smock of a worker, they were dressed in white, accompanied by a casket drawn by a horse; on their shoulders was written "1852" in large red letters. Twenty-eight "witnesses" refused to identify the symbolic pallbearers who shouted "Down with the reaction!"[14] In a few cases, prefects banned all carnivals and feast day celebrations, as in the Ardèche, placed under the state of siege in October 1851. Local ordinances, like that of the subprefect of Gaillac (Tarn), which banned all music in one town and limited the celebration of local feast days, were somewhat less oppressive measures.[15]

These "folkloric" political manifestations reflected the political-cultural time lag suggested by Agulhon, as widening horizons and political consciousness reached into villages in the "red" departments and were reflected in traditional and often archaic forms of social behavior:

> A spontaneous collision took place between a new view which people unexpectedly discovered and the structures of social life which conformed to custom and were quite incapable, by their very nature, of rapid modification.

The peasants, therefore,

> lacking [the possibility of] legal political meetings, transformed folkloric festivals into red demonstrations ... they discovered democratic faith but evidently did not know how to suddenly 'defolklorize.'[16]

Two other traditional forms of collective "festivity," the *charivari* and collective singing, manifested signs of politicization during the republic. The charivari was traditionally a sarcastic serenade "offered" to someone who had broken a village norm. Noise, provided by shouting, playing musical instruments, or simply banging on pots and pans, loudly publicized the misdeed.[17] An example of a charivari from the July Monarchy illustrates its traditional use: in July 1844, four charivaris occurred in Vierzon after a widow of forty-eight married a twenty-two-year-old man.[18] Likewise, a girl from one village could expect to be "serenaded" after marrying a man from another village, thereby subtracting herself from the usually small local pool of eligible females. During the July Monarchy, charivaris given to unpopular local officials indicated that the institution was already becoming politicized. Similarly, real serenades, a symbol of respect, were offered to popular opposition leaders on their arrival in town.

As the grip of the repression tightened, the government invited local wrath in montagnard-dominated areas as the transgressor of the community sense of justice. Charivaris and group singing took on a more blatantly political character in 1850 and 1851,[19] particularly as "the most supercilious authorities saw the school of popular insubordination in the charivari under the window."[20] The prefect of the Lot received a noisy charivari from a crowd accusing local officials of falsifying military electoral ballots; visiting montagnards were often given the opposite type of reception, serenades in their honor.[21]

Songs played an important role in "these marriages of politics and folklore."[22] The widely diffused songs of Pierre Dupont and Alfred Durin added to the revolutionary repertoire long dominated by the "Marseillaise" and "Carmagnole". These verses of the "Chanson de Ledru-Rollin" offered montagnard ideology as well as solidarity:

> V Ledru-Rollin veut encore faire
> Pour dégager le prolétaire.
> Payer l'impôt au revenu,
> A bas Ledru!
> Mais le capital et la rente
> Remplaceront bien la patente,
> L'impôt du sel, l'impôt du vin,
> Vive Ledru-Rollin!

> VI Enfin, C'est la Démocratie
> Luttant contre la bourgeoisie
> Qui, de peur de perdre un écu,
> Honnit Ledru.
> Mais la bourgeoisie aura beau faire
> L'avenir est au prolétaire,
> S'il persiste dans son refrain,
> Vive Ledru-Rollin![23]

Le Démocrate de Vaucluse published the song "Aux rouges" which described the repression of political festivity itself:

> Un rouge ne doit pas chanter;—car, s'il chantait, il chanterait "La Marseillaise" qui est un chant prohibé.
> Un rouge ne doit pas crier, "Vive la République," car, dans la bouche d'un rouge, Vive la République! Cela veut dire vive l'anarchie.
> Un rouge ne doit pas danser—car sous la forme de polka il dansera la Carmagnole.[24]

The "Chant des paysans," "Chanson des vignerons," and "Chant des ouvriers" reached seemingly every corner of France, requiring not only persistence but a fine ear on the part of the gendarmes, like those who disbanded a singing group in Poitiers who swung into a seditious set. A country ball near Tournus (Saône-et-Loire) was similarly terminated when the Société philharmonique sponsored a "socialist manifestation."[25] Revolutionary songs, deemed seditious and legally punishable, became part of popular radical culture in areas of montagnard strength. As legal means of celebrating the republic disappeared, impromptu singing took on great symbolic significance as protest and as a means of rallying the faithful. Wool-spinners striking in Rethel (Ardennes) in June 1851, sang the "Marseillaise". The refrain echoed through the busy Sunday market, then as now, at the place Sernin in Toulouse, while the commissioner of police, struggling to get through the hostile crowd, vainly attempted to gauge the direc tion of the singing.[26] Montagnard songs, like "seditious cries," became one of the last means of dissident public political expression.

On some occasions in 1850 and 1851, the funerals of montagnards became symbolic revolutionary corteges and démoc-soc shows of strength. These political funerals accounted for twenty-nine of the "ideological disorders" in the Vaucluse between January 1, 1850, and the coup d'état.[27] In Nantes, a crowd of four hundred followed the casket of Bacherau, member of the

Club de l'Oratoire in Paris and founder of the Société fraternelle of Nantes, to the cemetery, although the police commissioner had forbidden political speeches. The death of an ex-revolutionary of 1793 vintage in Montpellier occasioned a demonstration by that city's many socialists and the Marseille montagnards who lined the streets as the body of a man implicated in the Plot of Lyon passed. In March 1851, an estimated seven to eight thousand "democrats" buried another socialist without the assistance of a priest. In the Lyon region, where the republic was being suffocated by the state of siege established in 1849, funerals assumed an obvious symbolic meaning and were one of the few means of public political expression. As a result, General Castellane established a maximum figure, of 300 people who could attend any funeral. Shortly thereafter, exactly that number laid a gunsmith to rest, but two thousand followed his casket through the streets of St. Étienne as an estimated twenty-five thousand (surely an exaggeration) solemnly watched the procession. The next day a scrawled placard warned:

> Castellane, you [tu] tell us in your order of disorder that only 300 democrats can participate in the funeral procession for a worthy citizen. As for me, I tell you that we don't need that many, that only '93 are needed to do our job.[28]

As the repression limited opportunities for planned political manifestations or shows of montagnard strength, the spontaneous protest, particularly against the repression, took on added significance. Violent protest against the closing of a café, the banning of a local celebration, or a political arrest were actions with a political and ideological component. In contrast, the collective disturbances in the first weeks of the revolution—those relating to forests, anti-Semitism, and even the forty-five centimes tax—were traditional protests accentuated by the revolutionary situation and the power vacuum caused by the virtual abdication of authority.[29] The first category qualify as "ideological disturbances"[30] and are more typical of "modern" forms of collective violence, while the "troubles" which followed the revolution seem closer to what Tilly has called "reactionary collective violence," the attempt by the rural community to reassert its traditional claims over resources, eroded by the impingement of the state and the centralized taxing apparatus (*fisc*).[31] Examples of ideological disturbances abound in the Midi in 1851, and they eventually led the authorities to place the Ardèche under the state of siege in October. Examples would include protests against the removal of liberty trees (the most serious incidents of this kind were in Paris, near Arts-et-Métiers in February 1850 and in Avesnes [Nord]); a pitched battle in Albi in July 1849 when a crowd attempted to free political prisoners (thirty-two persons hurt); a demonstration in Beaune in 1851 which commemorated the day in 1848 when members of the Society of the Rights of Man placed the symbol of Solidarité républicaine on a cliff overlooking the town; an attack by a crowd hurling rocks and insults upon the adjunct mayor in La Motte (Var), who prevented socialist meetings in January 1851; an incident in which troops were fired upon while they assisted the prefect who was making the rounds to close cafés in October 1851; and the "hostile reception" given to Louis Napoleon in several eastern towns on his tour in the fall of 1850.[32] Tax riots, widespread in 1848 after the imposition of the forty-five centimes tax, came to take on a political color, red, as the montagnard representatives rallied support on the issue of opposition to the hated indirect taxes and, in some cases, reimbursed those who had actually paid them. The most serious incident occurred in Issoire (Puy-de-Dôme) early in 1849 when several months of periodic disturbances partially centering around the town's feast day led to a confrontation. It began with a mocking serenade for a tax official, among cries of "Down with the bourgeoisie! Down with the Carlists! Down with everyone who supports indirect taxes!" and ended with the arrival of four hundred troops to bring order to the mountain town. Such incidents, Robert Bezucha argues, portrayed or acted out the popular montagnard song, the "Chanson des vignerons."[33]

Unlike less serious collective demonstrations, these sometimes violent conflicts were met with force. Troops were sent and garrisons established or expanded; the ultimate sanction was the state of siege, "the unique guarantee preferred by the bourgeoisie."[34] In some areas of the Midi, troops kept order in the cities, but only the coup d'état brought the rural regions under control. In the countryside the repression only intensified hatred of the government, and the montagnards were able to organize underground. These "ideological disturbances" were merely symptomatic of the remarkable organizational strength of the of secret societies.[35]

In an era when shouts of "Long live" someone or something and "Down with" someone else had serious implications, the "seditious cry" or shout emerged as one of the few possible public political manifestations, a chorus of outrage against repression and support for the democratic and social republic. Such acts of sedition, individual and collective, aroused official concern and ultimately hundreds of reports reached the desks of the ministers of justice, interior, and war. The shout "Long live the democratic and social republic!" a rallying cry during the June Days, was prohibited as a political statement. Indeed the decline of the republic was reflected in the evolution of what was considered seditious and legally culpable.

In March 1849, the minister of justice replied vaguely when asked whether the addition of the word "sociale" made any shout illegal. He ruled that use of the word could be interpreted as expressing opposition to the constitution, which established a democratic, but not a social republic. However, he left it to the discretion of his subordinates whether individual circumstances were sufficient to make the shout an "invitation to incite rebellion." The procureur général of Caen suggested that "parties who want a social republic necessarily want a modification in the principles and rights of the present society," which was true enough. General Bugeaud, who had fought the army of the social republic in June, agreed. Therefore, the end of 1849, the cry "sociale" was included among "all signs or symbols propagating the spirit of rebellion" and was prosecuted accordingly.[36]

Henceforth gendarmes leaned forward to catch the forbidden "sociale" at the end of Vive le République démocratique" at republican celebrations. "Vive la sociale" was, by .tself, illegal. Shouts of "Long live Barbès!" (who was suffering in prison), "Long live Raspail," "Louis Blanc," or references to others associated with the social republic were proscribed. General denunciations like "Down with the whites!" "Down with the aristos!" or "Down with the rabble of order!" fell under the regulations, along with more complicated slogans, harder to report accurately, like "I would rather be a good peasant than a bourgeois laggard!" "Louis Napoleon is a monarchist dog," and "The people are all brothers to us!"[37] In the Drôme, several men adorned in illegal red ties and ribbons were arrested after singing, "In 1852 we will play nine-pin. The heads of the rich will serve as the *boules*; those of the priests as the goals!" Conservatives associated such bravado with the events of 1793, symbolized by Robespierre and the guillotine, shouts for either being also illegal. There was nothing subtle about the people of St. Dié dragging a guillotine through the streets while singing montagnard songs in September 1850.[38] In June 1850 an unusually bizarre ritual took place in the Pyrénées Orientales (where montagnard demonstrations and symbolism thrived):

> [Jean] Batlle, the former justice of the peace of Arles, went . . . to St. Marsal, in the company of a forge-worker of Arles, and from there to Labastide, with (eight) other individuals from St. Marsal; there they had a meal and sang democratic songs; the nine of them returned to St. Marsal about six in the evening, carrying a young goat crowned with a red cap that they ate at St. Marsal on Monday morning, and drank the blood of the goat in turn, while singing songs suitable to the occasion and saying we will soon have "la rouge" and swearing war to the death with the whites.[39]

A more refined and equally illegal demonstration occurred in Vienne when cries of "Long live Marat!" echoed through the

Antique Theatre, while an appalled policeman observed an enthusiastic audience applaud "almost all of the terrorist tirades placed in the mouth" of the character of Marat in the play Charlotte Corday. A host of "Long lives" (Cabet, Blanqui, Barbès, and even Louis LeBlanc [sic]) greeted the production of A Voyage in Icaria or Communism in St. Maixent, in one of Cabet's former strongholds, the Deux Sèvres. Penalties for such offenses depended on the circumstances: officials often assumed, for example, that the influence of alcohol lessened the seriousness of purpose. But a carter in the Aisne received a two-year jail sentence for an inopportune yell of "Long live the barricades! Long live the guillotine!"[40]

Scrawled placards and signs, the written equivalent of the seditious cry, represented the gradual transition from an oral tradition to written propaganda in nineteenth-century France. The ancestors of political graffiti, placards articulated political beliefs which could not be expressed safely in public. As protest "modernized" in France, so did the placard. Half-literate but deadly serious threats against grain-hoarders and forest guards, embodying the popular sense of "doing justice" to powerful outsiders infringing upon assumed communal rights, gave way to placards with recognizably ideological sentiments in the Second Republic.[41]

Some placards were short and to the point, like "Long live Raspail!" or the rudimentary statement of the social economy, "Property is theft." Others were lengthy, written under the cover of night: "The people are sovereign and the republic is their work." "The tocsin sounds, the call to arms is given and the red flag flies everywhere!" "The republic is red, we will install it, dagger in hands!" "Apostles of liberty, let us preach, let us fight, let us die if necessary, heaven will do the rest!" The aggressive swaggering of such phrases was in some ways characteristic of popular culture at the time. Some were directed against certain transgressors in the social republic, similar to the placards during the agricultural crises that named hoarders and threatened them: "Down with the curé of Fougères!"[42] The oldest author of a seditious placard was undoubtedly a montagnard sympathizer

living in Morlaix (Finistère). "At eighty-five years of age," he
wrote, "I should know the priests and Norman counterrevolu-
tionaries." He posted this "republican prayer":

> Our Republic, which is in heaven . . . but let us
> not succumb to the inquisition, and deliver
> us from the nobles.

>   *   *   *

> I believe in the Republic, our all powerful
> mother, creator of peace and of justice; and
> in universal suffrage, its unique son, who
> suffered under Pontius Philippe, was crucified,
> died, and was buried . . . I believe in the holy
> principle and in the democratic cause . . . and
> in the resurrection of justice and peace. Amen.[43]

Symbols of the social republic were outlawed; most involved
the color red—red flags, red caps of the *sans-culottes*, red belts,
red ties, and red signs. Red flags recalled the June Days, and
reviving that memory may have been the intention of three tilers
in St. Symphorien-des-Bois caught tying the feared *drapeau
rouge* to a tree.[44] The Phrygian caps, recalling the French
Revolution's goal of social leveling, turned up as headwear in
the village carnivals and festivals acting out the story of the
republic and the repression. The one hundred leather-dressers
of Annonay (Ardèche) seemed dressed for revolution on their
feast day. Red hats turned up all over France: painted on a
tricolor presented to montagnard Representative Marc Dufraisse
by the peasants of Ribérac, for example, and in an oil painting
on a "figure of Liberty . . . a very mediocre painting, inciden-
tally," discovered by the subprefect of Gaillac (Tarn) in the
corner of a house on an isolated street.[45]

Red ties and ribbons, particularly prevalent in the Midi, were
officially prohibited by decree in the Drôme. Red paint could
also be objectionable: fifty troops were sent from Amboise to
a small town to remove from the bell tower of the village church
a weather cock which had been painted red. Several cafés were

also closed because their marquees were painted in revolutionary red.[46]

The repression of such symbols evolved into the repression of the republic itself. Most liberty trees were cut down by the end of 1850. The shout "Long live the republic" became a cry of defiance in the face of the attack on the institutions of the republic and its most ardent defenders. Verbal hostility towards Louis Napoleon was dealt with severely. By the middle of 1850, he was the "prince president" in many official reports. A carnival masquerade poking fun at the president of the republic outraged gendarmes (almost all of whom were former soldiers). Couplets such as "Voilà pour brûler tous les blancs, le président n'a rien fait pour la France" and references to "Little Badinguet" were as dangerous as "Vive la sociale." The cry "Down with Bonaparte" was unthinkable. One magistrate raged that *hommes en blouse* (workers) shouted "Long live Napoleon" with a "laughing air."[47] But while the symbols of the social republic could be repressed, as long as the government of France remained nominally republican, it was technically legal, though for all practical purposes ill-advised and considered subversive, to voice support for it.

By the time of the Second Republic, the café was already a social institution in France. In 1850, over 350,000 establishments were licensed to serve alcoholic beverages, 6,000 more than in 1848; in one year, 356 cafés opened in the rural department of the Doubs.[48]

Although notables and moralistic officials were concerned about the rise of drinking and blamed cafés and cabarets for the "demoralization" of the lower classes, authorities during the Second Republic had a more urgent concern: cafés provided convenient sites for ordinary people to get together and discuss politics. The role of the café was aptly described in the montagnard paper *La Ruche* of Périgeux in May 1849:

> The cabaret is the café, the club, the circle of the people. The people find pleasure there, because one can speak

openly and without risk; because one can find solace there, for one moment in the midst of the suffering of the week; because one can always hear intelligent discussions and make political decisions without the pernicious influence of the capitalist, usurer, noble, and fat bourgeois who believe we have disgraced them—they are so drunk with beer, punch, and champagne, they smell of the odor of the blue wine of the cabaret.[49]

As already mentioned, café provided an opportunity to read political newspapers, and complaints of public reading and political discussions were common. Innkeepers, publicans, and café-owners were often prominent montagnard activists whose occupation gave them both contacts and political influence. In 1852, 990 innkeepers appeared before the mixed commissions.[50]

In 1851 the minister of justice compiled reports from the procureurs on the political impact of cafés. From Nancy came this report: "The cafés are the scourge of the small towns; they have proven even better for the 'men of disorder' than the clubs." In the judicial district of Colmar, publicans were "the most active agents of socialist propaganda." Of sixteen communes of the canton of St. Amarin, ten had mayors who were innkeepers, and in the "socialist" towns the amount of bread consumed appeared to have decreased while more wine was consumed, particularly among the young men attracted to "the new ideas." In Rouen, electoral lists were drawn up in cafés along the waterfront, and the Lyon cafés seemed to be reading rooms. "Cafés," the procureur for Lyon claimed, suggesting that a law be passed to outlaw the reading of journals aloud, "are schools of demoralization."[51] Marshal Castellane claimed that the cafés of St. Étienne served ten thousand potential insurgents: "Each evening [there are] 722 meetings, where ten or twelve workers discuss the political questions while drinking and pass along instructions to each other."[52]

Many cafés became identified with the politics of their clientele and their owners: "the men belonging to demagogy always frequent the same cafés, the same cabarets." One gendarme expressed surprise that a visiting montagnard activist went to two different cafés in a town, because everyone knew that one of them attracted a more conservative clientele.[53] Like Frenchmen today, people then frequented the same café day after day without ever passing through the door of a nearby or even adjacent establishment. When the prefect of the Rhône closed the Cercle dit le Paradis, its members, without a place to meet, invaded a nearby café where they were confronted by the angry *habitués*, whom they had always called "aristos." Distinct clienteles, for example, could be found in insurrectionary Clamecy in the Nièvre, where one of the leaders was Denis Kock, "whose inn was for the workers what the café Gaumier was for the bourgeoisie."[54] Reference to political subversion of soldiers in cafés near their garrisons appeared frequently in the daily correspondence of the minister of war.[55] For example, it became known that soldiers engaged in political discussions in the small wineshop across from the Administration des postes in Paris. Gaité and Montparnasse, then on the outskirts of the capital, were already renowned for their lively café life, attracting the soldiers from the garrison. In Montrouge, soldiers sipping wine or beer could gaze at pictures of Barbès, Proudhon, and Marc Caussidière and join in the singing of montagnard songs. Below an unflattering engraving of Louis Napoleon, someone had inscribed on the wall, "Little Badinguet, who wants to overthrow the republic."[56] As a result, many cafés were placed off limits to soldiers.

The politics of café life in Toulouse are well documented, because "the followers of demagogy always frequented the same cafés and cabarets." While the police commissioner cited only two cafés in January 1850, socialists met regularly in small groups in eight more cafés by the end of the year, including one on the Place Capitole. A typical police report indicated, to cite one example, that "the Grand Café Barrié, at the corner of the Avenue Lafayette and the Boulevard Napoléon, is frequently the location of anarchist discussions" involving several workers, including members of the radical Association des ouvriers cordonniers. As of March 1851, no cafés or cabarets had been closed, except for the Cercle dit de l'union démocratique (rue de May), which doubled as a café. But in August, the prefect decreed the closure of a café which subscribed to *L'Émancipation* and had been the scene of political meetings after the February revolution. Outside of town, another café was closed because a bust of Ledru-Rollin, painted in red, was "habitually exposed" despite repeated warnings from the mayor. The rural guard (*garde champêtre*) claimed to have overheard people reading socialist journals aloud and eavesdropped on accusations that the rich wanted to reinstate the *dîme* to add to the profit they were making from the forty-five centimes tax.[57]

The law of June 19, 1849, gave the police the right to enter and to break up any meeting or gathering which could compromise the public peace. Furthermore, anyone making an inflammatory public statement in a café, or anywhere else, could be prosecuted if he were overheard by an official. But two circumstances hampered the prefects' repression of café political life. First, it was legal to discuss politics, and if nothing outrageous occurred, prosecutions seemed useless. Few police commissioners would risk antagonizing an entire community for the sake of a minor political arrest. It was also very difficult to catch people "at" café politics, unless commissioners spent a good deal of time in a café, or surprised a group "in the act." In 1851, a so-called "club" met in a café in Josselin (Morbihan) and a shoemaker read newspapers to sixteen to twenty townspeople. When the gendarme entered the café, the shoemaker lowered his voice, read neutral material, and because each participant had a cider glass in front of him and the café was a public place, the gathering could not be considered a political meeting.[58]

Local officials must have had an ambivalent attitude toward the campaign against the cafés. Closing a café was a provocative and grossly unpopular step which could set an entire community against those responsible for keeping order, and when the repression was particularly heavy-handed and clumsy, hatred of the government intensified in montagnard-dominated communities. Besides, the cafés allowed the authorities to note the comings and goings of montagnards and to ascertain the local political mood. For example, the police commissioner of Toulouse made it his business to know what went on in each of his city's suspicious cafés. On January 6–7, 1851, he reported: "Last night, at the red café called 'The European,' the conversation was very lively, on the subject of the resignation of the ministers . . . and of our [exiled] brothers in Geneva." Cafés were closed down only in exceptional circumstances; for example, when the café La Grandetasse of Saumur was visibly serving as a center of montagnard organization for the entire department.[59] The business of "building underground," although the cafés often facilitated recruitment and even initiation, required more secrecy than the public café could offer. In general, the café continued to provide a place for ordinary people to discuss political questions. The administration settled old scores only after the coup, when eighty cafés were shut down in Gers alone.[60]

Thus far this chapter has been primarily concerned with the means by which ordinary people expressed montagnard political belief, and the measures the administration took to suppress such dissidence. The repression of the radical apparatus, however, cannot be separated from the action taken against the montagnard leaders, the individuals who, by virtue of their organizational abilities, dedication, and charisma, were able to generate commitment to the democratic and social republic by linking national political ideology to local economic and social tensions, widening the horizon of ordinary people and "bringing politics to the village." Some of the montagnard activists had national reputations by virtue of their status as representatives or their experience as political militants during the July Monarchy or the first years of the republic. Officials must have experienced intense concern when Pascal Duprat, a representative, harangued a crowd of nine hundred peasants at a fair in the Gers, or Mathieu d'Épinal (called "Wooden leg") coordinated montagnard political organization in Épinal, Pont-à-Mousson, Toul, and Nancy.[61] The government struggled to limit the organizational efforts of such men and to counteract their influence on local political opinion. At the same time, lesser-known activists within the community presented what was in some way a more serious problem. The procureur général in Agen thus reflected on the mobilization of insurgent communities following the coup d'état: "In the midst of these lost men [are] dangerous leaders perverted by the doctrines of democratic-socialism . . . ; possessed by . . . ferocious instincts, they march resolutely toward social revolution."[62] The repression struck at any individual capable of generating collective political action.

During 1849, 1850, and 1851 the montagnard national leaders, despite the fact that many served as duly elected representatives of the people, were hounded as if they were common criminals. Detailed reports in the War Archives describe the surveillance of such men as Joigneaux, Théodore Bac, Martin Nadaud, Ollivier, Savatier-Latour, Pascal Duprat, Marc Dufraise, Mathieu de la Drôme, Noel Parfait, Charles Schmidt, Cassal, and Michel de Bourges, revealing minute information on their daily activities.

Few montagnards logged as many miles on behalf of the democratic and social republic as Madier de Montjau, a representative of the Loiret and a skilled courtroom defender. A national figure who could sway juries with his polished oratory, he seemed to draw a crowd each time he stepped from a stagecoach. However, the fact that Madier's appearance could revive the political hopes of ordinary people and confidence in the elections of 1852 made him a marked man. Comprehensive reports by gendarmes record virtually his entire schedule during the last three years of the republic. Because he could not travel anonymously he rapidly tired of "police spies who know when we are arriving before our friends do."[63] This kind of surveillance represented more than just harassment: influential montagnards attracted other activists and the rank and file, giving local authorities useful information for a collective biography of local democratic-socialists. For example, the travels of Bac, Crémieux, and Jules Faure to defend a number of those accused in the Plot of Lyon provided information on their political supporters in each town in which they stopped.[64] Representative Cassal of the Haut Rhin complained that his mail was being opened; other representatives found that the prefect had anticipated their arrival in a provincial capital and prevented local innkeepers from renting them banquet rooms.[65]

Watching the montagnard "stars" was relatively easy because

of their popularity and visibility. The surveillance of other activists was more complicated, though greatly facilitated by the passport system, which required that permission be obtained from the *mairie* to travel from one department to another. Reports reaching the prefect in Toulouse illustrate how authorities were generally able to keep one step ahead of traveling activists. The commissioner of police notified the prefect that:

> Sr Cazalas, Paul, aged 52 years, hat merchant, native of Pamiers (Ariège), living rue des Balances, no. 78, took out a passport today for Rhodez (Aveyron). Sr Cazalas is a red of the worst variety. He hangs around with only that kind of people, and, like all his political friends, he is waiting for the right moment to act. The trip of this suspect man appears to be related to some political goal; you may want, Mister Prefect, to alert Rhodez in order that his activities may be observed.[66]

The same prefect warned the prefect of police in Paris of the arrival of the former managing editor of *Le Proscrit*; at about the same time, a mechanic suspected of the "worst" politics left for the capital, where he was expected to visit montagnard Representative Joly and the usual "red cafés." Earlier the prefect of Haute Garonne had been advised by his colleague in Bordeaux that "an active agent of the socialist party in Lesparre," an attorney, had taken out a passport for Toulouse. Eventually the commissioner of police in the latter city could sketch the links in the radical apparatus involving Toulouse and twelve cities of the Midi.[67] A "chaud partisan" of Barbès traveling between Boulogne and Paris, a wealthy notary from conservative Dax (Landes), a former clerk at the Vésoul tribunal, the editor of *Le Républicain Breton*, and a public writer who worked near the Opéra in Paris were among the hundreds of people whose daily activities became the concern of the political police.[68]

Once suspicious travelers were on the road, normal gendarmerie surveillance and passport checks followed them. The arrest of a self-styled "man of letters" by police in Narbonne revealed the names of four socialists in the Tarn. A Hungarian refugee was stopped in Sarrebourg in August 1850, carrying a false passport and a letter from Madier de Montjau to a pastor of a reformed church asking his assistance in obtaining a valid passport for Piedmont. The usual search of the man's motley belongings produced copies of Victor Hugo's *Speech during the Discussion of the Proposed Electoral Law*, *The Sure and Peaceful Transition towards the New World*, and *Association as Offering a Guarantee against Misery*, which may have inspired the procureur général of Nancy to arraign him on charges of vagrancy and mendicity.[69] The surveillance of trains and diligences was, as noted earlier, easily routinized. Thus the subprefect of Lavaur (Tarn) learned that the diligence leaving for Nîmes carried an individual "who, in the course of the trip, manifested very radical opinions." Many such reports were inaccurate, but enough were useful so that officials were able to gather surprisingly dependable information on the comings and goings of montagnards.[70] Ultimately only ritualized secrecy could hide montagnard activities and activists, particularly in towns and bourgs. Police were able to identify and watch démoc-socs who assumed leadership roles, but finding a reason to arrest them was another matter.[71] Most of the leaders of the secret societies survived to lead the resistance against the coup d'état. Nevertheless, the repressors were relatively successful in identifying most influential montagnard activists. Constant surveillance and harassment (for example, thorough household searches on the pretext of checking for weapons, gunpowder, or caches of political pamphlets[72]) limited the organizational efforts of the most active montagnards, forcing the radical apparatus underground, into the ritual of secrecy in the seventeen departments where this network largely remained intact.[73]

In most of France, popular protest and organization had been stifled by the time of the coup d'état. The extreme left's means of collective organization and action had been severely curtailed. Only in the most rural areas of the most radical departments of the Midi and in a few departments of the Center (and here often only with the complicity of local authorities or only because the repressive forces were insufficient) were people able to parade their radical political loyalties openly. Elsewhere, organized dissent was largely impossible and limited to relatively harmless acts of "sedition"—a placard hastily scrawled in the night, the echo of the forbidden "Long live the democratic and social republic" from the interior of a café, an enthusiastic but cautious crowd gathering to welcome a montagnard activist under the watchful eye of the police commissioner who was ready to draw up an indictment at the slightest provocation.

This situation was only possible because of the assault upon the democratization of municipal political life which accompanied the revolution, an attack best symbolized by the law eliminating universal suffrage and by the purge of disloyal officials and National Guard units who were capable of "legitimizing" political dissent within a community by virtue of their official status. Not only had the revolution dramatically increased the possibilities for collective political action—the press, associations, political gatherings, freedom of expression—there were "new men" in positions of authority within communities capable of mobilizing political dissidence, as mayor, deputy mayors, municipal council members, schoolteachers, justices of the peace, National Guard officers, and even tax collectors. The purge of these officials was an essential and highly visible part of the repression, and it played an essential role in clearing the way for Louis Napoleon's rise to power.

5

Social Control: The Purge

The revolution brought Hippolyte Carnot, son of Lazare Carnot of the Committee of Public Safety, to a position of power in France as minister of public instruction. For a time, he was one of the most powerful men in the country and a symbol of the democratic republic which threatened to become "social." But more important to the citizens of Sardent (Creuse), the revolution also made, by popular acclamation (later confirmed by a summer election), Monsieur Junien mayor; it also made one of his politically radical friends commander of the National Guard. In nearby Soubrebost, their friend (and that of the Creuse mason Martin Nadaud) suddenly discovered that he too had political influence. Carnot, of course, was forced out of the ministry in August 1848, one of the most prominent victims of the reaction that followed the June Days. Many people in France knew of Hippolyte Carnot; few outside of a single canton in the Creuse had ever heard of Junien and his politically radical friends, but the elimination of all four men from their positions of authority is part of the same story. The revolution had democratized municipal politics, and with universal manhood suffrage many new men assumed positions of official responsibility, influence, and authority. The repression largely eliminated them from positions of power, particularly those who were capable of mobilizing and maintaining démoc-soc political sympathies if not organization. At the same time the government sought to purify and strengthen the "forces of order," it was moving to end the democratization of municipal politics, profiting from the law ending universal manhood suffrage.

The politically motivated dismissal of officials was instrumental

in the return of "men of order" to power in France during
the Second Republic. The early efforts of the counterrevolution
may be seen in the purge of the justices of the peace appointed by
the provisional government after the February revolution.[1] The
reconquering of the prefectures through politically motivated
dismissals paved the way for the repression. Although the
prefects helped define the nature and the severity of the repression
in each department, they realized that the security of their
positions, present and future, lay in their ability to follow instructions from above, particularly after the Ministry of October 31
(1849) was formed.[2] The purge of loyal republicans from minor
positions of authority within their communes was a characteristic
of the repression.

The February revolution temporarily altered French municipal
politics. The mayor and his deputy (he had two in larger towns)
could become political as well as administrative figures by virtue
of personal influence. Anticipating the advent of universal
suffrage, commissioners replaced mayors and deputy mayors
whose politics were blatantly Orleanist; in Haute Vienne 34
percent of the town halls changed hands during the first two
months of the republic.[3] The number of such replacements
varied sharply from department to department. The commissioners often lacked adequate political information on mayors,
many of whom, after all, had little or no political role during the
monarchie censitaire. Sifting through the piles of denunciations
from "patriots" was time-consuming. Thus while departments
like the Gers underwent real administrative purges after the
revolution, many commissioners were content with eliminating
those mayors and assistants viewed as most likely to be disloyal
to the republic. The summer renewal of municipal officials
(*renouvellement*) entailed a new election of councilmen who in
turn elected a mayor and deputy mayor from their number
(except in the 469 largest cities, where these officials were appointed). Almost exactly half of the newly elected mayors and
deputy mayors (32,657 of 65,231, or 50.05%) were new to their
positions.[4]

By the time of the elections of 1849, some prefects complained about the socialist political activity of municipal officials, particularly in areas in which the montagnards had been most successful, in the Côte d'or, Saône-et-Loire, Jura, Haute Loire, Dordogne, Haute Vienne, Gers, Aude, Hérault, Pyrénées Orientales, Var, Vaucluse, Basses Alpes, and Bouches-du-Rhône.[5] As would be expected, a positive association exists between departments with a relatively high (that is, over 50%) percentage of new mayors and deputy mayors elected during the summer of 1848 and political radicalization as reflected by the elections of May 1849. Several "radical" departments returned particularly low percentages of officeholders from the July Monarchy during the 1848 municipal elections, Basses Alpes (31%), Aude (28%) Drôme (38%), Var (27%), Saône-et-Loire (41%) and Pyrénées Orientales (24%). In other departments the revolution brought considerably less turnover in municipal offices, Côtes-du-Nord (62%), Finistère (59%), Indre-et-Loire (62%), Maine-et-Loire (62%), Sarthe (64%), and Seine-et-Oise (85%).[6] The Allier the most significant exception to this general pattern, returned 61 percent of its mayors and adjunct (deputy) mayors during the municipal elections, yet it became a radical department. In general departments evidencing montagnard support in May 1849 were those that had undergone a significant change in municipal leadership during the previous summer.

Prefects' assessment of the political activities of mayors in 1850 indicated a strong degree of regional variation. In the ten conservative departments of the west, mayors did not pose much of a political problem, although some "hardly [knew] how to sign their name and [were] incapable of understanding the simplest administrative details." In the north, many Orleanist mayors had been reelected, and prefects faced few problems with their municipal underlings. But in the eastern departments, "some [mayors had] abused their positions in order to propagate audaciously the most dangerous doctrines by their acts and their words." Several prefects mentioned that many mayors now seemed "independent" of their superiors and, believing themselves responsible to their constituents, manifested the predominant political feeling of their commune. As usual, the most serious problems were in the departments of the center and the Midi, where the revolution brought "a great number of disreputable, uneducated and hotheaded" men to positions of administrative responsibility. Of 107 communes in the Bouches-du-Rhône, 25 had "seen their municipalities invaded by a demagogic nominations."[7]

The following incidents, which brought prefectural requests for removal of municipal officials, have been chosen from numerous examples: The mayor of Luneau (Allier) was "the declared adversary of the higher government administration; he delayed the official posting of the repression in June 1848. He has resorted to disreputable maneuvers to influence the elections!" The mayor of Vallemoz (Haute Saône) refused to give gendarmes the names of workers in a sugar factory who were responsible for a number of "seditious cries." The mayor of Marciac (Gers) tolerated a "socialist club" and passed around a petition against the drink tax for his friends to sign. The deputy mayor of St. Pé (Hautes Pyrénées) sought to "flatter the working class by echoing the evil doctrines." In Corné (Maine-et-Loire) the mayor posted an article dealing with the misfortunes of peasants, clipped from *Le Peuple* of Paris. The deputy mayor of Crulai (Orne) was denounced as a friend of Garnier-Pagès, the minister of finance in 1848.[8]

Disloyal municipal officials could, by virtue of their formal and informal authority, legitimize political dissent and hinder the repression by obstructing or ignoring official measures. However, as "the most obvious instruments of political surveillance in the rural communes,"[9] the mayors were responsible to the prefects, subprefects, and, ultimately, to the minister of interior for enforcing the repression, for example, the laws regulating hawking and peddling, passports, or the closing of cafés. In the Midi, they had the unpopular obligation of enforcing prefectural decrees regulating or preventing carnivals, festivals, and dancing which tended to "degenerate" into montagnard festivals with seditious songs and symbols.[10] Thus the deputy mayor of Corneilla del Vercol in the Pyrénées Orientales lost his position when he urged the people of his community to disobey the prefect's stern injunction against dancing in the town square.[11]

The electoral law of May 31, 1850, resulted in many striking examples of the contradiction between the administrative duties of local officials and their informal positions within the community. Mayors were required to eliminate from the electoral lists citizens excluded by the law from voting. In practice, this stipulation meant that, particularly in the smaller communes, mayors might have to eliminate friends, acquaintances, or, worse, political allies. Many of them, hesitant to enforce the law, procrastinated. Some municipal officials tolerated or even sponsored petitions against the law, although they later neglected to circulate the officially approved petitions for the revision of the constitution to maintain the presidency of Louis Napoleon.

The democratization of municipal politics seemed to be destroying the principles of "moral authority and hierarchy."[12] Radical municipal officials could lend legitimacy to democratic-socialism within a community, especially where "monsieur le maire" was himself politically active. On the other hand, a mayor devoted to "order" could be an invaluable ally for the administration. The subprefect of Villefranche (Haute Garonne) noted that the new mayor of Caraman, the only commune in his arrondissement where "anarchist ideas have been actively propagated ... has accomplished his task with a zeal worthy of the greatest praise and, thanks to his help, I have good reason to hope that the socialist leaders will always be outwitted."[13]

In 1849 the administration began to "successfully reconquer [municipal government] by decrees of dissolution [of municipal councils] and dismissal requested on the authority of the president of the republic."[14] During the July Monarchy politically inspired replacements of municipal officials had been extremely rare— for example, there were only seventeen between 1837 and 1840.[15] During the Second Republic, such removals became common-place, reflecting the transition from the elite politics of the *monarchie censitaire* to "the apprenticeship of the republic."[16] In 1849, there were 48 dismissals of mayors and adjunct mayors; in 1850, 265; and during the first two months of 1851, 23. The

vast majority of these involved mayors. Prefects' requests for
dismissals were granted almost automatically in Paris: during
one period in 1850, 183 of 186 such requests were rubber-stamped.
Another 25 *révocations* took place in the 469 cities where the
municipal authorities were selected in Paris.[17] Those recalled
from their official functions ranged from the powerful mayor
of Grenoble, who founded the Association alimentaire in that
city, to an obscure adjunct mayor in Naftel (Manche), who
supervised the planting of a liberty tree in November 1850.[18]

In addition to those dismissals clearly marked in the records
as politically inspired, at least two other categories indicated
political considerations were involved, "abuse of power" (104 in
1849, 1850, and the first two months of 1851) and "refusal to
execute the laws and acts of the superior authority" (170 during
the same period). It also seems likely that another group of
révocations, "character problems and lack of harmony with the
municipal council" and "judicial condemnation" involved some
political motivation.[19] In sum, as table 5.1 indicates, political
dismissals easily accounted for the vast majority of the 852
replacements during this period. Possibly as many as 500 mayors
and deputy mayors were recalled for political reasons from
January 1, 1849, through February 1851 (after this period
information cannot be accurately compiled).[20] Some révocations,
of course, had nothing to do with politics (for example, the
mayor of Frayssinet, Lot, had a difficult time portraying himself
as a political martyr after being arrested for stealing chickens).[21]
Some dismissals were obviously influenced by the quest for
effective and absolutely loyal municipal officials.

Politically motivated replacements, however, were not always
the optimal solution. As one prefect argued, "A dismissal, . . .
often too late and far from being a sufficient means to repression,
only augments the unfortunate popularity of the functionaries . . .
and the harm, far from being diminished, gives the scandal a
noisy and misleading publicity and makes them seem to be
political martyrs."[22] Frequently the municipal council, if it was
completely or partially dominated by montagnards, would
simply elect another adamant republican. Some prefects were

Table 5.1 The Purge of Mayors and Deputy Mayors in Selected
Departments, January 1, 1849, through February 28, 1851

Department	Total Dismissals	Reason		
		Overtly Political	"Abuse of Power"	Refusal to Execute Laws or Acts
Ain	9	0	0	0
Aisne	12	4	1	1
Allier	34	23	2	5
Alpes, B[s]	8	6	0	1
Ariège	10	5	1	3
Aude	35	17	3	8
Bouches-du-Rhône	10	5	1	2
Cher	6	4	1	0
Corrèze	10	7	0	1
Côte d'or	50	10	9	14
Creuse	9	2	0	4
Dordogne	27	8	1	8
Drôme	2	2	0	0
Finistère	3	1	0	2
Gard	11	6	3	2
Garonne H[te]	7	3	2	0
Gers	26	7	8	5
Gironde	21	10	2	2
Hérault	34	12	3	12
Indre	11	2	5	0
Isère	5	2	0	2
Loire, H[te]	14	6	5	1
Loiret	3	2	0	0
Lot	13	7	0	3
Manche	10	1	0	5
Marne	1	0	0	1
Moselle	8	2	2	1
Nièvre	19	6	1	3
Nord	3	2	0	0
Puy-de-Dôme	27	12	4	3
Pyrénées Orient.	31	19	2	6
Rhin, Bas	14	9	1	1

Table 5.1(contd.)

Department	Total Dismissals	Reason		
		Overtly Political	"Abuse of Power"	Refusal to Execute Laws or Acts
Rhône	11	1	1	2
Saône, H^{te}	13	4	1	1
Saône-et-L.	51	24	7	12
Seine Inf.	13	0	3	5
Somme	5	0	2	0
Tarn	10	5	0	1
Var	17	9	2	3
Vaucluse	20	14	2	3
Vendée	1	0	0	1
Vienne, H^{te}	8	2	2	1
Yonne	12	7	2	1
Total (all depts.)	852	336	104	170

SOURCE: AN C 977, "Tableau par département du nombre et des causes de révocations de maires et adjoints prononcées en 1849, 1850, 1851 (janvier–février)."

compelled to tolerate republican mayors in the interest of administrative efficiency.[23] In addition, at least twenty-four times between April 1849 and the coup d'état, a municipal council reelected the official that had been dismissed.[24] This act of protest, as the council understood, entailed its immediate dissolution by decree.

Between April 1849 and the last day of February in 1851, 276 municipal councils were dissolved by official edict. Several motives for dissolution can be differentiated (see table 5.2). Of the 188 dissolutions that took place in 1850, 62 were recorded as having the "bad composition" of the council as the motivating factor, indicating that a majority of the members were suspected of being montagnard sympathizers. (Councils had ten to thirty-six members, depending on the size of the commune; most commonly they had ten to twelve.) Some of the dissolutions recorded under

Table 5.2 Municipal Councils Dissolved,
April 18, 1849, through February 28, 1851

Department	Dissolutions	Motives for Dissolutions
Pyrénées Orientales	1	Call to civil war
	1	Participation in disorders
	1	Collective resignation
	2	Refusal to assist superior authorities
	4	Hostility towards superior authorities
Haute Vienne	5	Renomination of revoked officials
	1	Illegal deliberation
Gers	1	Participation in disorders
	1	Petition against the electoral law
	1	Abuse of power
	1	Lack of harmony
	1	Impossible to organize council
	2	Refusal to organize itself
	2	Hostility
Saône-et-Loire	2	Participation in disorders
	2	Hostility
	1	Refusal of assistance
	1	Illegal deliberation
	3	Impossible to organize a municipal administration
	3	Reelection of dismissed officials
	1	"Bad" leadership
	1	Incapacity
Total of All Departments	1	Call to civil war
	16	Participation in troubles or disorders

Table 5.2(contd.)

Department	Dissolutions	Motives for Dissolutions
	11	Anarchist intrigues
	55	Hostility towards the government
	25	Reelection of dismissed officials
	2	Petitions against the electoral law
	9	Fraud in elections
	1	Fraudulent acts
	15	Refusal to meet
	54	Impossible to organize a municipal administration
	29	Misunderstandings among the council
	12	Incapacity
	5	Council "in disrepute"
	43	Other
Total	278	

SOURCE: AN C 977, "Résumé des décisions rendues par le conseil d'état sur les propositions de révocations depuis son entrée en fonctions le 18 avril, 1849 jusqu'à 28 février, 1851."

the category "abuse of power ... disobedience of the laws and acts of the superior authority, and internal disagreement," probably also related to radical politics.[25] For example, in October 1849, the municipal council of St. Clar in the Gers was dissolved on the request of twenty-five bourgeois of the town, who claimed that the council did not "represent the community" despite the fact that the mayor had been elected to the council with 280 of 300 possible votes. The prefect appointed a temporary council, which lasted until a subsequent election, in which the "reds" abstained.[26]

Some collective resignations represented a political protest, such as those precipitated by political révocations. Members of the municipal councils of Mamers and St. Calais (both Sarthe)

116

Table 5.3   Dissolutions and Dismissals (Mayors, Deputy Mayors,
and Municipal Councils) Enacted by the Conseil d'état,
April 1, 1849–February 28, 1851

Reason Given	Number of Cases
Participation in troubles or disorders, directly or by tolerance	160
Anarchist intrigues	88
Hostility	65
Petitions against the electoral law	55
Resisting superior orders	42
Refusal to assist authorities	40
Abuse of power	38
Violation of laws and regulations	28
Call to civil war	11
Condemnation for political acts	5
Others	183
Total	715

SOURCE: AN C 977, "Recapitulation de révocations."

resigned, with one member of the Conseil général in protest of a June 1851 law extending the term of municipal councils without elections. In St. Jean-de-Losne (Côte d'or, where most municipal councilmen seemed hostile to the administration), seven members of the council resigned. When fourteen councilmen in Grenoble called it quits, the minister of interior noted to a colleague, "I don't even have to tell you that this originated with the demagogic party."[27] Indeed, such municipal, officials kept the administration busy. As table 5.3 shows, between April 1, 1849, and the end of February in 1851, the Conseil d'état carried out 715 acts of dissolution of municipal councils and dismissals of mayors and deputy mayors.

At the same time, official correspondence concerning the dismissal of mayors and adjunct mayors and the dissolution of municipal councils indicates the thoroughness of the prefects' investigations into the politics of virtually every municipal councilman, mayor, and deputy mayor in the country. While

politically motivated replacements of officials were the exceptions, careful surveillance represented the standard response
of the bureaucracy when confronted with the threat of the
democratization of municipal authority. Communal politics
became the business of the prefect, accounts of the political and
personal rivalries and influence within small communes crossed
his desk. Subprefects compiled reports on their communes,
pinpointing trouble spots, naming disloyal officials, and making
recommendations. A report of the subprefect of Lavaur (Tarn)
on his communes is illustrative. The mayor of Puylaurens,
Monsieur Vergues, a *proprietor*, had "good political principles"
but evidenced "a slight tendency toward the advanced ideas."
Although he was highly regarded in his commune, Vergues
allowed himself to be manipulated by M. X., a wealthy socialist
democratic-patron (fortune of 200,000 francs) and his deputy,
"a very bad but intelligent socialist" who was active, capable,
and also relatively wealthy (600,000 francs). Worse, the deputy
mayor was influential among artisans and workers "with bad
tendencies." The subprefect had been instructed to evaluate the
"politics," "fortune," "influence," "personal worth and capacity" of every mayor, deputy mayor, municipal councilman, tax
employee, and schoolteacher in his arrondissement.

In St. Sulpice, another commune of the arrondissement of
Lavaur, the administration had little to fear politically despite
the bitter rivalry between the mayor and his Orleanist predecessor. The tax collector was "a man of order, his political principles
are sound," and he was "capable enough" as evidenced by his
"fortune" of 16,000 francs. The schoolteacher seemed politically
moderate, without influence, and very poor.[28]

The purge of disloyal officials depended on just such detailed
information. The procureur in Bordeaux stated the official
policy; the government will "always repress the abettors of
disorder no matter what high positions they occupy." Official
dismissal touched justices of the peace, tax collectors (like the
tax collector of Montargis, a political friend of Madier de
Montjau, who was transfered to Langres), rural guards (a
political propagandist in Borée, Ardèche, for example), a number

of rural postmen, and even an occasional gendarme (such as one in November 1850, in Largentière, Ardèche, the scene of serious troubles in the fall of 1851).[29] Even where relatively few officials were purged, intimidation aided the repression. Clearly no political opposition would be tolerated, particularly in the town halls. Prefects had already begun to call for organizational changes to take the choice of mayor and deputy mayors away from the municipal councils, and then from the communes. In August 1851, a number of arrondissement councils supported a return to the 1831 law permitting prefects to choose municipal officials. By the time of the coup d'état, which made any debate over the proposed law meaningless, the administration had wrested control of the mairies which had fallen to the montagnards, an important step in uprooting the republic from the village.

George Duveau's chapter "L'Illusion lyrique" in *Les Instituteurs* portrays the optimism of both republicans and schoolteachers (*instituteurs*) that their mutually profitable relationship would form a basis of the Second Republic's development. The teachers of industrial Sotteville, outside of Rouen, pledged their loyalty to Frédéric Déschamps, revolutionary commissioner for the Seine Inférieure:

> Filled with the importance of our mission in the work of regeneration which our republican principles are going to accomplish, we ask you to believe, citizen, that we will outdo ourselves in effort and zeal to make the children entrusted to us understand the importance of the symbols on which the future of our immortal republic rests: Liberty, Equality, Fraternity.[30]

The provisional government in Paris dreamed that schoolteachers would become the auxiliaries of the republican government, instructing the people in their obligations and rights as citizens and relaying their complaints, hopes, and aspirations to the concerned central government. Even though in some backward areas they were barely literate, they would be the "brokers of republicanism" in their communities. Malardier's 1848 brochure, *The Gospel and the Republic, or the Social Mission of Schoolteachers*, offered a clear message: "It is up to you, teachers, to replace the priests who have abdicated."[31]

Some schoolteachers were enthusiastically active in the 1848 electoral fray. Arsène Meunier's *L'Écho des instituteurs* and the Comité central républicain de l'enseignement supported republican candidates, following the instructions of Hippolyte Carnot, the new minister of public instruction. Some of the teachers' post revolution "civic manuals" attacked the influence of the clergy. One, in the form of a republican catechism, asked the student, "Does there ... exist a means to prevent the rich from being idle and the poor from being eaten by the rich?" In Dijon, a mathematics professor headed an electoral committee of teachers. The commissioner of the Moselle called upon the president of a cantonal conference of instituteurs and reminded him that it was his duty to support the government's strong republican candidates in the elections; the commissioner of the Marne reprimanded his department's primary schoolteachers for endorsing a relatively conservative slate.[32] Alfred Cobban pictures the April election as a victory for the curés over their secular rivals and the Falloux Law of 1850 as the logical consequence of the active participation of schoolteachers in the election. Adolphe Thiers's fear that each village would have a phalansterian schoolteacher reflected the anxiety of the men of order that teachers would become a force for political and social radicalization.[33]

Indeed, the revolution had thrust many schoolteachers into the limelight in their communities, as interpreters of the electoral *professions de foi*, as readers of official proclamations, and as instant political sages. One Morer of Thuir in the Pyrénées Orientales recalled the advent of the Second Republic when he was professor at the Collège de Perpignan in 1886. In 1848, Morer remembered, he considered himself "a very liberal republican ... imbued with the great ideas so well summarized by the beautiful republican motto." He began, at the mayor's request, a mutual-aid society for "sick and disabled workers" and presided over a political club. "I was astonished," he remembered, "to learn that I had acquired a certain influence over the population." The club, which included workers and "workers [travailleurs] of the soil," met nightly, at least until the election. Morer was also named, "in spite of himself," secretary of a departmental association of schoolteachers and charged with drawing up its statutes and presenting them to the commissioner. The organization continued through 1848 until the prefect ordered it disbanded. It then tried unsuccessfully to regroup and circumvent administrative disapproval by naming as its president an ex-imperial soldier, justice of the peace, and member of the departmental general council. A rival, a private teacher with, if Morer is to be believed, the "imperialist band," kept Morer from his teaching position until late in the life of the republic.[34]

Was Félix Ponteil correct in asserting that "the revolution made schoolteachers political men"? Did they become the "priesthood" of republican virtue as *L'Émancipation de l'enseignement primaire* predicted one week after the disappointing April election?[35] They were often blamed for montagnard gains in May 1849, like those in the Dordogne, where they had played no political role the previous year but had assisted the victory of Marc Dufraisse the second time around.[36] Printed montagnard political statements demanded salary increases for schoolteachers, who, poor in legend and fact, receiving only lodging, two hundred francs per year, and whatever expenses the general council saw fit to vote annually. *L'Ami du peuple* of Montargis, *Le Messager du Nord*, and *La Feuille du village* urged all teachers to support the montagnards. In Paris, the Association fraternal des instituteurs et professeurs socialistes (rue Rambuteau) planned six courses a week for the poor (despite a rather modest beginning enrollment of two students) and looked forward to a socialist primary school in each commune with a "red alphabet" and socialist prayers for children.[37] None of this came to pass. But how many instituteurs in provincial France underwent the prise de conscience of the primary-school teacher in Grans (Bouches-du-Rhône), legitimist in 1815, liberal in 1830, and socialist of 1848?[38]

In 1850, prefects reported that some teachers had been discharged because they had exerted influence in the May 1849 elections in favor of the extreme left.[39] But in the Eure-et-Loir, only 2 of 400 primary schoolteachers were accused of being "advanced"; in the conservative Mayenne, "not a single" case had been cited to the prefect. The teachers of the Tarn-et-Garonne seemed to have "abandoned their advanced opinions" and those of the neighboring Tarn had avoided "traps of all kinds laid in their path, irrealizable but seductive promises ... made to them ... everyone expected them to regenerate society." But in some areas, the prefects' reports were less optimistic, and the situation, from the administration's point of view, deteriorated during 1850. The military administration in the Ain suspended thirteen instituteurs under the requirements of the state of siege. The prefect obtained the suspension of twelve and the removal of fifteen schoolteachers in the Marne, while one of every twelve teachers in the Ainse was in some way compromised in "political matters." In Haute Vienne, they seemed subversive in two arrondissements of four and only a "just severity" improved matters in the Hérault. Ten dismissals and fourteen suspensions reflected a serious problem in the Allier, and in the Dordogne, 22 of 383 schoolteachers faced disciplinary action of some kind.[40]

In 1850, the repression struck schoolteachers exhibiting montagnard sympathies. The so-called petite loi of January and the Falloux Law passed during the summer put France's school-teachers under the control of departmental supervisory commit-tees (comités supérieurs) and made it easier for prefects to obtain révocations.[41] The repression eliminated about 1,200 "dangerous" schoolteachers. (Michelet's figure of 8,000 is incredibly exag-gerated.)[42] Significantly, those who matriculated in 1848 sometimes appeared to be the most politically active. When the communal teacher of Uzay-le-Venon in the Cher lost his job, his correspondence revealed political contacts with eight col-leagues in the Cher and the Nièvre, two departments in which the secret societies were taking root in 1850 and 1851. All of these instituteurs were already under suspicion. They had matriculated from the *école normale* at the end of 1848, and "consequently . . . [had] been subject to the particular excitations and seductions of that era."[43]

The "subversive" political activity of primary schoolteachers in the rural Gers (where the illiteracy rate was 75%) and subsequent repression have been well-documented. The sub-prefects and the supervisory committees who were responsible for the conduct of the department's 333 primary schoolteachers suspended or terminated 42 of them, 26 for specific political offenses ("socialist propaganda," "demagogic deviation," "seditious talk," and so on). One report indicated that, "since February, schoolteacher Eugene Daure of Barran has gotten into the habit of reading the most dangerous newspapers to the peasants gathered around him each Sunday."[44]

J. Dagnan also recounts the dismissal of Monsieur Bazerque, instituteur of Montclar in the arrondissement of Condom. The process was apparently typical. Bazerque received a letter from the underinspector of primary schools accusing him of being a socialist and ordering him to report to the subprefect and the supervisory committee of Condom. Before leaving, he went to see the mayor, curé, and sacristan of his commune, requesting a letter or certificate of "competence and morality" which presumably would help his case and perhaps avert suspension. All three refused him. The curé attacked him as "a man outside of the Church" who read "anarchist journals" and supported "democratic" candidates in the elections. But Bezerque enjoyed considerable influence in the community (which undoubtedly had contributed to his undoing) and obtained a petition of support from the village property-owners and the "fathers of families" which the mayor "legalized" by signing it on the bottom. Thus armed, Bezerque travelled to Condom to confront the committee and the charges of "propagating socialist ideas," "uttering a seditious cry at the meeting of one hundred people," "leading his school with laxity," "not assisting at the divine offices of the Church," and "frequenting dangerous societies." Dismissed, he moved to Auch to give private lessons, and was reinstated at his own request in 1851 because of good political behavior. But in October, the prefect and the supervisory committee again ordered his suspension. The mixed commission of the Gers deported him to Algeria after the coup d'état.[45]

Bezerque's experience typified that of many schoolteachers cashiered in 1850 and 1851, and such dismissals occasionally led to angry confrontations between officials and townspeople.[46] Many other idealistic teachers abandoned republican politics of any shade rather than run the grave risk of losing their job. Once fired, most instituteurs had little hope of earning a living. A schoolteacher needed a certificate of morality in order to open up a private school, and by 1850 few mayors would dare grant one if the teacher had been dismissed. Curés, reveling in the passage of the Falloux Law, would be of no help here. The local rector and academic council could prevent any school from opening; illegal and sometimes clandestine instruction was discovered and punished. Mathieu de la Drôme organized a national subscription for dismissed teachers, sponsored by montagnard newspapers, which pictured these teachers as victims and martyrs.[47] The meager funds raised, however, could hardly sustain an unemployed teacher. Reprimands and temporary suspensions usually sufficed to terminate the brief political careers of the idealistic schoolteachers of the Second Republic. Selected acts of révocation intimidated the survivors and publicized the ultimate sanction.

At the same time, the increase in the minimum wage of primary schoolteachers contributed to the lessening of their political ardor, and it took an issue away from the montagnard representatives. The inspection process, formalized by the Falloux Law, also proved effective. The prefect of Cantal, where primary schoolteachers had posed a political problem, reported that the "worst arrondissement" of Aurillac had required relatively little attention by the supervisory committee.[48] Although the mixed commissions after the coup dealt severely with 261 instituteurs,[49] French schoolteachers did not become political men en masse during the Second Republic. The purge eliminated the core of montagnard activists from the schools, and those who remained heeded the lesson.

The Falloux Law also strengthed the repression in lycées,

collèges, and universities. Paul Gerbod cites the voluminous
correspondence between the departmental rectors (*petits rec-
teurs*) responsible for surveillance and discipline: from September
1, 1850 until April 1, 1851, 353,628 letters were exchanged,
almost 4,000 for each rector, or about 23 per day.[50] Although
there was a personnel turnover of about one thousand during
this period, final révocations were rare. Politically motivated
transfers to less prestigious posts seem to have been the common
way of dealing with political dissidence in higher education: a
professor at the Châteauroux lycée was transferred to Ajaccio
because of his "demagogic imprudences"; another in Tulle, one
of the leaders of the "parti rouge" in the Corrèze, to Millau and
finally to the Finistère; three young regents in Digne, "friends
of Langomazino [*sic*]," fired in September 1850; a lycée professor
dismissed because he allegedly told his charges that praying was
unnecessary; a regent at a collège in the Isère sent to Gap because
"he paid too much attention to those known as the reds of the
region"; and the nephew of montagnard Representative Daniel-
Lamazière sent to another lycée. At least three hundred professors
were the specific victims of their political allegiances during 1850
and 1851, as the repression purged the higher institutions as well
as the rural schoolhouses.[51]

Michelet was the most famous political martyr in French
academic life during the republic. Although his course had been
suspended by the Orleanist government shortly before the revolution of February, he found that the republican government of
Louis Napoleon was no more sympathetic to his views. In 1850
and 1851 police took more notes than did students during his
history lectures, in which he presented obvious allegories on
the demise of the republic. After one lecture in February 1850,
a police spy noted that "the political allusions of the professor
in the course and the lesson were welcomed with frenzied bravos."
Two weeks later, cries of "Down with the Jesuits" and "Long
live the political prisoners of Versailles and Bourges!" interupted
a lecture. Police reports on Michelet's class resembled those
concerning any potentially threatening political demonstration.
Michelet spoke of "the glorious destinies of humanity, that is

to say, socialism" and attacked the Church. During one lecture, students passed around a petition against the electoral law of May 31, 1850.[52]

During the spring of 1851, police became more apprehensive about Michelet's impact when he responded to personal attacks in the newspapers by accusing the clergy of blocking all ideas of progress. On February 20, 1851, he suggested that the press should deemphasize the frivolous serials because "the people need a stronger and more substantial nourishment, that of the good man, M. Robespierre." "Revolution," he argued, "alone has changed the world." One week later, an immense throng of twelve hundred, twice as many as there were seats, turned out to hear Michelet, and the police agent in attendance described the professor as "a most dangerous enchanter, who seduces enthusiastic youth with his marvelous and beautiful language." Michelet left the lecture hall amid thunderous applause and shouts of "To the Bastille! Let's go and visit our brothers!"[53]

This was clearly too much for the administration, and they suspended his salary and his course. Michelet refused to accept any of his remaining stipend and followed many of the purged schoolteachers he had described in a recent lecture into a forced retirement.[54]

The army was the ultimate force of repression, called out when gendarmes and local officials could not handle disorders or when real or at least possible insurrections loomed. At the time of the coup, eight departments were subject to martial law, the state of siege—five in the Lyon region (June 1849), and the Ardèche, Nièvre, and Cher in the fall of 1851. Although the revolution of 1848 carried with it the expectation that the National Guard would take on the role of dealing with internal disorders, troops were a familiar sight in the countryside, particularly in the Center and Southwest, during the first months of the republic. Called in to quell civilian disorders, by suppressing tax riots or halting the pillaging of forests in the name of lost rights, the army's actions set a significant precedent for the republic: "Appliquée à l'intérieur, l'armée ne savait que réprimer."[55]

During the first months of the republic, the army's political reliability was very much in question. About eighty officers were "retired" by the provisional government because of their obvious monarchist sentiments. The army had been ineffective during the February journées, and an "epidemic" of desertions followed the proclamation of the republic. P. Chalmin has described three stages of the army's reaction to the revolution: "disarray" was followed by a period of "reconquest" of discipline, and then a general lull, or return to normalcy, broken only by the intrigues among the top officers in Paris.[56] The June Days marked the beginning of the "divorce . . . between the troops and the people," ending any illusion that the alliance portrayed in optimistic engravings showing the fraternization of troops and ordinary citizens on the barricades might actually come about.[57]

And yet the montagnards persisted in their attempts to find allies among the junior officers and rank and file. Montagnard candidates received some support from soldiers in the 1849 election. Troops based in the capital sang the "Marseillaise" on the way to vote, and it seemed that troops from Paris, regardless of where they were based, tended to vote for démoc-socs. The minister of war suspected other soldiers with proletarian backgrounds had similar voting preferences. Three sergeants, popularly compared to the Four Sergeants of La Rochelle, who were executed conspirators of the restoration, were elected montagnard representatives from the Seine, Bas Rhin, and the Nièvre. Subversive propaganda directed at the army seemed to be achieving some success.[58]

The tone of these montagnard appeals consistently reminded the soldiers that the army was merely the extension of the "people." Félix Pyat's speech "To the Soldiers! To the New Army!" was widely disseminated in April 1849, before the elections: "No! No! The army will not forget that it is the daughter of the people, it will not forget that the three colors include blue, the color of work."[59] A popular contemporary lithograph proclaimed, "The people are the heart of the army; the army is the arm of the people." Another popular drawing published in Paris and Lyon showed the worker and the soldier standing together with Progress, represented by the symbol of the republic.[60] Something like thirty thousand copies of *To the Electors in the Army* urged soldiers to support the montagnard candidates in the March 1850 elections, and some of these pamphlets offered suggestions for improving the soldiers' lives, for example, a retirement fund. But when the repression tightened, the most prevalent theme became "Soldiers, don't be gendarmes, support the people and their rights" (from Pierre Dupont's "Le Chant du Soldat"). *Soldier Loup-garou*, written by the Limoges journalist Ernest LeBloys, describes the political prise de conscience of a young soldier called upon to kill Paris insurgents.[61] Montagnard papers sent free copies to soldiers; four hundred copies of *Le Peuple* were distributed outside of a Paris garrison. Officers checked soldiers returning to the barracks and searched their living quarters.[62]

Yet there were at least 223 separate reported incidents of socialist influence in the army. Commanders wrestled with the problem of preventing contacts of garrisoned troops with social- ist "subversives." Cafés, the most frequent point of interaction, were often placed off limits. Nevertheless, some touchy situa- tions occurred. In Saumur, two "bourgeois" wined a number of thirsty troops, telling them, "You are our brothers; we are among the suffering people, but our turn will come soon. Is it not in 1852 that the violated constitution will be restored?"[63]

With such problems in mind, the minister of war rotated gar- risons in cities like Lyon and Limoges to avoid any prolonged contact between soldiers and workers. Quartermasters carefully selected campsites and lodgings for troops on marches and on temporary duty in towns without barracks. The billeting of troops in private homes, still a common practice, caused resent- ment. Soldiers traveling in the Haute Loire were put up in barns because the local military authorities suspected the politics of the potential hosts. In Gex, near the Swiss border, officials avoided lodging soldiers "chez les anarchistes."[64]

Individual soldiers suspected of propagating subversive doc- trines were subject to surveillance and discipline. One soldier on leave in Paris faced arrest because he "visited socialists of a low level and unreliable subjects who make up the clientele of

the bars of the Latin Quarter." Another soldier fell under suspicion because he "professed the most revolutionary opinions."
Three junior officers in Toulouse were watched because they were
seen "fraternizing" with a radical worker, while the political
opinions of another were blamed on his mother, who lived in
the faubourg St. Antoine in Paris.[65]

Penalties for dissidence were severe. One grenadier was sent
to North Africa "for professing anarchist principles" and another
"because it was necessary to tear him away from his bad political
relations." Five soldiers seen in "bad" cafés soon joined them.
In June 1850, 136 soldiers left for Africa for disciplinary reasons
related to their political opinions; among them was a soldier
reported for wearing a Phrygian bonnet at a local carnival.
Seditious cries earned offenders banishment, as did signing or
passing petitions against the electoral law. Troops who sang
socialist songs while marching ("We Need Another '93" or
"Chanson de Ledru-Rollin," sung by troops marching through
the Gironde) were marked for disgrace.[66]

But acts of major collective sedition were rare as most of the
army fell into line. The 220 soldiers killed in April 1850, when
a bridge fell into the swirling Loire, had been singing the "Chant
des vignerons" and chanting "Long live the democratic and
social republic!" The most serious incident occurred in Salins
(Jura) after a soldier was arrested during an altercation with a
junior officer. A mutiny began when the soldiers tried to force
his release. The company was officially dissolved, one captain
forced into retirement, the battalion commander sent to a warmer
climate, and ten soldiers court-martialed, five of whom received
the death sentence.[67]

However, these incidents were exceptional; Bonapartism did
appeal to the army. The mass of French soldiers were peasants.
Isolated from their villages and shaped by the army, they became,
for the most part, loyal followers of the imperial dream. With
this in mind, Rémi Gossez generalized that it was "the proletariat
who made the revolution and the peasantry who liquidated it."[68]
Louis Napoleon's first plebiscite following the coup appealed
to the army, by then purged of unreliable elements and ready to

serve another Bonaparte. The Napoleonic legend was nurtured by small rewards for good service (fifty francs to gendarmes who faced a mob in the Ardèche, extra wine to army units for exceptionally heavy duty, etc.) distributed on December 10, the anniversary of the 1848 election.[69] The gendarmerie, made up of retired soldiers, was a dependable repressive force. Gendarmes served in their native region, although usually in a neighboring department. Some were old enough to remember fighting for another Napoleon.[70]

The shuffling and strengthening of garrisons facilitated social control during the latter years of the republic and ultimately guaranteed the success of the coup d'état. The essential strategy —hold the cities—did not change, even during the coup. Even if the repressive forces were never able to maintain what they considered to be perfect order in the countryside (though the Cher, put under the state of siege in October 1851, may have been an exception among the montagnard departments[71]), they did secure the cities and the potential urban "army" of insurrectionaries. The ministers of interior, justice, and war sized up the strengths of the montagnards in each department and contingency plans were distributed to administrative and military personnel in case of an insurrection. Troops were sent to some departments—Gard, Gers, Yonne, and others—where the prefects were able to demonstrate that the need existed.[72]

Not all of the military measures were directed against possible domestic unrest. At least sixteen hundred French political refugees in Geneva formed a community of exiles close enough to the frontier to peer across at the nervous French guards and to think about raising an army with the help of German and Italian revolutionaries. Geneva hummed with political intrigue. The French government received little help from the Swiss authorities. Even though the exiles were supposed to be confined to the canton in which they lived, they wandered about as they pleased. The new steamboat on Lac Léman increased their mobility. The Swiss government seemed more likely to respond to pressure from the exiles than to appeals from the French government, and an occasional search was about all the French could expect.

The Geneva authorities forbade any uniformed soldiers to enter their territory.[73]

Thus free to indulge openly in the démoc-soc rituals of fraternity, the exiles held political rallies, songfests, elaborate political funerals, and even a lottery for their own benefit. They tried their hand at publishing a newspaper and entertained montagnard leaders who still resided in France, particularly those from the adjacent departments of Ain and Jura. The French authorities kept informed by sending police spies across the border to check for false passports, socialist literature, and gunpowder (although this task was complicated by the fact that Swiss hunting powder was very much in demand in France). The most important precaution remained the maintenance of a sizable and mobilized armed force in the garrisons near the frontier.[74] Here also, social control remained in the hands of professionals and the army was the surest repressive force.

The reconstitution of the National Guard during the first few months of the Republic was often met with wild enthusiasm. Because at least in principle it formed the second line of defense against foreign invaders or brigands and marauders, the National Guard of the Republic symbolized the citizens' exercise of their rights and obligations. Small towns in which the Guard had only existed on paper now petitioned the provisional government for weapons. Guard units who possessed only a few ragged uniforms and rusty weapons proudly participated in the symbolic rites of the republic, the planting of liberty trees and the proclamation of the republic on May 4. A few people on this occasion might have recalled the words of Robespierre: "To be armed for self-defense is the right of all men without distinction; to be armed for the defense of the fatherland is the right of every citizen."[75]

In most of France, few disturbances accompanied the reorganization of the National Guard. Democratic elections of officers threatened to end the stranglehold of the privileged on the socially prestigious officer positions. In most communes, the most serious problem seemed to be that of armament. For example, in Haute Vienne thirty-nine communes petitioned the provisional government for arms. The commune of Pierrebuffière, near Limoges, had a population of thirteen hundred and two companies of guardsmen, but only thirty guns. Guns were expensive, and many of those distributed in similar circumstances eighteen years earlier did not work, a fact later demonstrated by an inspection of arms in 1850. In Vayres several former soldiers reorganized the Guard, but the commune of twenty-five hundred could not find a single serviceable weapon. The mayor of Oradour-sur-Glane, now remembered for the massacre of its civilian population by Nazi troops in 1944, complained that he had been shortchanged in 1830 and that only fifty guns were available for two hundred Guardsmen.[76] In the spring of 1848, Oradour-Sur-Glane was better off than most communes in France in terms of National Guard armaments.

The provisional government had sent as many guns as possible to arm provincial National Guard units during 1848, an act much regretted by the government of Louis Napoleon Bonaparte. The National Guard, despite several memorable occasions when it demonstrated a reactionary spirit, provided an organization capable of mobilizing militant republicans and of supplying them with weapons and an excuse to meet regularly. Some prefects, remembering the disloyalty of the Paris National Guard in 1827 and 1848,[77] anticipated a dangerous armed enemy within France. Already suspect from the point of view of efficiency, the National Guard did become a political problem in communes dominated by the montagnards. The administration responded by dissolving the offending units.

During the Second Republic, there were at least 286 such acts of dissolution, ranging from a single company to the entire Guard in twenty or thirty communes within a single department. Of these dissolutions, 36 occurred in 1848, beginning with the National Guard of Limoges, a conservative force. Most of these dissolutions were based on technicalities with the acts marked "immediate reorganization." Yet a few cases provided omens for the future of the Republic. In Essonnes (Seine-et-Oise), for example, the Guard refused to clear away the barricades from the route to Paris. After the socialist successes in the May elections of 1849 and the June uprisings of the same year, almost all dissolutions were politically motivated, resulted from an overt act of disloyalty, or were based on the prefect's determination that the entire Guard of a town or an important part of it had been "corrupted by the mauvais esprit" and posed a "threat to order." Some examples illustrate this purge. The National Guards of Sisteron, Manosque, and Volonne (Basses Alpes) were dissolved and disarmed in July 1850 for their "bad spirit." The Guard of Le Blanc (Indre) faced demobilization because the "arms [were] placed for the most part in dangerous hands." In Montpellier, two companies of "anarchists" were broken up. The "hostile composition" of the Moissac (Tarn-et-Garonne) Guard determined its fate. The minister of interior dissolved one battalion in Bordeaux because "most of the national guardsmen have socialist opinions." The last unit to be dissolved before the coup, in Bagnères (Hautes Pyrénées), had exhibited a mauvais esprit in November.

Cases of sedition or open defiance of the administration by entire units graphically demonstrated the potential danger of armed and disloyal units. Examples include the "hostile reception" offered Louis Napoleon by several units officially called upon to welcome him in 1850 (Joigny, Châtellerault, and Pont-à-Mousson), the illegal distribution of weapons (Barbaste, Lot-et-Garonne), and the participation of the National Guard of Sèvres in the June insurrection in Paris in 1849. The Guard of La Charité (Nièvre) "paraded in the town in uniform displaying a flag on which was printed the egalitarian triangle" and then held a banquet. Red hats completed the uniforms of some Toulouse guardsmen, and "anarchist shouts" were featured in an "unauthorized" parade in Semur. In Marseille, seditious chants were heard at a review. In Charolles, the Guard refused to escort the unpopular subprefect to an official function; in La Loupe (Eure-et-Loir), the Guard refused to repress disturbances caused by the turbulent railway workers of that canton, which was in an otherwise quiet department; the Guard of Belfort included an artillery company which continued to support the recently purged mayor; the Guard of Lodève did not help close a club, and so on.[78]

A law passed in June 1851 aided the repression by permitting a two-year delay in the reorganization of those units which had been dissolved by order of the minister of interior. It also stipulated that all guardsmen carried on the active rolls in a cantonal capital must own a uniform, recalling the June 1847 crisis in Limoges discussed in an earlier chapter. Henceforth an administrative council, half to be selected by the prefect and half by the municipal council, would supervise the Guard, further removing it from local control. Prefects recommended which units could be safely reorganized and which were to be completely dissolved.[79] Some officers protested these changes with collective resignations both in large cities like Grenoble and in small towns like Lannion (Côtes-du-Nord) and Boissy-Fresnoy (Oise).[80]

The law gave prefects virtually unlimited power to disarm and dissolve units. Voluminous correspondence discussed measures to be taken, and detailed reports had to account for every weapon in the possession of a National Guard. In Montargis 544 guns, 6 sabers, and 6 old muskets were taken from "the inhabitants of this town, [who] are animated by a mauvais esprit" by soldiers lodged in the inns and cabarets.[81]

The experience of the National Guard of St. Junien (Haute Vienne) seems typical for montagnard areas. The February revolution caused a rush to enroll; M. Roche, popular among the lower classes, was elected captain (in 1846 he had received but one vote, perhaps his own). Roche emerged as a montagnard organizer and the prefect blamed him for the leftist vote in the vicinity in 1849; he "was a man animated by the most hostile sentiments!" In February 1851, Roche refused to send a delegation to the perfunctory celebration of the twenty-fourth, claiming that the event would be a mockery of the revolution. Instead, he led a group of guardsmen through the streets chanting and singing. The prefect thereupon asked the minister of interior to order the dissolution of St. Junien's National Guard. On March 24, the prefect arrived with the commander of the departmental gendarmerie and a company of soldiers, who joined three brigades of gendarmes in front of the town hall. A decree was then posted ordering all National Guard guns into the town hall by five in the afternoon. It was a measure of which all "men of order" approved. De Mentque, the prefect, hoped that the example of St. Junien would be salutary in a department which "socialism has developed such deep roots." Henceforth, perhaps the hopes of the president would be realized in St. Junien, "that the good are reassured and the wicked tremble." The National Guard units in nearby St. Yrieix and in St. Léonard were also disbanded and disarmed in 1851.[82] A short time before the coup, the authorities could account for all of the guns in Haute Vienne, including those distributed after the revolution.

At about the same time Haute Vienne was effectively disarmed, the minister of interior moved to eliminate most units in the Gers, Drôme, and Isère. In the Loire, all but ten communes were without a National Guard; in Hérault, only the unit in St. Pons, "which has always shown itself to be a friend of order," survived.[83] Between January and May 1851, the National Guard was eliminated in seventy-six communes of the Gard.[84] In October, twenty-one National Guard units in the Lot were demobilized. Thus, before the coup d'état, most of the troublesome National Guard units in France already had been disarmed and dissolved.[85] As an institution, the Guard proved incompatible with a highly centralized, authoritarian bureaucracy. In montagnard regions, the Guard offered a legitimate means of organization as a republican institution and placed weapons "in the wrong hands." Instead of being a means of social control, the National Guard became another of its targets.

The National Assembly took the most notorious step in the disarmament of the laboring poor when it passed the law of May 31, 1850, ending universal suffrage. Noting that the workers of Rouen voted "as one man" for the montagnards and fearing that any major economic deterioration might convert the peasants of the Seine Inférieure to socialism, the procureur général voiced the sentiments of many of his colleagues:

When it consented to the periodic renewal of political power
by election, society committed a type of suicide, in that it
thus placed a weapon that could be used against it in the
hands of enemies. By offering the communists the possibility
of becoming kings one day by a "coup de scrutin" we have
offered the most irresistible encouragement for the propagation of their doctrines. . . . the repression becomes insufficient protection for the country as, however energetic
we can be, we can never neutralize . . . the hope of con-
quering the leadership of society and all its advantages . . .
legally and without much waiting. As long as the government
lacks the force and toughness necessary, as long as we are
without powerful barriers against the invasion of communism, the country will continue to be in the hopeless
and ruinous grasp of the social evil delivered to us by
1848.[86]

Startling successes in 1850, notably Eugène Sue's election
in Paris and the unexpected victory of Ducoux over Louis
Napoleon's personal secretary in Haute Vienne, indicated an
increase in montagnard influence. Of the latter election, which
reflected démoc-soc sympathy among the peasants and petty
bourgeoisie of Haute Vienne, the procureur général in Limoges
warned: "what more terrible threat than this revolt of the lower
classes, armed with universal suffrage, against the necessary
condition, against the eternal laws of human society."[87]

The law of May 31, 1850, stipulated that all electors had to
have had at least three years residency in their communes, must
never have been convicted of any illegal act, and must be "eligible" to pay some personal tax. The importance of this measure
of social control, which destroyed one of the foundations of the
republic—universal manhood suffrage—lies both in the fact
that it virtually disenfranchised whole urban and working-class
communities and in the measures of repression taken to counter
the petition campaign to protest the law. The measure eliminated
3,126,823 voters, or 31.4 percent of the total eligible to vote in
the May 1849 elections.[88] This legislation affected the cities more

than the countryside, eliminating, for example, seasonal migrants and the unemployed people who were forced to leave town in search of other work. In Rennes, the number of voters eligible dropped from 9,500 to 3,500 (a 68.1% loss); in Nancy, the figure dropped from 9,531 to 4,100 (57%). About two-thirds of the potential voters in the industrial Nord lost the right guaranteed by article 23 of the constitution.[89]

A petition campaign, reminiscent of the Chartist movement in England, protested the "attack against the security of the country and the sovereignty of the people." *La Voix du peuple* urged a "revolution of petitioning" and forty other papers followed, printing petitions that had been signed in markets, cafés, and workshops, or had been mailed to subscribers. In the Doubs, 154 petitions circulated and there were 92 in the neighboring Jura. More than 500,000 signatures were collected in seventy-eight departments.[90]

Léon Faucher attempted to discredit the petitions, correctly noting in the National Assembly that very few "men with a substantial political or social role and some influence among their fellow citizens had signed." In the commune of Savonnières eighty-six people had signed, but all but ten had used an "x". To discredit the petitions, the administration tried to prove that most of them were fraudulent. The prefect of the Cher claimed that signatures in the arrondissement of St. Amand had been falsified, because they included names of "honorable citizens . . . true friends of order." There were indeed cases of fraud, or ignorance. In Paulhiac (Lot-et-Garonne), some men had allegedly been forced to sign. A "dangerous" joiner near Grenoble enthusiastically signed fifteen times, and thirty-three of those who had "signed" could neither read nor write. A few signatures were obtained by guile, others were attributable to excessive "compliance or ignorance." One man who had been dead for ten years "signed" in the Hérault. Belgian workers were enlisted to sign in the cabarets of the Nord. Four "militaires" who signed in Riom turned out to be convicts in the military prison. Officials in some regions were ordered to attempt to validate every signature in a commune. For example, in Moulins it was determined that of 199 signatures, 47 were fraudulent, 49 "without value," 12 had been obtained under false pretenses, and 91 were "sincere." Of 175 signatures in Condom (Gers), 8 were "false," 30 could not be traced, 20 were the signatures of those who had signed to oblige someone they knew, 7 were the signatures of minors, and 1 was that of a *failli* (indicating a bankrupt person or a scoundrel). Six people disavowed their signatures, stating that either they had been led to believe that they were signing a petition against the drink tax or that they had signed because they feared trouble. The other 103 signatures were valid.[91]

But these were exceptions, particularly as the reports noted only the most flagrant cases. The ministry of justice, which had undertaken seventy-eight prosecutions, had won only six condemnations by the time of the report. There were also forty-three cases involving peddlers and hawkers who passed the petitions, and nineteen against printers who did not initial their work. Finally, there were six trials in which the wording of the petition appeared to violate the law by "inciting citizens against each other"—one was drafted by Emile de Girardin, glorying in his new role as a montagnard representative from the Bas Rhin. Prefects studied the gendarmerie reports on the petitions searching for any officials who had signed. At the same time, the success of the petitions in some communes gave administrators a general indication of the evolution of local politics.[92]

The law of May 31 lessened, but it did not remove, the possibility of a socialist electoral victory in 1852. "Is there not reason to believe," asked the procureur général of Limoges, "that socialism is marching to an electoral victory?"[93] The year 1852 was above all the year of the elections, and "1852" was the montagnard rallying cry in 1851. Despite the purge and the generally successful repression of the political activities and organization of ordinary Frenchmen, until the coup, there seemed to be even some hope for the elections, particularly if universal suffrage was returned to the people.

6

Repression in Urban Areas: Limoges and the Nord

The means of collective action utilized by ordinary people after the revolution of 1848 were national phenomena, but the mechanics of the repression itself varied from department to department and from region to region. In some regions, where the organizational and mobilizational capacity of the extreme left was limited, the repression was superfluous; in others, it was extremely harsh. The repression, for example, was obviously more visible and severe in the Dordogne than the Côtes-du-Nord because the left was far better organized and more powerful in the Dordogne. But the repression's goals varied in another important way, from city to countryside, following the real or potential balance in the coalition of the démoc-socs. By "cities" we do not only mean communes which qualified (by virtue of a population greater than 2,000 in the main settlement) as "urban areas" by mid-nineteenth century French statistical definition. Nor do we include all bourgs, which, as Margadant shows, served as marketing centers facilitating not only the entry of rural artisans, for example, into the market itself, but also their exposure to new ideas and organization.[1] The bourg is an important unit for understanding the growth of montagnard political commitment among the laboring poor. But an even simpler distinction will better serve the present discussion, the difference between the repression in largely urban areas and that in predominantly rural areas. Cities had special properties which made them potential bases for the regime's opponents. The initial goal of the repressors, who were well aware of these characteristics, was the destruction of the radical ap-

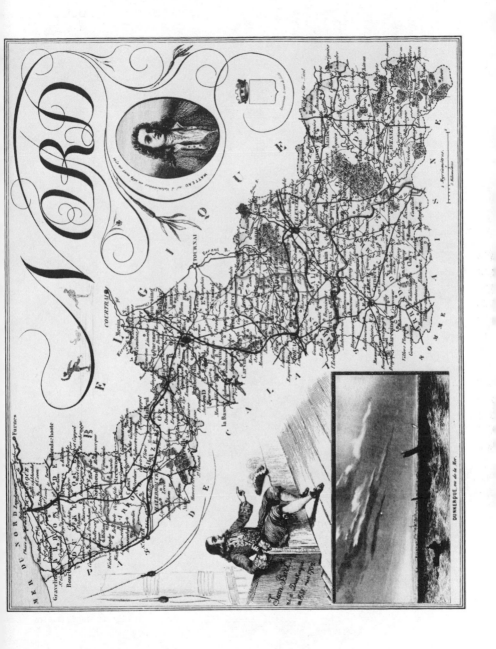

NORD

DUNKERQUE, vue de la Mer.

paratus in cities, and they were almost completely successful in France as a whole.

Population concentration, however, is not sufficient explanation for the cities' importance for both political organizers and repressors. Cities provided *organizational* opportunities. They had coteries of radical lawyers and journalists (with presses churning out papers unthinkable before the revolution), halls large enough for club and election meetings, street-corner hawkers, and large markets and fairs facilitating the dissemination of written and oral propaganda. Urban workers, who either lived in districts segregated by class or rubbed shoulders with a hostile bourgeoisie in mixed quarters, had already formed workers' associations during the July Monarchy. In an earlier chapter, we have seen the workers of Limoges and Rouen in action, allied with an influential group of bourgeois democratic-patrons against the majority of the bourgeoisie of those cities. Equally good examples are Troyes, Nantes, or one of a number of other cities, including Paris, where there were major urban disturbances after the revolution. Such disturbances were indicative of the rise in organized social conflict in which electoral associations, newspapers, clubs, workers' associations, and National Guard factions played important roles. Such organization could not be found in the countryside in April 1848. The countrypeople who arrived to vote in Limoges in the election of that month were intimidated and harassed. As would be expected, they cast votes for conservative candidates whose social and economic domination obviated any need to "organize" political support. One year later these same gentle *campagnards* were likely to pick up socialist propaganda on their trips to market. In the city's faubourg cafés, they listened to the political counsels of the same angry workers who had taunted them at the customs barrier a year earlier.

Cafés, workshops, factories, and markets provided regular gathering places and fertile ground for political proselytizing among the laboring poor. As we have seen, the development of workers' mutual-aid societies and associations provided an organizational foundation for working-class militancy in Lyon, Nantes, and Reims and elsewhere as well. We also noted the development of the propaganda network in Toulouse, centering upon workers' associations and cafés and spreading out into its hinterland, linking the radical organization in Toulouse to other Midi cities and to the rural arrondissements of Haute Garonne. Colmar, Nantes, and Nancy offered examples of cities where the offices of militant démoc-soc newspapers provided the nexus for the regional montagnard political organization. Urban bourgeois radicals, like Mangin and Guépin in Nantes and Bressy in Reims, used their influence in workers' associations and the press to help create radical constituencies with the organizational potential to engulf the hinterlands.

The repressors feared the specter of urban revolution, remembering the fall of recent regimes to motley groups of revolutionaries in Paris in 1830 and 1848, major insurrections in Lyon in 1834, the June Days and the unsuccessful insurrections in Paris and Lyon in 1849.[2] The Affaires of Limoges and Rouen demonstrated that the possibility of urban insurrection was not limited to France's largest and traditionally most unruly cities. When officials uncovered some conspiratorial links in the Midi, they automatically began referring to the "plot of Lyon," because they assumed Lyon's second city was about to rise again. They thus underestimated the extent of montagnard opposition in the rural Midi. The law of May 31, 1850, which curtailed suffrage, was intended to strike at the cities more than the countryside. Because it assumed that concentration bred militancy, the government prepared to hold the cities at all costs, a policy it later followed during the coup d'état. The government miscalculated the amount and nature of the resistance which would follow the coup, but it had fortified the cities against "the enemy within." The cities remained relatively calm, despite the insurrection in Paris and attempts in other urban centers. The defense of the democratic and social republic came from the hinterland, and the cities remained armed camps.

The experience of two urban areas, the city of Limoges and the urban department of the Nord (particularly the Lille, Tourcoing, Roubaix agglomeration) will illustrate the application of the mechanics of repression in specific cities, where it severed the links of the radical apparatus and broke up the revolutionary coalition which formed in 1848.

Despite their basic similarities, relatively advanced large-scale industrialization and influential democratic-patrons, Limoges and the relatively urbanized department of the Nord manifested important differences. The repression began earlier in Limoges, in the aftermath of April 27, 1848. Always much stronger in Limoges than in Nord, the montagnards constituted what Alain Corbin has called the "gauche limogeoise," contributing to the "red legend" of the city. They were largely responsible for the radicalization of most of Haute Vienne, particularly the small towns of St. Junien and St. Léonard in the valley of the Vienne.[3] The working class of the Nord was more amorphous (linguistically, for example) and more geographically mobile. The workers of Limoges included a reasonably militant group of artisans, principally shoemakers, which the Nord lacked. Because of these differences and similarities, an examination of both areas during the Second Republic will illustrate the experience of the repression in major urban areas.

At the end of April 1848, Limoges was under the control of its workers and a provisional committee of administration. Between the Affaire de Limoges and the elections of the following year, montagnard political organization, based on a coalition between the small elite of bourgeois socialists and the city's workers, spread from Limoges into its hinterland, changing the political profile of Haute Vienne. *Le Peuple* of Limoges predicted:

> The social question has been posed on the barricades of February. Be convinced of this: it will receive a solution. . . .
> We will not have to wait eighteen years for France to be socialist as it is today republican.[4]

With such confidence and enthusiasm, the démoc-socs produced a stunning electoral success in May 1849, when all representatives elected from Haute Vienne were socialists. The montagnards won 60 percent of the Limoges vote and dominated the election in eighteen of the department's twenty-seven cantons.[5] Théodore Bac, Marcel Dussoubs-Gaston, Michel de Bourges (who opted for another department), and other montagnard candidates defeated a conservative slate by effectively utilizing the benefits of the revolution—press freedom, the right of popular assembly and association, and universal suffrage—and by profiting from the influence of some devoted republicans in official administrative and judicial positions in the department.

Briefly, there were at least five important reasons for the montagnard success in Haute Vienne: the efficient organization centered in Limoges, working through the press and other propaganda organs, of which electoral committees, *Le Peuple*, and the oral propaganda of the candidates, were especially important; the general social, economic, and ideological division between the rich and the poor (the montagnards' opposition to indirect taxes was attractive to the laboring poor, in sharp contrast to the vague assertion of immutable "principles" by conservatives), the relative weakness of the notables in Haute Vienne, a characteristic of the Limousin; the ability of the Limoges socialists to find allies among the petty bourgeoisie of the smaller towns of Haute Vienne; and the heavy-handed repression which began immediately after the Affaire de Limoges and widely publicized the events of April 27, 1848. The timing of the trial of those indicted after the Affaire, which took place in Poitiers during the spring of 1849, made martyrs of those found guilty and heroes of the acquitted.[6]

How then was Limoges, the organizational center of montagnard success, ultimately demobilized? The repression began when a new commissioner, Duché, finally reached the troubled city shortly after the workers had seized power. Duché appointed a new municipal council and took action against the Société populaire, depriving it of a meeting place by ensuring that municipal and privately owned rooms became unavailable.[7] The July decree effectively limited political meetings, but though the club disbanded, its leaders, according to the procureur général, "continue[d] to exercise an influence on the rest of Haute Vienne and even beyond the department."[8] The municipal workshops, another urban symbol of the revolution, also disappeared. First the commissioner regulated the hours of work, then the numbers of eligible workers. From April until June, the workers on the rolls declined from thirty-seven hundred to one thousand. An enlarged garrison discouraged any disturbances or protests when the workshops were finally disbanded.[9]

Even without the organizational structure provided by their club, Limoges radicals managed to elect a municipal council of which half of the members were socialists, despite the division of the city into electoral districts which gave disproportionate strength to votes in the elite districts. The Orleanist paper *L'Ordre* still saw the political power of the "men of order" slipping away: "On April 27, the National Guard was disarmed by a riot; today, the riot has again disarmed the men of order by depriving them of the positions they should hold in the municipal council."[10] The city's vote for Louis Napoleon in December 1848 did not contradict this assessment of the political mood. Raspail and Ledru-Rollin had very little chance, although they received the votes of some workers. Cavaignac, the butcher of June, was the real enemy. Louis Napoleon seemed to be a republican and he was a Bonaparte; he was apparently interested in the fate of the people (had he not written on "the extinction of pauperism?"). The procureur général caught the mood of the city:

> The situation in Limoges has changed little. The city is still divided into two completely distinct classes, the workers, imbued with principles borrowed from communism and socialism, and those residents who . . . want to keep [what they have] . . . the workers, voting with great unity, obtained the election of all their candidates . . . on the other side, the manufacturers, the property-owners, and all those who are called bourgeois, still strongly resent the events of April 27, the forced loan which threatened them and the disarmament of the National Guard. This last measure, carried out with violence, profoundly humiliated them; it was an affront, and its memory does much to maintain in some [bourgeois] feelings of a vexatious fanaticism.[11]

Yet the sweeping socialist victory in May 1849, based upon returns from the entire department, surprised and horrified conservatives, who had been confident after the moderate result of the April 1848 election. The legitimist paper *La Province*, expressing the shock of the "good citizens," accused the Limoges socialists of calling out "the jacquerie."[12] At the same time, the paper blamed the administration for not having adequately coordinated the repression. Not until Pierre Paul Edouard de Mentque became prefect of Haute Vienne did the Ministry of Interior have the right man for the job in Limoges.

Commissioner Duché, who had been made prefect in June, was replaced in August. His successor, Monsieur Titot, a wealthy manufacturer who was in poor health and already planning his retirement, demonstrated to conservatives that he would not be an acceptable guardian of order with his initial proclamation, in which he noted that "democratic institutions represent progress compatible with the existence of family and property." Viewing Louis Napoleon as "antidemocratic," he favored the porcelain workers' efforts to organize a producers' cooperative. Worse still, he wrote that "the bourgeois party seems to me to be struck with an exaggerated terror; the town remained in the power of the workers for two weeks without any attacks on persons or property."[13] De Mentque, with two decades of Orleanist administrative experience, arrived to run a prefecture that just one year earlier had been headed by a provisional government which included workers and had only recently been vacated by a prefect who sympathized with them.[14] Most of the Limoges bourgeoisie approved of de Mentque, who pledged to defend "the unshakable maintenance of the sacred principles of family and property."[15]

The radical press became de Mentque's first priority. The return of the caution laws during the summer of 1848 had driven Limoges's two left-leaning papers out of business.[16] The black-bordered final issue of *Le Carillon républicain*, which had had a circulation of fifteen hundred, appeared on July 11 and contained an epitaph by the political cartoonist, songwriter, and editor, Alfred Durin, for its satirical antihero, Prefect Duché:

> Ci-gît le fameux Jean-sans-Peur
> Le Chansonnier Carilloneur,
> Ça loi sur le Cautionnement,
> L'a fait mourir subitement.

Le Peuple, which had closed down about the same time, returned on October 19, 1848, with a new editor, a former disciple of Pierre Leroux and his "religion of humanity." The paper, which in many ways appropriated the organizational role vacated by the Société Populaire, defended the "democratic and social republic" and the accused at the Affaire de Limoges trial in Poitiers in the spring of 1849. Enduring confiscations and court convictions, *Le Peuple* survived until after the elections; its editor then joined the political exiles in Switzerland.[17]

In November 1849, the montagnards twice attempted to revive the radical press in Limoges. *Le Carillon républicain* briefly returned as a monthly, a stratagem to avoid paying caution money. Simultaneously, it was announced that other editions of *Le Carillon* were to appear alternately in Poitiers, Angoulême, and Périgeux, so that, in effect, *Le Carillon* would be a weekly *sans caution*. For their imagination, all nominal editors were condemned by the Limoges appellate court for their "fraudulent declaration." Alfred Durin continued his career as a political cartoonist in prison. His conviction was announced by the single issue of a new newspaper. Its publication landed the editor, a dismissed schoolteacher, in jail with his friends.[18]

But the montagnards persisted, overcoming multiple press convictions. *Le Républicain du Centre* first appeared in November 1849, the inspiration of Marcel Dussoubs-Gaston. Its first issue was confiscated because of an "offensive" article, "Letter from a Sharecropper" (of which there were many in Haute Vienne). The nominal editor, a cooper, faced prosecution, and the court ruled that he could not possibly be the "serious" editor because he was "incapable." During these events, de Mentque obtained a list of subscribers in Haute Vienne, valuable information in view of the role of the literate in the diffusion of political propaganda among the illiterate (considerably more than half of the department).[19]

As an election in March 1850 approached (to replace Daniel-Lamazière, convicted by the High Court of Versailles for conspiracy), *Le Salut du peuple* supported the candidacy of an influential local montagnard radical, Ernest LeBloys. However the extreme left decided to run Ducoux, a former deputy from the Loir-et-Cher. His opponent, handpicked in Paris and aided by the prefect, was Louis Napoleon's personal secretary, a veteran of the Boulogne fiasco in 1840. After assisting Ducoux's victory, *Le Salut du peuple* disappeared.[20]

Finally, in November 1851, *Le Travailleur*, a newspaper of the "democrats, socialists, workers, peasants, workers of the land and industry, living from our intelligence and the labor of our hands," was begun with the financial backing of public subscriptions undertaken in Haute Vienne. Its third issue announced that it would be the last: de Mentque threatened to collect some old court costs if the paper continued. Thus, despite persistent efforts, the Limoges montagnards were without a paper when the final blow came on December 2, 1851.[21]

Like his colleagues, de Mentque opposed the other types of propaganda which appeared in Limoges. Much of this originated in Paris where Théodore Bac and Martin Nadaud, the mason and representative of the people from the Creuse, were instrumental in the founding of Solidarité républicaine.[22] De Mentque and the prefect of the Creuse believed that the propaganda was being brought back from the capital by the seasonal migrants returning home each fall. However, some pamphlets and brochures were illegally printed in Limoges, including *Gifts of the Democrats, or the Police Commissioner of Limoges*, written by a socialist lawyer, which described, with the scenario of an imaginary banquet, the harassment of workers' associations, electoral meetings, and montagnard leaders by the police.[23] To control démoc-soc propaganda, de Mentque exchanged information with other prefects, authorized household searches, and ordered the surveillance of the roads into the city and the markets and fairs. He seems to have been more successful than many of his colleagues, in whose departments copies of Pyat's *Toast to the Peasants* were as common as official almanacs and notices.

Of equal concern was oral propaganda, "developed by reading journals out loud, by seditious speeches"[24] at electoral meetings, banquets, cafés, and marketplace discussions. The club law forbade any kind of meeting which could "compromise the public peace" and anyone could be prosecuted for "inciting one group of citizens against another group," or its logical extension, "inciting civil war."[25] After June 1849, de Mentque adopted the minister of justice's interpretation and forbade "in an absolute manner, clubs or public meetings which concern themselves with the discussion of public affairs."[26] These laws applied to electoral meetings in 1850 and to banquets celebrating republican anniversaries and the visits of Haute Vienne's representatives. Like authors of political pamphlets, speakers or readers could be prosecuted, even in Limoges's "veritable clubs,"[27] cafés where ordinary people gathered to read newspapers or listen to them be read aloud. Although he generally preferred to leave cafés open (a visiting police spy or police commissioner could come up with all sorts of interesting and useful information there), de Mentque did close the Café des prolétaires, with its bright red marquee, because masons returning from Paris had been distributing propaganda there.[28] The police became expected but unwelcome habitués.

Workers' associations felt the weight of the repression. The *Gifts of the Democrats* pamphlet described the harassment of the Fraternal Association of Bakers' Apprentices, which was founded in April 1849, but later failed as a producers' cooperative. The shoemakers association came under official scrutiny when its members organized a fund drive for *Le Travailleur* and were implicated in various attempts to subvert the garrison politically. During a search, police uncovered some guns and a small supply of ammunition in the possession of the shoemakers. One Limoges radical who died on the Paris barricades in December 1851, had been in the capital, it was alleged, "on behalf" of the shoemakers association.[29] In August, a number of shoemakers had been convicted of political crimes; the court ruled that their association was a "secret society" intended to "fortify and spread socialist ideas of the worst variety." At the time of the coup, de Mentque also ordered the prosecution of the porcelain workers' association, barely tolerated since its creation in 1850. The Perfect Union, a bourgeois lodge, was dissolved for discussing "dangerous political theories" after it had come under the domination of Limoges's socialist lawyers.[30]

Almost folk heroes in Limoges, and identified with the interests of the people, the démoc-soc leaders faced official harassment. Because they linked Paris's political organization to Limoges, and Limoges to its hinterland, these bourgeois radicals had to be isolated if the repression was to be successful in countering montagnard strength in the department. A strong current of populism pervaded the organizational efforts of Limoges's radicals, whose missionary spirit is reflected in this passage from a letter written in prison by one of the convicted participants in the Affaire de Limoges:

> What you tell us of Haute Vienne and the progress made by the social ideas in the countryside fills us with joy. If Jacques Bonhomme can finally understand the revolution, it will be three-quarters made; it is he, the mistreated, robbed, and beaten, who holds the doors to the republic. He can open or shut them at will.[31]

In addition to limiting the radicals' organizational potential, the prefect orchestrated a propaganda campaign to challenge their informal authority by cultivating "order" as the official ideology. Louis Napoleon emerged as the ultimate symbol of conservative order; the allusions to the "president of the republic" faded.[32] The "anarchists" and "socialists" were identified with insurrection, turmoil, and chaos. Strong executive authority was posed as the only alternative to the "disorder" symbolized by the Affaire de Limoges and the June Days. The montagnards might very well be preparing an insurrection far worse than the June Days, another "1793." Several committees of "order" (as distinguished from the monarchist "men of order" who shared the same sentiments but had a different solution in mind) were organized in Limoges, similar to the Committee of December Tenth belittled by Marx. The Central Committee of General Lugnot, an old imperial soldier, was such an organization. Léon Faucher, no stranger to Bonapartist sentiments, addressed this committee in 1849 and hardly disguised his attack upon the republic:

> Hardly had the republic been declared in the streets of Paris than the government paved the way for attacks on property by giving gifts to the workers of the barricades ... Socialism

was begun here, as everywhere, by men whom I will call the
junior officers of the industrial army ... above all, we must
fortify authority and place it above all attack.[33]

A committee circular in 1851 warned of a coming insurrection by
the socialists in 1852: "The orders have been given, posts are
assigned, and each soldier of demagogy waits for the sound of the
bell which should blot out even the memories of '93."[34] The
legitimist paper *La Province* proved an invaluable, though often
unfriendly, ally for the prefect by attacking universal suffrage and
picturing each arrest for "seditious shouts" as evidence of a
massive plot.[35] Fear spread among the Limoges bourgeoisie in
1851 as a series of fires in the woods near the city in June sparked
rumors that "anarchists" were preparing to rise.[36]

In 1850, the word "democrat" had the same meaning for prefects and procureurs as "anarchist" and "communist" and the
yell "Long live the democratic and social republic!" was construed as an apology for the "crimes" of June. "Long live the
republic!" approximated, in official reports, a seditious shout.[37]
Municipal authorities prevented the celebration of February 24,
which *La Province* described as "this day forever infamous ...
of insurrection, pillage, and violation of all rights ... a day of
mourning which should be scratched from the official calen-
der."[38] In 1850, many officials routinely referred to the "prince
president." In February 1851, one gendarme reported with obvious satisfaction that he had heard some citizens say that 'they
could not understand how people could rejoice in having a
republic' and 'that only the nomad workers' wanted one. Many
administrators had written off the republic long before the
coup.[39]

The repression eliminated a number of montagnard leaders by
jailing them or forcing them into exile, some in 1849 for their
involvement in the Affaire, others for later political indiscretions.
This process of skimming off the top of the radical leadership led
to the participation of more ordinary people.[40] In Limoges, part
of the original leadership, including bourgeois and some porcelain
workers, survived. At the same time, there was some evidence

that the workers became determined to "go it alone," shunning bourgeois patronage. However, political organization was no longer possible; public and private meetings were too risky. When Nadaud arrived in 1851, gendarmes followed him and attended each gathering, which usually consisted of twenty-five or thirty "democrats" who met in a certain café. On another occasion, police dispersed a meeting Michel de Bourges had planned for two to three hundred porcelain workers in a factory. That same night the police broke up another meeting organized by Denis Dussoubs, younger brother of the representative. Denis Dussoubs had just been released from prison after serving a two-year sentence for his part in the Affaire. Police watched the home of Patapy, a socialist lawyer and organizer of the Democratic Committee for the 1852 elections who was assuming increasing leadership responsibility.[41] The police seemed to be everywhere and to know everything, leaving no doubt in anyone's mind about the danger inherent in maintaining contacts with radicals and the determination of the prefect and procureur général to eliminate montagnard organizational strength in Limoges.

While de Mentque weakened socialist organization, the Ministry of War strengthened the Limoges garrison and concentrated on selecting reliable troops. The army became the ultimate political sanction. Two weeks after the Affaire, three thousand troops entered the city; never again would Limoges's garrison be as easily neutralized as it had been after the February revolution. The workers of Limoges seemed resolutely socialist and possibly insurrectionary. The procureur had no illusions: "Limoges is still threateningly and profoundly divided by the most obvious cause of disorder, class antagonism. There must be no illusion about this. The evil is not subsiding, it is spreading."[42]

After first protesting the quartering of the occupying army in private homes (the result of inadequate space in the barracks), the workers began to subvert the garrison. Early in 1850, the subdivision commander in Limoges requested the transfer of troops because of their long exposure to the socialism of the Limoges workers. Many of the troops were Parisian-born and from working-class districts and most had voted for montagnard candidates in the elections. An incident on April 1, 1850, confirmed the general's fears. When word reached the barracks that three junior officers had been demoted and that three others were to be sent to Africa (the usual penalties for dissident political opinions), forty soldiers protested and went to town to find support among the workers, particularly among a group popularly known as the "sectionnaires." All forty were court-martialed and their penalties ranged from death to service in Africa (which could amount to the same thing). A military investigation uncovered close contacts between the garrison and the workers of Limoges, particularly those porcelain workers and shoemakers, who, if one report is to be believed, were providing soldiers with "wine, woman, and journals." A small fund collected by popular subscription tempted soldiers to desert or disobey orders. The Forty-sixth Line Regiment left Limoges, and was replaced with units drawn from less proletarian environments which proved to be more reliable.[43] The army, to whom the first plebiscite was directed immediately after the coup in December 1851, became the faithful servant of Louis Napoleon.

The existence of Volunteers of Haute Vienne further resolved the question of social control in Limoges. This elite corps, the former National Guard of the July Monarchy, had bitter memories of their humiliation after the revolution. The National Guard, theoretically open to all active citizens, was dissolved after the Affaire and was never reconstituted during the republic, and Limoges thus became the first of more than one hundred cities and towns during the Second Republic to lose its National Guard for political reasons.[44] The Volunteers, the remnants of the Orleanist Guard, received special authorization from the minister of interior because of "their excellent social composition" in a city where "the bourgeois class, the men of order, are in the proportion of one to three or four workers, [who are] more or less corrupted by socialism."[45] Once the workers' districts were disarmed, the Volunteers controlled virtually all of the guns that were not in the garrison; they drilled regularly (sometimes three days a week), inspected by junior army officers. A census council maintained the exclusiveness of the Volunteers by admitting only those respectable citizens "whose views guaranteed the maintenance of order." The Volunteers were a permanent part of social control in Limoges. One of their responsibilities was patrol of the workers' districts; an undated plan of defense against insurrection shows a carefully coordinated sharing of responsibility with regular troops. Several brawls reflected the hostility between workers and the bourgeois Volunteers. The editor of *Le Peuple* was convicted of a violation of the press laws for serializing a satiric attack on the Volunteers ("Note Fallen from the Pocket of a Volunteer of Haute Vienne"). The existence of nearly two thousand Volunteers showed that the bourgeoisie had rapidly closed ranks after the February revolution.[46]

As December 1851 approached, the Limoges montagnards confidently anticipated the 1852 elections, despite the effects of the law of May 31, 1850, which deprived over 40 percent of the Limogeois, almost all workers, of the right to vote.[47] As the minister of the interior surveyed a map of the departments and pinpointed spots where trouble could be expected, Haute Vienne seemed to be, particularly in comparison to its situation earlier in the republic, a relatively safe department. Only a few fragments of the démoc-soc network, successful in the 1849 elections, remained. A strong montagnard showing in 1852 was probable, but resistance to the coup d'état another matter.

The timing more than the fact of the coup caught the Limoges radicals by surprise. After hurried meetings, about fifty delegates went into the department on December 5 to sound the tocsin and organize a massive march on Limoges. A counterorder soon followed from the montagnards gathered at Patapy's house— news from Paris had been discouraging, including as it did the report that Denis Dussoubs had been shot while asking troops to remember that Louis Napoleon had taken an oath to obey the law. Only one column of peasants formed in Haute Vienne, passing through the villages of St. Paul, St. Bonnet, and Linards (where the mayor had been purged and National Guard dissolved) before being dispersed by a platoon of twenty-five soldiers. While there were two other smaller disturbances in the department, the troops and bourgeois Volunteers kept perfect order in Limoges.[48]

December 2 brought immediate repression of the last fragments of the montagnard political organization. *Le Travailleur* was banned, while the legitimist editors of *La Province* put their columns at the prefect's disposal, congratulating Louis Napoleon for saving France from civil war. Prefectural decrees closed two Limoges cafés, one because the socialist representatives gathered there with their friends, the other because porcelain workers sang seditious songs written by Alfred Durin. The owner of the latter café, a porcelain worker, had been arrested in the commune of Nexon, where he had hoped to mobilize peasants after the coup. Four workers' associations were dissolved at the request of the police commissioner; the shoemakers association, an association of sabot-makers, the Society of the Philanthropic Porcelain Workers (four members of which were involved in the Linards march), and an association of dressmakers known for their political contacts with Nadaud and Michel de Bourges.

The Mixed Commission of Haute Vienne concluded the task of dismembering the montagnard movement, dispensing penalties ranging from deportation to Cayenne to simple police surveillance. One hundred thirty-two people were found guilty and those from Limoges, of course, dominated the statistics. Their penalties, which in eighty-eight cases involved some sort of exile from Haute Vienne, reflected the officials' perception of the threat of their radical political activism and organization.[49]

By 1848, the Nord was undergoing large-scale industrialization and had a large work force of proletarians. Ten thousand miners worked the Nord coal basin; half of them were between the ages of ten and twenty. Lille, joined to Paris by railroad in 1846, was a depressing and unhealthy town of over 75,000. There, when times were relatively good, about twenty thousand workers spun cotton and linens. Although there were thirty-eight textile factories, cottage industry was still prevalent.[50] Nearby Roubaix, whose twenty thousand workers were mostly weavers, maintained a more rural character. Tourcoing lay a few kilometers to the north at the Belgian border. In 1845, a year before the economic crisis initiated a depression, about eight thousand men, five thousand women, three thousand children, and five thousand temporary or seasonal workers were employed in the woolen industry in that city. There were other pockets of industry in the department, including Avesnes (wool weaving), Le Cateau (spinning), and the mines of the Valenciennes region. The department of the Nord offered an industrial concentration unmatched anywhere in France.[51]

To these urban areas, the two northwestern arrondissements of Hazebrouck and Dunkerque, divided from Lille by the Lawe River, provided a marked contrast—they were essentially rural in character and had a largely Flemish-speaking population. Linguistic and cultural duality also characterized the industrial arrondissements; Belgians made up 14.4 percent of the population of the district of Lille and about 40 percent of the population of Roubaix.[52]

The presence so many Belgian workers, including those commuting to work from across the border, exacerbated social tensions in the department. Belgian weavers, ditchdiggers, bricklayers, and agricultural laborers would usually work for lower wages than French workers. Brawls between French and Belgian workers and French demands for the latter's expulsion reached epidemic proportions in the Nord, particularly during years of economic crisis.[53]

The February revolution ended any hope that the economic crisis begun in 1845 might subside. Half of the Tourcoing work force (92% of the wool combers) and 15,000 workers in Lille were unemployed by the end of the summer; of Roubaix's 34,000 people, 15,000 were on public charity.[54] Dissatisfied workers confronted the provisional government. There were attacks against Belgians; a worker's statement in a Lille club typified the xenophobic outbursts of March, "We want work; to get it, the foreign workers must be sent away." Several days of disturbances shook the Lille region in March and again in May. In Lille the workers sang the "Marseillaise" and rioted against an unpopular employer, and the miners of the coal basin were able to force "certain important concessions."[55] Strikes in March led the provisional government to set wages and the length of the work day; several agreements enacted between employers and workers after the revolution were still bitterly contested in 1851.[56]

The Nord's bourgeois radicals felt understandably optimistic about forging a successful revolutionary coalition with the department's proletarians. Their organizational strength derived from an active montagnard press with "socialist" papers in each of the Nord's eight arrondissements, and their goal was to expand their influence through the help of workers' associations, whose members numbered well over 40,000 workers. [57] The goal of the repression was to keep what became the montagnard leadership isolated from its potentially vast constituency.

Alphonse Bianchi emerged as the leading montagnard organizer in the Nord. A former plaster molder and occasional poet, Bianchi founded *Le Barbier de Lille* with his friend Achille Testelin in 1843, and three years later the paper became *Le Messager du Nord*. Bianchi, an "old republican" who had been active in the reform movement in Lille in 1847, became president of the Société républicaine de Lille following the revolution; in 1849 he preside over the Société des montagnards.[58] From the offices of *Le Messager du Nord*, which appeared seven days a week and had a regular circulation of over a thousand,[59] Bianchi organized the montagnards of the Nord. The procureur's description of Bianchi fits other democratic patrons of the Second Republic:

> The office of *Le Messager du Nord* is the source of all of the evil doctrines being spread in the region. M. Bianchi, one of the salaried editors of the paper, is also its inspiration. His influence, nil among the intelligent, enlightened, and moral faction of the arrondissement, is still very great among the workers, who consider him their defender, their father.[60]

Le Messager obtained the election of four candidates running for the conseil de prud'hommes. Bianchi developed considerable influence with the workers' associations (there were sixty in Lille), including the mutual-aid societies and the colorful "carnival societies"; "they thus form a type of network and all of the strands lead to Bianchi.[61]

Bianchi's political power in the Nord, at least on the left, was matched only by that of Charles Delescluze, another "old republican" to whom the revolution presented a chance for political power. Implicated in the 1835 plot against Louis Philippe, he lived in exile in Belgium until 1840, when he moved to Valenciennes and collaborated on *L'Impartial du Nord*. Declaring the republic in that city in February 1848, Delescluze served as the Nord's commissioner until May 22. After another brief fling at editing toward the end of the year, Delescluze headed for the capital and edited *La Révolution démocratique et sociale* and served as the general secretary of Solidarité républicaine. Tracked by the police after the journeé of June 13, 1849, he escaped through Valenciennes into Belgium. But Delescluze remained a force in local politics, albeit from London, where he edited *La Voix du proscrit* and conspired with Nord socialist leaders.[62]

Breaking the links of the radical network entailed the isolation of the leaders from the mass of workers, the curtailment of their influence through the press, and the prevention of the politicization of the Nord's working-class associations while limiting the political activities of Bianchi, Testelin, and Delescluze. Press prosecutions, routine surveillance of political activities, and searches were ultimately effective. The household searches seemed particularly important to the repression in the Nord. As the procureur général admitted, their purpose was much more "to produce a salutary moral result and to intimidate their leaders . . . than [to obtain] a judicial condemnation."[63]

The proximity of Belgium and the French exiles who resided there complicated the task of the police. At one time, eight thousand brochures were seized at the border as they were about to be smuggled into the Nord. The Paris police complained that Ledru-Rollin's brochures and pamphlets were coming into the capital with passengers on the Lille-Paris train.[64] Even boats from England had to be watched and information gleaned from the comings and goings of ordinary people. Confiscated letters from

London and Brussels added names and details to the prefect's information on the démoc-soc network in the Nord. The fact that the Belgian border was just a few kilometers away from the Lille-Roubaix-Tourcoing agglomeration presented a special problem. After his expulsion from France for political activities, (his political gatherings were dubbed the "club Piscart") a Belgian, Doctor Piscart, set up a café in Mouscrou, just across the border from Tourcoing. Despite the formal protests of the French minister of foreign affairs to the Belgian government, démoc-socs from the Nord crossed into Belgium to gather in Piscart's café, which was within hailing distance of the Tourcoing factories.[65] At the time of the coup, three police spies were investigating the links between Piscart, Bianchi, and their friends, and the miners of Anzin who were protesting a new and dangerous dig in the Cave d'Osse. The spies, generally useful to the prefect (except when they requested more money), were sent to ascertain the local influence of the editor of *La Voix du proscrit*, who had recently moved to St. Amand. They had succeeded in identifying three nonminers active in the vicinity: a locksmith, a butcher called "Big Eyes," and a charcoal-burner.[66]

The montagnards' organizational ventures were intended to prod the workers into political consciousness. They placed their hopes, as the prefect quickly discovered, in the workers' associations and the conseil des prud'hommes. *Le Messager* stressed the importance of elections for the conseil des prud'hommes and supported leftist candidates, including its secretary, Femy. Police uncovered a small nucleus of working-class leadership in the associations: Desiré Debuchy, president of the Société fraternelle des fileurs de Roubaix, who slipped back and forth across the border for meetings in Belgium, received ten months in prison for his activity in a strike in 1849; Leloir, the general secretary of the largest working-class association, L'Humanité (similar in some ways to the Association rémoise); and Delatombe, an appropriately named miner. But the Nord's administrators blamed the radical bourgeoisie for corrupting the workers. For example, the police commissioner of Tourcoing wrote that, because of this most pernicious influence, the worker "is forsaking

the docility which the worker owes to his master." The workers
of Tourcoing profited from a law of 1848 regulating the hours of
work and were now trying to force adoption of a new wage rate.
It was reported that Leloir, their leader, was not even a spinner,
and he and his friends were trying

> to erode the intimacy which should exist between the master
> and the worker. Then, finally, they obtain their goals—in-
> subordination, threats, and votes against [the workers'] true
> convictions. We should consider the workers' societies exist-
> ing in Tourcoing, under the patronage of the ultrademocrats,
> as conspiracy workshops, functioning principally at election-
> time, when the unfortunate workers, duped because of their
> naivete, send the government's enemies to the Chamber.[67]

The workers' riots in the spring of 1848 and several strikes in
1848 and 1849 frightened both officials and the industrialists. The
prefect resorted to dissolution as a means of eradicating any
political instincts the mutual-aid organization might possess.
The Société républicaine des fileurs de coton de Lille was closed
after a strike in August 1848. Other organizations disbanded
included the Société des fileurs of Roubaix and its counterparts
in Tourcoing, Lille, and St. Saveur (St. Saveur was the most
wretched district in Lille); the Société des malades of Saint Roch
and that of St. Antoine in Tourcoing, and the Cercle du Nord.[68]
   The most active workers' association was the cooperative and
mutual-aid society L'Humanité, founded by eighteen Lille workers after the revolution. Like similar organizations in the north
of France, L'Humanité sponsored four cooperative butcher
shops which soon spread to the suburbs of La Madeleine and
Wazemmes, as well as associate organizations in Tourcoing,
Loos, and Comines. L'Humanité brought together spinners and
the usual assortment of craftsmen, especially shoemakers. In the
first year of the republic, members of republican political organizations, La Solidarité and Bianchi's Société républicaine, joined
L'Humanité, giving it a political taint which it never lost. L'Humanité was allegedly organized into the groups of twenty and
one hundred characteristic of a secret society (though this was

never proven). L'Humanité, like L'Association rémoise, was banned in July 1851.[69]

Other types of popularly constituted voluntary associations fell under prefectural interdiction. The prefect dissolved a society of "montagnards rouges" in Sars-Poteries after its president and vice-president ordered red caps from an Avesnes hatmaker. The Société philharmonique des montagnards of Dunkerque (authorized, presumably under another name, in 1846) was disbanded when its seven members stood accused of political ties with Parisian radicals. A decree banned a Société des amis réunis in April 1851, and the authorization of the Société des marchands was terminated in February of that year, because it was "accused of benevolence towards the red republic."[70]

As should be clear, the development of voluntary associations, part of the social and economic evolution of the Nord, influenced the everyday life of a great number of ordinary citizens. There were at least one hundred workers' associations in Lille with a total of nearly five thousand members; there were also many interesting leisure associations—such forms of "sociability" were not limited to the Midi.[71] When voluntary associations threatened to influence the political development of the department, the administration repressed them, preventing democratic-socialism from obtaining more than a foothold in the Nord.

Just as the prefect curtailed the activities of the workers' associations, the law of May 31, 1850 "disarmed" more than half of the Nord's workers by depriving them of the right to vote. The law worked to perfection in the industrial Nord. In Lille alone, 10,438 workers lost the right to vote and more than half of the electorate in Valenciennes was eliminated. In Roubaix the number of eligible voters declined from 5,510 to 1,085 (a loss of 80.3%); in Tourcoing, only 1,521 of 5,091 voters survived (a loss of 70.3%). Even in rural Hazebrouck, the capital of the Flemish-speaking arrondissement of the same name, the number of eligible voters dropped from 1,900 to about 600 (a 68.4% loss).[72]

At the same time, politically inspired dismissals eliminated a number of montagnard sympathizers from positions of authority. The mayor of Lysoing was suspended after twenty years on the job because his commune did not sponsor a petition favoring the revision of the constitution to allow Louis Napoleon another four years as president. The communal schoolteacher and two tax collectors joined him in official disgrace. Four rural mailmen were fired for political indiscretions in 1850; the prefect replaced the mayor and deputy mayor of Louvil for similar reasons, the police commissioner of Roubaix was required to leave because he was not up to his task; the justice of the peace of Douai canton, because he was a socialist; and several other minor government employees, because they committed assorted political indiscretions.[73]

The politically festive were as active as the politically organized. At Mardi Gras, 1849, a parade in Lille featured young men in red hats and a woman representing Liberty. Cries of "Masquerade of Carnival" greeted the subprefect of Avesnes who had dissolved a singing society; the impromptu carnival moved into a café where a worker dressed as Ledru-Rollin pretended to ask another, dressed as Louis Napoleon, to reestablish universal suffrage. When "Louis Napoleon" refused, a rope was passed around his neck, and those in the café sang:

> Let us love the Republic,
> Love it well,
> And God will bless us!

For this minor melodrama, three workers (a spinner, a lace-maker, and a book-worker) were arrested, but they were later acquitted by a local jury.[74]

And, as elsewhere, funerals of montagnards provided the occasion for démoc-soc processions. The Cercle des ouvriers démocrates turned out in force for the funeral of a political radical in March 1850. Three hundred socialists, including a number from the Pas-de-Calais, attended the final rites of a charismatic café-owner at Quesnoy. Thirty members of a Douai mutual-aid society followed the casket of a locksmith in July 1851, stopping from a liberty tree on the way to the cemetery to sing the forbidden "Marseillaise".[75]

These few rebellious incidents and the necessarily secret meet-

ings of démoc-soc leaders represented not the political radicalization of the department but the endurance of its activists and the
efficiency of the repression. Socialism seemed to be making the
most headway in 1851 in the predominantly rural arrondissement
of Avesnes. Only small pockets of montagnard followers remained in the Nord: a former schoolteacher turned peasant, a
shoemaker, and a brewer (and former justice of the peace) in
Millonfosse: a wigmaker, a carpenter and part-time farmer in
Orchies; the artisans of Le Cateau, and so on.[76] The mass of
workers were increasingly indifferent to the montagnards' overtures. The miners of Anzin perhaps were an exception: in
September 1851, they resisted the industrialists, and their seizure
of the town hall and the National Guard's guns after the coup
was the most serious act of resistance in the Nord.[77]

The end of the worst of the economic depression aided the
work of the repression. Although the mining industry suffered
until the end of 1852, the textile situation improved in 1850 and
1851. Wages rose to about the 1847 level by 1850, and officials
assumed that relatively high wages would mean working-class
docility. While wages in 1851 were not quite equal to those of
1847, the cost of living, particularly the price of staples, was
lower.[78] However, an industrial slump in the spring of 1851,
principally affecting the weavers of Roubaix and Tourcoing,
brought gloom to workers, capitalists, and government officials.
In June, justices of the peace were dealing with numerous minor
disputes, as "almost everyone owes his landlord and baker." But
by the fall the crisis subsided. The Roubaix spinners, more concentrated and, the Nord's chief magistrate assumed, therefore
more exposed to the "seductions of socialism," feared a "return
to the disorders of 1848 and the cruel miseries which that year
brought in its wake."[79] The workers of Tourcoing still appeared
to be religious; in fact, the persistence of some religious attachment among Nord workers may help explain their growing lack
of interest in politics during the Second Republic.[80]

Harassed and facing increasing indifference, the montagnard
leaders made little headway once the workers' associations they
had influenced were dissolved or became apolitical. Few working-

class leaders or militant artisans provided literate guidance to assist or to succeed the bourgeois politicos under fire. Bianchi was an exception, agitating in November 1851 while *Le Messager du Nord* carried on. *La Voix du proscrit*, the continuation of Ledru-Rollin's journal in London, moved to the Nord in 1851 and immediately faced a series of prosecutions. Convictions were obtained when the manager of the paper illegally signed an article (he was in jail at the time) and when the newspaper violated "periodicity" (several editions were missed because of legal proceedings). A new managing editor was in jail by December 1851.[81] But the "high style" of *La Voix du proscrit* prevented it from being understood by the few workers who could read.[82] At the time of the coup only the Anzin miners and bourgeois-worker coalition in the small industrial town of Le Cateau offered officials reason for concern.

When the coup came, there was a small demonstration in Lille. Bianchi hid in a border village and went into exile, officially deported *in absentia* because his parents were both Italian. Montagnard Representative Testelin was expelled at the same time.[83] The montagnards were unable to effectively mobilize their logical constituents, the workers. This was hardly the stuff of a proletarian prise de conscience. Without sufficient working-class leadership, either from the ranks of artisans or from the factories, montagnard ideology meant little in the face of the repression. The subsiding of the economic crisis aided the government of Louis Napoleon. The germinal of working-class militancy awaited a future generation.

7

Repression in the Countryside: The Creuse, Ariège, and Finistère

Louis Napoleon's officials were just as eager to root out montagnard influence in the countryside as in the cities, although they may have exhibited less concern about the rural areas because they miscalculated démoc-soc strength and because the specter of recent urban uprisings and revolutions was more haunting than that of the fabled jacquerie. In rural areas, the repressors faced a somewhat different task because the existing or potential revolutionary coalition presented different components and strengths. The fact that the insurrection of 1851 was largely a rural phenomenon indicates the extent to which the government had underestimated the durability of the radical apparatus. However, the nature of the insurrection—which was spearheaded by the secret societies—also demonstrates that in many rural areas the repression had succeeded either by completely breaking the montagnard organization or by forcing it underground. The coup finished the job, although it was by no means an easy task.

This chapter is exclusively concerned with the repression in rural areas. Three case studies will allow us once again to apply the earlier findings on the mechanics of the repression to specific regions. Without attempting to construct a typology of rural radicalism, we can identify certain common characteristics which, although the combination of factors varied, still determined both montagnard strengths and the goals of the repression. We have had the chance to see all of these factors at work before, particularly in the discussion of the repression of collective protest and the purge.

First, the democratic-socialists drew strength in rural areas from the local influence of a radical political elite which had strong ties to the national political scene. This elite was capable of discerning and expressing the relevance of montagnard ideology to local social and economic grievances; conversely, the weakness or abdication of the local notables could increase the influence of this new elite brought into local and often national prominence by the revolution. The proximity of an urban center was also important—it provided a source of newspapers and propaganda and supplied a base for electoral organization and influence.

Second, the democratic-socialists needed local allies in positions of formal or informal authority. Compromised officials included radical justices of the peace, mayors, schoolteachers, or even tax collectors, particularly those appointed in 1848; their local allies with informal influence were petty bourgeois, radical shopkeepers, small town lawyers, innkeepers who subscribed to the montagnard press, and also the lionized artisan of myth and reality. These people, who would gather to welcome the diligence carrying a popular montagnard organizer in a small bourg, were capable in a more personal and everyday sense of linking social tensions and economic grievances to national political questions and elections.

Third, the rural community, or at least a sizable and cohesive segment, had a strong sense of solidarity on social and economic issues. Montagnard allegiance, or consensus, developed in many communities through the political awakening that arose from resistance to taxation (especially the forty-five centimes tax). This kind of resistance was particularly evident in the Massif Central and Midi. In addition, the erosion of communal economic liberties (forests, water, land) intensified fundamental tensions between the poor and the notables. Resistance to and contempt for the repression often nurtured what officials called "the spirit of opposition." It festered in communal associations (societies, popular circles, chambrées, mutual-aid societies) and at the regular meetings of other groups (National Guard, electoral committees, and municipal councils) as well as in cafés. Outward

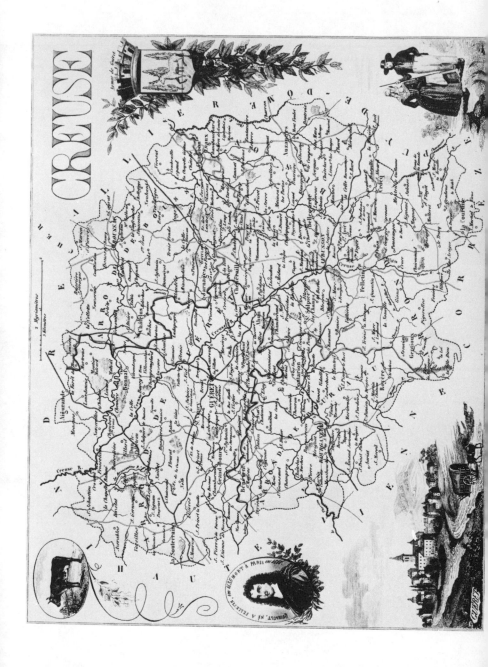

CREUSE

manifestations of this "moral disorder" or "mauvais esprit" included hostile demonstrations of opposition to the government or its representatives and support for the montagnards and the "democratic and social republic." These ranged, as we have seen, from staging confrontations with gendarmes to waving red caps in carnivals, from demonstrations around liberty trees to seditious singing and shouting. Such activities placed the government in the role of a hostile intruder who represented essentially different values.[1] The repression moved to counter this political mobilization of ordinary Frenchmen.

This chapter will offer a sketch of the repression in three departments where it succeeded: the Creuse (arrondissements of Boussac and Bourganeuf), the Ariège, and the Finistère. The first two departments qualified as "radical" both according to the results of the elections of May 1849 (returning all montagnards save one in the Creuse) and according to official appraisals of their "public spirit" during 1850 and, to a lesser extent, in 1851. In the Finistère, on the other hand, there was only minor activity. The Creuse and the Ariège had strong leaders, which included the elected montagnard Representatives and their allies, the mayors and schoolteachers who translated local grievances into the vocabulary of national politics. Both departments had traditions of resistance against taxes. Guéret in the Creuse was the scene of the bloodiest revolt against the forty-five centimes tax in France, and the Ariège peasants habitually battled the hated tax apparatus, as well as the notables and state administrators who were shutting them out of the forests. Seasonal migration made the Creuse unique, furnishing a steady contact with Paris, indeed with working-class Paris, and with other urban areas. The urban center nearest the Ariège was Toulouse, on the doorstep of the Pyrénées. In the Finistère, a strong sense of community existed, but its base was religious, conservative, and Breton; the repression here had only the most limited needs and objectives.

The Creuse has always been one of France's poorest regions. In 1848, it had only three small pockets of industry—in Aubusson and in Felletin (textiles, including the famous tapestries) and in

Bourganeuf (porcelain production). A region of bare subsistence agriculture characterized by small units—almost 60 percent of all farms had fewer than ten hectares, and two-thirds of those had fewer than five—its land was of such poor quality that in some cantons herding was necessary for survival. Two-thirds of the inhabitants were illiterate; nearly all were debt-ridden and in-adequately clothed. Their diet reflected their grim poverty; most ate only poor-quality rye bread, chestnuts, and potatoes, and they had meat only four or five times a year. The Creuse could not support its population. As early as the seventeenth century seasonal migration played a major part in the local economy, giving the region a distinctive character.[2]

In certain cantons seasonal migration was particularly heavy, involving up to 60 percent of the active male labor force. Most seasonal migrants went to France's urban centers, particularly Paris, where they worked in the construction industry as masons, tilers, stonecutters, and day laborers. The geographical and occu-pational patterns of this migration dated from the eighteenth century. For example, two townships, Lépinas in the canton of Ahun and Rougnat in the canton of Auzances (988 and 2,250 people respectively), provided most of the slaters from the department. The village of Alleyrat (canton of Aubusson) sent all of its seasonal workers to the north, to Paris, Troyes, and Auxerre, while the sixty-two workers from nearby St. Amand went east to Montluçon or Clermont.[3] Martin Nadaud's fas-cinating memoirs provide an unforgettable and graphic view of the life of the seasonal migrant who returned to the Creuse each November with some degree of relative prosperity, full of the tales of the sights, frivolity, and dangers of the capital.[4] The urban world offered a striking contrast to the Creuse, but the seasonal migrant remained part of both.

As the new republic desperately needed the political support of the enfranchised masses, the regular links between the Creuse and Paris (and, to a lesser extent, between Creuse and Lyon) took on political significance: the creusois workers living in Paris brought the revolution back home. Parisian radicals with provincial ties took it upon themselves to "force [their] brothers of the countryside to accept the glorious heritage of [their] brothers in Paris; the latter shed their blood, the former gave their sweat."[5] After the revolution, Nadaud met with a group of masons from the home department, formed a club, and returned to the Creuse, as emissary of the Club of Clubs and, at the same time, as "candidate and worker" on the "list of candidates proposed by the workers and laborers of the Creuse in Paris."[6] But Nadaud and the other revolutionary delegates had little luck at home. The few clubs formed after the revolution were far more conservative than their names indicated (they were called "democratic societies" in Guéret, Ahun, and elsewhere). Members of the small republican clubs in Bourganeuf and La Souterraine were resisted by many of their reticent fellow citizens. The Club des ouvriers in Bourganeuf, led by a schoolteacher, opposed the club under the sway of Emile de Girardin, the powerful legitimist journalist. Nadaud and another delegate from Paris were run out of town by the Aubusson textile workers who accused them of "having tried to spread communist ideas" and of opposing the "philanthropic intentions" of the textile magnate Sallandrouze.[7] Purged Orleanist officials, including the former prefect, lent their influence to a list of conservative candidates. They were helped by the forty-five centimes tax, a "calamity, a general frustration, and, for the elections, an immense mistake" which accentuated local opposition to the republic. In the most serious protest against the tax in France, sixteen peasants were killed in a confrontation with the Guéret National Guard.[8] The April elections resulted in a split between conservatives and moderate republicans. Nadaud found support only in the cantons near his village; the other radical candidates took an even worse beating.[9]

But by May of 1849, helped by a massive oral and written propaganda effort and by the relative weakness of local notables, Nadaud, Pierre and Jules Leroux, and their friends were well-known political figures in the Creuse, and they were popularly identified with the interests of the poor.[10] They benefited from their contacts with the seasonal migrants in Paris and the political organization and propaganda of the capital. They also received assistance from local officials, many of whom had received positions after the revolution.

The printing presses of the family of Pierre Leroux, who had moved to Boussac in 1844, provided a vehicle for montagnard propaganda in the arrondissement.[11] At the first news of the revolution in Paris, Leroux, the founder of the "religion of humanity," had been carried triumphantly on the shoulders of the townspeople to the town hall and declared mayor. The Leroux family influenced the outcome of the election of May 1849 in the Creuse, as an estimated 25,000 copies of the political platform of Jules Leroux, Pierre's victorious brother, circulated in the department:

> I am of the people. I am a printing worker, living like the poor, the peasants, the workers, my brothers and comrades ... I have never stopped fighting ... against *les Gros*, the bourgeoisie, the rich, the powerful.[12]

His program appealed to the poor, calling as it did for the reimbursement of the forty-five centimes tax, increased pay for schoolteachers, "free justice," a progressive tax, the abolition of the taxes on salt and drink, and the proclamation that work would be the equal of "property." He also demanded amnesty for those jailed after the June Days ("the honorable civil war"), and many of those incarcerated were in fact from his department —the Creuse, with the Vosges, had the largest number of its citizens arrested during the journées outside of the Paris region. Leroux, Nadaud, Gustave Jourdain, and "Ratier, seasonal migrant," addressed an appeal to the "true electors, peasants and workers." Their circulars, exhibiting the same populist appeal as Félix Pyat's famous "Toast to the Peasants," originated in Boussac, printed by the Leroux family.[13]

To counteract Leroux's influence, the prefect of the Creuse pressed for the rejection of Leroux's application for funds from the 3 million francs allotted by the National Assembly for the development of industrial associations. The government refused to subsidize "antisocial doctrines."[14] In July 1849, gendarmes searched the printing workshops hoping to find hidden guns and ammunition; three months later, Leroux's printers were prosecuted for bringing people together for "the political instruction of the peasants" and for attacking the concept of "property." Leroux's son-in-law went on trial for allegedly organizing an effort to aid the insurgents of Lyon. Those accused were all acquitted, causing the procureur to complain that no local jury would convict Leroux's followers. This did not prevent St. Amand, the prefect, from closing another of the Leroux printing enterprises in nearby Chambon. Pierre Leroux's *L'Éclaireur* ceased publication during the same year, and he left the area in 1850.[15] That October the commander of the departmental gendarmerie was pleased to report that "the Leroux family no longer appears to command the same credit; the peasants appear more disposed to follow the counsel of their landlords."[16]

In the arrondissement of Bourganeuf, Martin Nadaud, from Soubrebost in the canton of Pontarion, was elected as "the standard-bearer of the workers of Creuse" and "candidate of the Committee of Creusois in Paris . . . member of the working party of the department."[17] Nadaud's personal popularity and incessant propaganda, written and oral, largely contributed to the montagnard success in this region, which gave the highest percentage of votes to the radical candidates in the Creuse. Nadaud's experience during the remainder of the Second Republic was typical of the montagnard representatives, who had been legally elected by the people but were treated like ordinary criminals. His followers in the bourgs and villages of the region were harassed, and their meetings and banquets were prevented from taking place. His two most influential followers, the lawyer Gustave Jourdain and the notary Adrien Rouchon were, like Nadaud, followed by gendarmes and police spies. Household searches intimidated most of Nadaud's friends and relatives.[18] Because Nadaud's influence appeared strongest among the seasonal migrants, the prefect tried to turn the peasants against him by suggesting that their interests were in conflict with those of the seasonal migrants. A newspaper backed by a committee of men of order began in 1851 with the supervision and support of the prefect; *Le Conciliateur* warned:

> What will happen in 1852 . . . when Nadaud will have voted in a project which will consist of covering our soil with phalansteries with the help of a forced tax of two-thirds of revenues? The masons will be able to pay, but the peasants?[19]

Agricultural prosperity was thus equated with political order, a strategy bound to have some impact in the relatively "sedentary" arrondissement of Bourganeuf, whose four cantons had relatively low percentages of seasonal migration.[20]

At the same time, there is evidence that the conservative propaganda written for the seasonal migrants served its purpose. Although the prefect tended to blame the seasonal migrants returning home each November "perverted by the evil doctrines which they acquire in the large centers of population" for the diffusion of "the detestable maxims of socialism," there does not appear to have been positive association between high percentages of Montagnard votes in May 1849 and high percentages of seasonal migration. In fact, there seems to have been a negative association. Thus, the canton of Evaux (arrondissement of Aubusson) where over 60 percent of the active male labor force migrated seasonally in 1846, had the lowest percentage of démocsoc votes in 1849.[21] This could indicate that the administration's propaganda effort to identify "disorder" and economic crisis was paying off; in 1848, there had been only limited migration because the revolution occurred just before the migrants were to leave for the cities. Workers from outside Paris were, in principle, excluded from the national workshops. The construction industry suffered. As mayors granted few travel passports, the representatives from the Creuse successfully pleaded for special permission for the seasonal migrants to leave for Paris in 1849.[22] Therefore, the negative association in the canton of Evaux may reflect the fact that, in 1849, the large number of seasonal migrants had already left for the north and therefore did not vote. Whatever the reality, the officials hoped that migrants as well as peasants would see a relationship between revolutionary political upheaval and their own economic hardship. When gendarmes estimated the number of seasonal migrants leaving in the spring of 1851 at between 30,000 and 40,000, they assumed that this would help undermine the influence of the montagnards in the Creuse.[23] They were quite probably correct.

Although seasonal migrants did provide creusois radicalism with its leaders and its ideological exposure to the social question, other factors had their effect on the left. For example, in the canton of Bourganeuf, which gave 59 percent of its vote in May 1849 to the démoc-socs (only about 10 percent of its active male labor force migrated seasonally),[24] the porcelain workers and Nadaud's personal influence in his home region were important factors. Furthermore, as Corbin has demonstrated, the more sedentary regions of the Creuse were hardest hit by the crisis of 1846–47.[25] In addition, a group of communal officials, who had come to power in the wake of the revolution, seemed to be radicalizing their own communes. The prefect and his subprefects, aided by almost unlimited power to have officials dismissed, moved to root out these dangerous influences who were seemingly legitimized by the tricolor sash of official authority. Minor dramas of accusations, denunciations, official notices, and bitter rivalries were acted out in hundreds of French townships.

The administrative structure of the commune was simple enough to manage, once the ministers of interior and justice knew something about the politics of the man at each desk. The justice of the peace, with cantonal responsibilities, had considerable formal and informal authority in the communes of his canton; ten of the Creuse's twenty-four justices of the peace were brought to power by the revolution.[26] In each township, the influence of the mayor (and his deputy) increased with universal suffrage; for the first time in recent memory, the identity of the mayor mattered and national political questions thus influenced communes of relatively small size. The postrevolution purge of 19 percent of the department's mayors sometimes left the town halls in the control of those who became politically unreliable; most of these, and some other new men, were elected by the municipal councils during the summer of 1848. Schoolteachers with considerable local influence also seemed to be "artisans of disorder" in the region. Literate men in largely illiterate communities, they could wield political influence, for example, by serving as the mayor's secretary. Creusois schoolteachers took a more active role in the May 1849 elections than they had in those of the previous year.[27]

In the arrondissement of Bourganeuf, the disloyalty of ten of the forty-two mayors worried the subprefect.[28] Some communes divided into two factions, with the "revolutionary" mayor opposed by the former mayor and his friends—purged officials were understandably bitter and deeply hated the republic. As we have seen, a loyal mayor was essential for the administration, much more so than in the days of *censitaire* politics, when only a handful of close friends or confirmed enemies voted. Under pressure from the Ministry of Interior, disloyal, slow-moving, or incompetent mayors were removed and the town halls were turned over to surer hands. In Bourganeuf, the mayors of Augurès, Royère, and Soubrebost, Nadaud's commune, were fired because they were friends of the Creuse's most popular statesman.[29]

The commune of Sardent, canton of Pontarion (population 2,506 in 1846) is a case in point. The mayor who served during the July Monarchy was replaced following the February revolution by a noted "red" republican, Monsieur Junien. During June, he had to deal with disturbances against the forty-five centimes tax, yet, as Nadaud's friend, he had no trouble being elected by the new municipal council. Junien enthusiastically got out the vote for Nadaud, which was his political undoing. His authority ended on August 29, 1849, nominally because he had read an article "injurious" to Louis Napoleon at a communal meeting. Three weeks later, the "socialist" municipal council reelected him. The council was dissolved, and in the subsequent municipal election, the prefect managed to obtain a council of "more suitable" composition, despite Nadaud's efforts on Junien's behalf. But Junien's influence in Sardent continued, seemingly unabated. When Jules Leroux came to town, he stayed with Junien; gendarmes therefore searched the house. At the end of 1850, the "spirit of disorder" still persisted in the commune. The minister of interior ordered the dissolution and disarming of the National Guard, which had elected a montagnard commander and continued to meet long after the guns of most rural units were left to rust. The new mayor, even with the subprefect's assistance, proved unable to infuse "moral order" in Sardent; he was also inefficient. "Doubtful" voters remained on the rolls for the 1852 elections.[30]

Similar political dismissals occurred in the communes of the arrondissement of Boussac. In the canton of Jarnages, where the montagnards won an impressive 73.4 percent of the 1849 vote, thirteen mayors were recalled for political reasons during 1850 and 1851; two of these had attended a banquet for Nadaud.[31] The dissolution of the municipal council of Jarnages followed its reelection of a cashiered mayor. The justice of the peace of the same canton, a postrevolution appointee and friend of Pierre Leroux, lost his position. A club member in Boussac after the revolution, he assisted Jules Leroux in the electoral campaign of May 1849. His replacement, who had held the same position in La Souterraine until he was fined by the provisional government, had appealed to the minister of justice for another position. Like other officials replaced in March and April 1848, once he was again in power he was eager to do battle with the republic which had humiliated him. No more loyal ally could be found for Louis Napoleon Bonaparte.[32]

Beginning late in 1849, five schoolteachers in the arrondissements were fired (including those of Royère and Soubrebost, where the mayors were also replaced).[33] These changes, combined with warnings from the prefect and the regional inspection committees created by the Falloux Law, helped impose a voluntary limitation on the political activities of schoolteachers. Once suspended or dismissed, a schoolteacher's career was finished unless he could be reinstated—few alternative employment opportunities existed in a poor department like the Creuse. The rise in salary probably also lessened the commitment of teachers to the montagnard cause.

By 1851, neither arrondissement, nor the department as a whole, was considered politically dangerous to the administration. Socialist activity was limited to minor protests against the repression in Bourganeuf. Several small meetings took place to protest the promised revision of the Constitution. On February 24, lights were left burning at night to celebrate the birth of a republic whose primary and most representative institutions were being destroyed by its government.

When the National Guard of Bourganeuf refused to present arms, it subsequently faced dissolution and disarmament. Occasional "seditious shouts" or scattered placards nailed up in the night were the only reminders of montagnard strength: "Long live the democratic and social Republic! ... Down with the Chouans of Boussac!"[34]

When the coup d'état came, resistance in the Creuse seemed pathetic, particularly when one considers its seemingly vigorous attachment to the montagnard cause only two years earlier. Two hundred peasants marched from the communes of Aulon and St. Dizier to Bourganeuf. The radical notary Adrien Rouchon had organized a meeting of one hundred socialists at a bridge near that town on the road to Limoges. Delegates were sent to Limoges, and returned with the order to march. A secret provisional administration was established with Rouchon as mayor; emissaries to Aulon and St. Dizier began the feeble insurrection which was easily put down by the gendarmerie and one hundred twenty national guardsmen just organized by the conservatives in Bourganeuf. As the crowd cried "Long live the republic!" for the last time, seven were arrested. Troops from Limoges arrived the next day.[35] In Paris, Nadaud had been arrested in his apartment on the rue de Seine at 6:00 A.M., December 2. All of his personal papers were seized, including a manuscript for a book he was writing on Louis Napoleon's conspiracies to seize power during the July Monarchy. His confiscated letters reflected his confidence in the coming triumph of "democracy" in the 1852 elections.[36] The mixed commission of the Creuse finished the repression, trying those "considered dangerous for public security," even if they were not involved in resisting or protesting the coup.[37]

The department of the Ariège in the Pyrenees provides a second example of the repression of rural radicalism. Like the Creuse, the Ariège had a relatively strong radical elite with national political ties and influence. The department returned all montagnard representatives in the elections of May 1849. Similarly, some local officials played a critical role in the political radicalization of communes where economic issues were of paramount importance. The dialectic from "traditional" to "modern" applies almost too easily to this region[38] where peasants disguised "à la carnival" as women (and therefore known as "demoiselles") chased charcoal-burners and forest guards from the forests in 1829 and 1830.[39] The advent of the republic offered the Ariège peasants political means to express traditional grievances. In the elections of 1849, the Ariège supported montagnard candidates who promised to return their forest rights and end the onerous salt tax. Among them was a popular former subcommissioner of 1848, Clément Anglade, known in the department as "l'homme de la sal (sel)," because he had supported the abolition of the salt tax during the July Monarchy. The communal solidarity evidenced in the 1830 "War of the Demoiselles" became the basis of rural radicalism expressed in the political terms of the Second Republic.[40] Peasant communities, believing themselves wronged by the forest code of 1827 which deprived them of the rights of usage in "their" forests,[41] began to see the world in political terms for the first time and followed the leadership of the montagnard representatives and influential spokesmen within their communities. Universal suffrage, even if it only provided a more modern way to express traditional popular economic grievances, threatened the hegemony of the powerful Ariège notables.

Overpopulation had long characterized the Ariège; the 37.7 percent increase between 1801 and 1846 put even more pressure on the department's meager resources.[42] Aside from the forges,

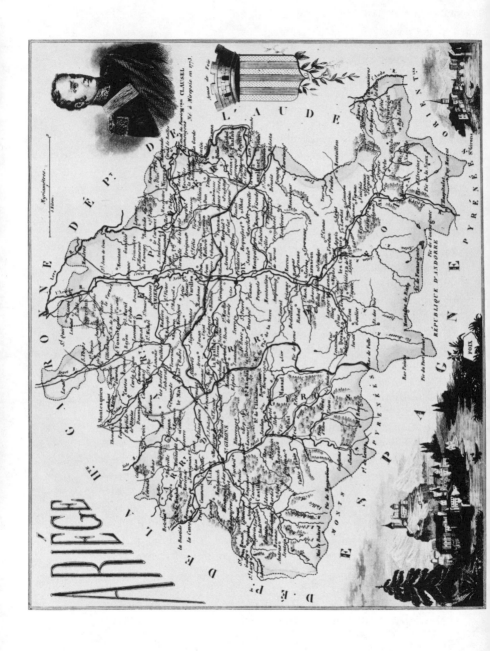

whose number and productivity were already declining, few industries survived: some cloth production in Mirepoix canton, the
digs that occupied 340 "half-savage" miners in Rancie in the
valley of Vicdessos, some weaving in Saverdun, and a number of
quarries. Lavelanet remained the most "industrialized" canton,
with about 2,000 manufacturing textiles (the industry, however,
suffered from overproduction and competition from the north),
tending forges, or woodcutting. Even the livelihood of the 240
workers producing a rugged mountain cheese in the canton of
Vicdessos was threatened by the spread of Roquefort.[43]

Almost all ariègeois were totally dependent on the resources of
the land. At the lower elevations, a poor agricultural economy
survived, but most cantons had relatively little arable land. Taxes
and usury weighed heavily on small property-holders.[44] The vast
forests formed the principal resource of the department, particularly in the arrondissements of Foix and St. Girons where
livestock could be raised and wood cut for fuel and housing to
lessen the effects of the harsh and lengthy Pyrenees winter.

However, the forest code of 1827 restricted the amount of forest
which the Ariège communes could use. The notables and the
state hired guards to keep the peasants out of the woodlands. As
a result the number of forest "crimes" jumped from 415 in 1827
to 2,340 by 1844.[45] The peasants of the mountainous regions
recalled a halcyon age when they had had virtually unlimited use
of the forests. As one justice of the peace noted, the people certainly had more "freedom," as they defined it, during the so-called
feudal regime before 1789, since to them, liberty meant the
unlimited use of the forests.[46] Most ariègeois, who spoke patois
and were largely illiterate (85–90%), hoped that the republic
would "return the forests to the people."[47]

The February revolution, like that of 1830, sparked attacks
against the property of notables and tax collectors. The most
serious disturbances took place in the canton of Quérigut where,
in 1847, the people of one commune asked the bishop of Pamiers
"to bless their misery and their hopes."[48] Peasants there had
steadily lost rights of pasturage, withdrawn by the crown and the
leading property-owners led by one Jean Abat, called "King of

the Mountains" and the "Iron King." In February 1848, at the calling of the tocsin, peasants stormed the houses of the leading property-owners, some of whom also happened to be tax collectors, and pillaged the forest guards' residences. From February to July, the peasants of Quérigut remained "masters of the forest." The canton was "a sort of pastoral republic comparable to Andorra" until enough troops could be sent to restore at least the appearance of order.[49]

But as in 1830, the "liberty" promised by the revolution in Paris brought not a return of the forests to the peasants but only more taxes: the forty-five centimes tax was surely one of the great political blunders of the century, particularly in view of the fact that so little of it was ever collected. By the end of July, only 15.6 percent of the Ariège assessment had been taken (only in the Lot were the authorities less successful, which is to say that the peasants there were even more successful).[50] Largely because of the tax, staunchly republican candidates made only an average showing in the elections because "radical" doctrines had no "echo" in the Ariège. Victor Pilhes, at thirty-one a veteran of the secret societies, friend of Barbès, Pyat, and Proudhon, and a former medical student and traveling salesman, lost because the presumed advantage of being commissioner disappeared with the forty-five centimes tax.[51] Pilhes, Anglade the "Salt Man," and their friend Théophile Silvestre (commissioner until forced out by his bourgeois enemies, allegedly because he danced with a woman worker at the prefecture) found virtually no following in a department that showed little sign of political agitation either before or after the February revolution.[52]

But, by May 1849, the Ariège returned the entire montagnard list of candidates, despite vigorous opposition from two electoral committees, the Friends of Order and the Friends of the Constitution. One losing candidate, former Orleanist deputy Firmin Darnaud, "a candidate from the ranks of the bourgeoisie," accumulated only half the votes he had gathered in April 1848. Montagnard success in the Ariège contrasted sharply with result in the neighboring Haute Garonne, where the radicals won only 23 percent of the vote.[53] The reasons for the démoc-soc victory in the Ariège were evident to official observers: "The peasants of the mountains wanted to protest: (1) the 45 centimes, (2) the forest regulations, (3) the salt tax."[54] Montagnard candidates promised the reimbursement of the forty-five centimes tax and harped on the indirect taxes. The Ariège became a montagnard constituency. The subprefect of St. Girons, whose predecessor twenty-two years earlier had tried to repress the archaic violent protest of the "demoiselles," wrote: "Should we be surprised that these peasants ask the government for help and scornfully abandon the cult of Napoleon? Socialism easily exploits this situation."[55] According to rumor, Pilhes, a commissioner in 1848, had authorized pillage in the forests; this belief was probably popularized because the commissioners had promised amnesty for forest offenders. Peasants continued to pour into the forests, pasturing their animals and taking wood at will, "in a complete state of independence," believing that it was "not the peasant who [was] committing a crime, but the government which [was committing] sacrilege."[56] The army feared that any montagnard insurrection would find support in the department. The minister of the interior warned his colleague at the War Ministry that 540 troops in Foix were insufficient: "The Ariège is one of the departments of France where the population has been the most stirred up by the apostles of socialism."[57]

The prefect, P. M. Piétri, less ruthless than some of his colleagues, faced a pressing but relatively uncomplicated task of repression.[58] Montagnard strength in the Ariège did not reside in the relatively modern political organization found in urban areas. Instead it was a mood of uncompromising hostility and opposition used to advantage by the radical elite with the assistance of a few key local officials. The only montagnard paper, Le Républicain de l'Ariège, shut down in early 1850. Despite the proximity of Toulouse, newspapers had little impact and needed only minimal surveillance. Of the 635 copies of political papers reaching the arrondissement of Pamiers, which was closest to Toulouse and by far the most literate of the department's three regions, only 218 were considered to be of the "opposition."[59] The clubs which began in a few small towns after the February revolution had long since quietly disbanded. Only the club in St. Girons had manifested a slight radical inclination. A single mutual-aid association in the same town could hardly be considered to manifest the threat of "association" in a region still dominated by exclusively communal ties. The National Guards were the only potentially dangerous organizations. Piétri's routine surveillance of public gatherings, preparations for elections, the few workers, and political propaganda, coupled with the administrative purge, were quite sufficient.[60]

Purging disloyal men from positions of authority within Ariège communes, where they seemingly legitimized dissidence by virtue of their official functions, was Piétri's most important task. By linking national politics and communal solidarity over the issues of the forests and taxes, such men could justify or even unofficially authorize rebellion and mobilize the communal electorate while maintaining the indigenous "spirit of rebellion." They might even inspire insurrection.

One justice of the peace, from Castillon, had, with the help of his friend the former schoolteacher, "protected" the montagnard representatives.[61] Mayors, some of whose predecessors had been "demoiselles" during the 1829–31 period, could foil attempts to enforce the forest code by refusing to draw up the indictments for violations.[62] During the Second Republic, eleven justices of the peace and at least seven mayors, six deputy mayors, and two police commissioners were replaced for political reasons. The dismissal of five more mayors and five deputy mayors at the time of the coup almost certainly indicates that their politics had been officially suspect. The number of justices of the peace purged seems particularly high, which undoubtedly relates to their role in policing small crimes in the forests.

The first politically motivated dismissal occurred in Le Bosc, where a "mairie populaire" had been constituted spontaneously after the Revolution. The mayor, François Portet, suspected by the provisional government in May 1848, lost his job the next month. In August, the new municipal council elected Pascal Portet, surely a relative, whose authority ended when the prefect ordered the municipal council dissolved in November 1850. Likewise, in Labastide de Sérou, where the community opposed the noble Sérou family over the use of the forests they legally owned, both deputy mayors were replaced in January 1850. The municipal councils of Junac, Le Sautel, Mas d'Azil, and Mirepoix were also dissolved.[63] In Rimont, the deputy mayor and a tax collector who had "abused his functions for a long time to pervert the spirit of the population" provided political leadership and were dismissed. The circulation of Proudhon's brochure *Property Is Theft* in the commune, provided by a toulousain lawyer, seemed to prove "mauvais esprit" and hostility to the administration. The municipal council of St. Girons, where the police commissioner had to be replaced as a means of furthering the repression, survived despite complaints that it was "almost entirely composed of workers" with a "naturally democratic spirit."[64]

Finally, the National Guard, the only legitimately organized means of communal opposition to the government, was dissolved in five towns. The Guard of Massat, insurrectionary in 1829–30, still participated in political meetings; that of Varilhes, a commune on the road from Pamiers to Foix, took part in "grave disorders" which included yells of "Long live the Montagne" and the physical beating of a rural guard; that of Foix was animated by a "mauvais esprit" which reflected the radicalization of the petty bourgeoisie; and the Guard of Pamiers, where there were serious tax riots in 1830, manifested a similar "state of systematic insubordination."[65]

The administration struck at every visible means, symbol, or sign of montagnard organization in the Ariège, and no invisible, underground organization emerged in defiance of the repression. As everywhere, the montagnard representatives were watched and harassed. The démoc-socs might have counted on votes in the 1852 elections, although the law of May 31, 1850, had eliminated 26.1 percent of the Ariège's electors.[66] A "democratic and social republic" might yet mean the return of the forests to the people and freedom from taxes and conscription. With the removal of political radicals from key communal positions, however, démoc-soc electoral success was uncertain.[67]

After the coup, the montagnards met at the home of Pilhes in

Tarascon; sixty radicals gathered in a St. Girons café to decide what to do; and a "tumultuous procession" of two to three hundred persons formed in Pamiers. But while the petty bourgeois radicals of the towns agitated in vain, the Ariège's traditionally rebellious communities were quiet.[68] The forests were not going to be returned to their former users. Migration, not politics, represented the only hope of the economically marginal inhabitants. Emigration accelerated, and although the "demoiselles" occasionally appeared as late as 1872, open resistance to the forest code and taxes decreased.[69] The first experience of mass politicization in the Ariège, despite its promise of political transformation, ended. The poor of the Ariège resented the government, but they did not organize against it. Elimination of the most articulate and popular voices of dissent from positions of authority within their communities ended the hopes of the démoc-socs for the Ariège and broke the tenuous links between national politics and the archaic solidarity of the Ariège peasant community.

During the Second Republic, very little activity of political importance occurred in the Finistère; the administration did not have to dismantle a démoc-soc organization—none existed. The prefect's task was to keep the department, which lacked an indigenous montagnard leadership, isolated from outside socialist influence, and this proved to be relatively easy. Throughout the Second Republic, the Finistère seemed completely secure. There were few disturbances during the years of the republic and not a single arrest at the time of the coup. Hence, "repression" in the Finistère took the form of prevention, and it succeeded very well.

The Finistère remained largely rural and staunchly religious. Brest, a major port of about 40,000, formed an urban and French enclave in a foreign land, with its French bourgeoisie and a relatively large working class surrounded by the mass of Breton-speaking peasants.[70] Any new prefect must have come to the Finistère as an amateur anthropologist, ignorant of the most elementary facts about the region. Brissot-Thiran had been the director of "sanitation and lighting" in the capital before assum-

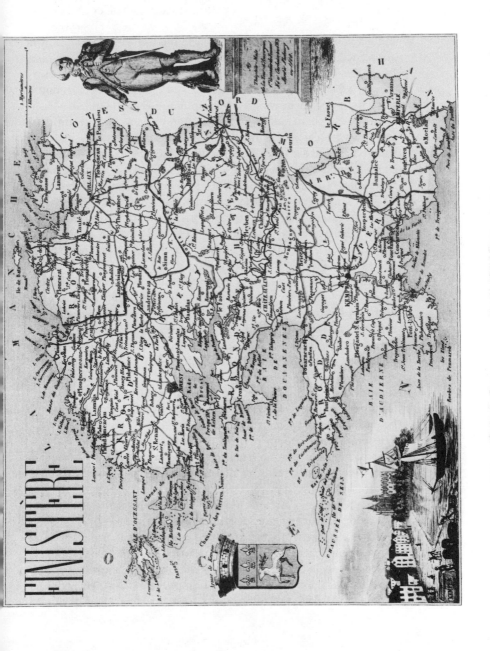

FINISTÈRE.

ing his new post in October 1848. He died in May 1850 and was succeeded by Bruno-Devès, a wealthy gun merchant who had twice served as president of the tribunal of commerce in Bordeaux.[71] Nothing in the administrative experience of either could have prepared them for an overpopulated Breton land they considered less than half-civilized, dominated by very traditional legitimist nobles and earnest, if not exactly lettered, curés. The Finistère seemed no more likely to embrace democratic-socialism than French taxes. The administration and the montagnards were almost competing colonists in a region in which even the French language had made few inroads.

From its beginning, the republic had little impact in the department. The legitimist elite did not welcome a republic, although they did not mourn the Orleanists. The population, apathetic in the spring of 1848, took the revolution in stride. The bishop of Quimper sent a moderately phrased letter to his priests asking God's help. A liberty tree was planted in Brest while a short-lived club, La Fraternité, sang the "Marseillaise." A few enthusiastic republicans complained about the attitude of the clergy toward this solemn if secular event. Some mayors, determined to weather the political squall and maintain their positions, addressed letters to the commissioner in Brest, expressing their attachment to the republic. A small "workers' club" gathered briefly in Morlaix, led by a wigmaker, whose father, in the words of the procureur général of Rennes, had provoked "murder and pillage" in 1793. The only troublesome electoral incident in the republic's first year occurred when the frustrated loser in a municipal election threw the electoral urn out of the window. A brief "correspondence" transpired between a Société dite l'union in Brest and some workers in Lyon and Marseille during 1848. A few hundred national guardsmen traveled to Paris at the time of the June Days and a few stalwart citizens attended the Fête de la fraternité. The tiny working classes of Landernau, Morlaix, and Quimper, composed largely of artisans, left only one small trace of their mobilization—a petition of ten merchants and thirteen workers ("honest workers") to the commissioner in March that protested the competition of master tailors from the garrison working for lower prices (a complaint also directed against prison labor, often echoed in the 1848 Inquiry into industry and agriculture).[72] These were the exceptions, with apathy the rule.

Finistère supported Cavaignac in December 1848, and legitimists in the two legislative elections. The montagnards gained almost no influence. When the serious business of monthly political reports began in November 1849, Brissot-Thiran wrote that socialism was popular only among the few "workers" and several idlers of the towns.[73] In Quimper, socialist ideas seemed "antithetical" to the ideas of "religion, family, and property." In nearby Quimperlé, a socialist literary circle failed; other unspecified political "overtures" to workers were rejected. Because of total indifference, a commemorative banquet on February 24, 1850, in Morlaix was cancelled. Subprefects (including Brissot-Thiran's protégé in Quimperlé who wrote "Mon cher patron,... merci mille fois" upon his appointment) dutifully sent boring monthly reports almost totally devoid of politics.[74] The subprefects discovered during tours of their districts that five gendarmes could easily control an entire canton. Social tensions which the montagnards might turn to their advantage, such as the feud between the sardine fishermen of Douarnenez and Concarneau and the merchants, seemed easily resolved.[75]

Without Montagnard leaders with national political ties, influential local citizens with socialist sympathies, an organized working class, or troublesome communal economic issues, the repression had little work to do. Because of the inevitable rumors of outside agitators, gendarmes checked travelers. On the alert for the invasion of montagnard propaganda, they arrested several hawkers distributing brochures or songs printed in Breton and were wary of contacts between Brest's few socialists and rural Finistère. The isolation of the department facilitated surveillance; roads running north and south along the coast had been built by the intendants of the eighteenth century for the purposes of defense, but communications with the interior of the department were primitive—the road from Brest to Rennes had been completed only in 1837.[76] The occasional political intruder invariably found a "cold reception"; the department was unlike other regions where business and social contacts allowed montagnards to blend into the everyday scene. When a friend of Mangin, the démoc-soc organizer and journalist of Nantes, arrived in the department, he was observed until his contacts were noted, then arrested. A Swiss socialist turned up in March 1850, and he too was easily identified and incarcerated. A certain M. Robinet, socialist propagandist, arrested as a vagabond in Douarnenez, was even less fortunate. He was housed, for lack of more suitable facilities, in a mental asylum.[77]

Most of all, gendarmes were on the lookout for "insiders," political radicals among the Breton population, such as Mignier, the rural postman who owned a little cart and distributed mail in Faou, and the employees of the customs stations who received Le National de l'Ouest, sent without charge from Nantes, supposedly to provide navigational information. Officials feared that a situation might develop "when a demagogic peasant, living in their midst, speaking their language, sharing their misery, would want to exploit this state of things."[78] Officials routinely observed the activities of the usual range of minor officials and employees of the Ponts-et-Chaussées. The few activists, an occasional schoolteacher, a Faou locksmith, a private teacher in Quimper with "advanced" ideas, and a few others had, outside of Brest and Landernau, absolutely no followers.[79] Because the Bretons were already renowned for heavy drinking, cafés and cabarets fell under suspicion; the subprefect of Quimper observed that "it is especially in the state of drunkenness that our Bretons become communicative and any attempts to stir up trouble would begin among the lower classes."[80]

Just as most attempts at montagnard political organization came from the outside, so did the ambitious antisocialist attempt to prevent the corruption of the population. In July 1849, the Association for Antisocialist Propaganda and for the Amelioration of the Condition of the Laboring Populations, founded in Paris, had several members in the Finistère.[81] The association intended to spread "popular songs dedicated to the workers, friends of order," portrayed in one highly recommended ditty:

Leurs orateurs au lieu d'battre la campagne
Pour honorer le suffrage universel
D'vraiement profitant du vote de la Montagne
Dans leurs discours, mettre un peu plus de sel

Crime ou folie étant leur véhicule
En se montant à leur diapason
Puisqu'on n'atteint qu l'blâme ou l'ridicule
Préferons tous l'honneur et la raison[82]

The association asked the prefect's assistance, proposing an inexpensive paper which would appeal to the people of the countryside. Its motto was to be "Conserve while Perfecting." *Le Dimanche* was, of course, to defend "religion, family, and property and to enlighten the workers [*travailleurs*] on the goals and consequences of the subversive doctrines which the apostles of social upheaval preach to them." But the administrators of the Finistère responded that the peasants were really too poor to purchase even the regular almanacs, which were standard rural fare. Furthermore, the whole idea was rather pointless as the peasants sang only in Breton and a socialist paper in Breton had already failed. While such an inexpensive Breton newspaper devoted to order would seem to be a fine idea, a subscription would cost about 6.5 francs per year, and 6,000 subscribers would be needed to ensure its success. Few peasants could afford that kind of money. Even the bishop of Quimper, still asking God's help, could only scrounge up thirty-eight citizens to contribute. A Breton almanac also was scrapped for lack of finances. Although some socialist songs against the "clergy and property" printed in Breton did circulate at the fairs and markets, the department remained infertile ground for political propaganda of any shade.[83] While montagnards and the men of order competed for political support in a region still essentially legitimist, the administration was already entrenched and easily rebuffed the démoc-socs.

After the coup d'état, a new prefect, promoted from the subprefecture at Morlaix, reported on only thirty socialists. Fourteen of these lived in Landernau, and they included a shoemaker who served as the National Guard's drummer, a café-owner, a boat captain, a property-owner, two doctors, a clerk for the justice of the peace, a baker, a merchant, and a veterinarian. In Brest, 85 of the 101 socialists dismissed as "imbeciles," were the blind followers of three montagnards—a watchmaker, a naval engineer, and a weaver.[84] The mixed commission of the Finistère met but decided not to consider any cases. Police reports trace the few "demagogues" into the first years of the empire, and then they disappear.

8

The Repression Incomplete: The
Yonne

In our studies of the mechanics and general objectives of the repression and in the case studies presented in the last two chapters we have seen how the repression largely attained its goal of demobilizing the extreme left. However, in at least seventeen departments, radical organization survived the repression and secret societies took root among the laboring poor, who resisted the coup d'état.[1] The experience of the department of the Yonne, little more than seventy miles southeast of the capital, exemplifies this particular sequence, which was most typical of the Midi: radicalization, repression, insurrection, and the final repression. In the Yonne, a predominantly bourgeois elite in Auxerre and Joigny provided ideological patronage and the nucleus for montagnard organization. Commitment to the politics of the extreme left spread among the poor of in these arrondissements and in part of Avallon. This pattern was most characteristic of cantons with a considerable proportion of rural workers reduced to penury by the long-term decline of local industries, a situation exacerbated by the economic crisis. When the repression eliminated or limited open montagnard organization, the increased risks of political opposition rendered the bourgeois socialist groups impotent or forced them to abandon their activism. However, the repression failed to break completely the links of the radical apparatus at the communal level, especially among many rural artisans and proletarians. The secret societies of the Puisaye, the department's most impoverished and illiterate region, participated in the insurrection of December 1851.

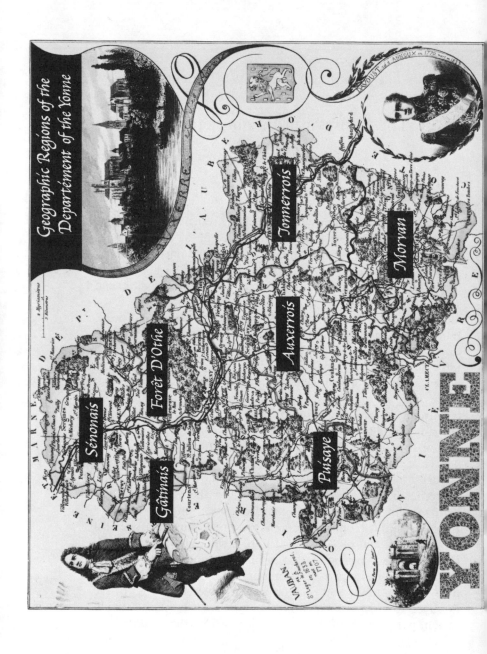

Geographic Regions of the
Département of the Yonne

Sénonais

Gâtinais

Forêt D'Othe

Tonnerrois

Auxerrois

Morvan

Puisaye

YONNE

The Yonne was principally an agricultural department, "infinitely divided" in the words of G. E. Haussmann, repressor of Montagnards and future rebuilder of Paris. More than half of the land and 65 percent of all employed labor were devoted to agriculture. The arrondissements of Sens (roughly corresponding to the traditional region of the Sénonais), Tonnerre (Tonnerrois) and part of that of Auxerre (the Auxerrois, fed by the Yonne River) were characterized by relatively prosperous grain economies, supplemented in the Sénonais and the Auxerrois by vineyards. These three regions were much wealthier than the rest of the department. Parts of the arrondissements of Sens and Joigny comprised the Gâtinais, an underdeveloped forest region of poor soil quality and limited communication with the outside, which extended into the department of the Loiret. Within the arrondissement of Avallon, the hilly Morvan supported only the cultivation of secondary cereals and the potato. Finally, most of the Joigny district and part of that of Auxerre included the Yonne's poorest and least agricultural region, the Puisaye. In this forested area, large landowners owned two-thirds of the land and dominated a considerable population of rural artisans, day laborers, and sharecroppers.[2]

The only industries of any consequence in the Yonne were either declining from the impact of outside competition, principally from Paris, or severely weakened by the economic crisis. Competition had ruined the small tanning industry in Villeneuve-sur-Yonne and limited the production of cloth in the canton of Brienon, a few kilometers up the Yonne River from Joigny. The Inquiry of 1848 repeated the theme, finding that all industries had been ruined in the cantons of Seignelay and Toucy, which had featured the most diversified economy in the department; that the quarries of Tonnerre were unable to market their products; and that champagne had almost disappeared from the region. Wine sales had been hurt in the cantons of Vermenton, Tonnerre, Auxerre, and Chablis, where opposition mounted against the drink tax.

The economic crisis of 1846–47 and 1848 also damaged the mining and forest-related industries centered in the arrondissements of Auxerre and Joigny. In good times, thousands of workers were employed as saw-pit workers, woodchoppers (2,000 in the canton of Aillant), charcoal-burners, and log-drivers (*flotteurs de bois*) on the department's navigable rivers. The mines and quarries of the cantons of Ancy and Cauzy in the arrondissement of Tonnerre, Pont-sur-Yonne near Sens, and St. Sauveur southwest of Joigny provided work in the construction industry to 3,000 in the canton of Brienon. The Tonnerre region contained four large forges and another small, dying textile industry. The growing numbers of unemployed or underemployed day laborers living in pitiful conditions in the Puisaye suffered from the economic malaise. A constant flow of "vagabond workers" passing through the Yonne on the way to or from the capital and 2,000 workers building the Paris-Lyon railway added to the numbers of rural proletarians.[3]

The revolution and militant republicanism in the Yonne began as urban phenomena in 1848. Auxerre and Joigny became "foyers démagogiques," politically dominated by a radical bourgeoisie of "old republicans" supported by the artisans of those towns.[4] Marketing, administrative, and judicial centers for their arrondissements, they emerged as montagnard bases of operation with the revolution, spawning propaganda and encouraging organization.

When the managing editor of the opposition newspaper *L'Union*, Claude Colas, armed with news of the revolution of Paris, brushed aside a bayonet and took control of the prefecture, the revolution began in Auxerre; the "old republicans" of forty-eight were to become the Montagnards of forty-nine.[5] Three commissioners quarreled over policy, intrigued, and dashed off to Paris to confer with Ledru-Rollin. The first, Théophile Robert, won the support of the population by ordering the immediate suspension of the unpopular municipal customs tax (*octroi*) and the drink tax, which were locally known as the "trop bu" and the object of two large demonstrations because "they burdened the laboring classes."[6] On this reputation, Robert was elected representative of the people in April and again the following year, until his death from cholera deprived the Yonne of one of its leading montagnard spokesmen. A second commissioner, Jules-Patrice Uzanne, a merchant and once president of the tribunal of commerce, was elected mayor during the summer of 1848.[7]

Five clubs, given a "great unity of action" by a miniature version of the ineffective Parisian Club of Clubs, met in Auxerre during the months following the revolution. The club leaders of the springtime became the montagnard activists of the republic: Colas, president of the Club des travailleurs; Berthelin, innkeeper; Pierre-François Savatier-Latour, Auxerre-born journalist and representative in 1849; Pompier, who became director of the primary schools in the arrondissement after years of political persecution during the July Monarchy; and Eugène Germain, a young attorney's clerk from Bléneau in the Puisaye. The clubs seemed on the verge of aiding the Paris insurgents during the June Days. An unsympathetic observer, the departmental archivist Quantin, condemned the clubs, where these "orators . . . stir up the population and the most dangerous doctrines are presented."[8]

Auxerre's artisans, many living in wretched poverty, exhibited what M. Quantin called a "mauvais esprit" by helping elect a municipal council whose composition, indicative of the widening of the political process, included five vine-dressers, a number of artisans, and several bourgeois socialists.[9] Several political leaders developed among the artisans, notably François Levêque, tailor, and Auguste Pujos, turner; the town soon had its own "worker-poets" in the tradition of the Paris cobbler Savinien Lapointe, born in Sens and popular in the Yonne.[10]

The leftward drift of politics in Auxerre continued after the municipal elections. In September, Colas, Berthelin, Savatier-Latour, and the others formed the Association démocratique for "the defense of the interests of the people . . . the development of the democratic republic based upon universal suffrage, the freedom of speech and the press, and the right of assembly and association." Delegates from other towns arrived for the first meeting as the association planned corresponding committees. Because the July decree forbade affiliations between clubs, the new prefect overruled the radical mayor's authorization for his friends to meet. Strikingly similar statutes for a Société démocratique de la commune d'Auxerre were also rejected at first. Ultimately many of the eighty prospective members, including Colas, Eude Dugaillon, and Uzanne, joined a Cercle industriel et agricole which was more concerned with politics than either of the interests mentioned in its name. It was dissolved by prefectural decree.[11]

At least one club, which met in the small church of St. Pélerin, survived. By April 1849, this *Club de la propagande démocratique* outgrew its meeting place and moved into the more spacious but poorly lighted banquet room of a café-owner. Its members discussed the "social question," including the general irritation that Auxerre's artisans felt concerning indirect taxes. At one session Berthelin held forth on the "just needs and the democratic and social society," while Charles Paulevé, a journalist and "man of letters" influenced by Proudhon and perhaps also "a little bit mad," read from the works of Saint Simon. The suffering of Barbès in prison, an emotional issue noted in Flaubert's *Sentimental Education*, also reached the attention of the club members.[12]

When the clubs closed, the editorial offices of *L'Union Républicaine* (née *L'Union* in 1844), edited and managed by Claude Colas and his brother-in-law, Eude Dugaillon, became the headquarters for the political activities of the extreme left. Dugaillon, a former officer in the army sent to Spain in 1823, had been converted to "democratic ideas by the revolution of 1830." He and Colas and Savatier-Latour "flattered the most evil passions of the population" with their "powerful" biweekly paper. *L'Union républicaine*, after playing an instrumental role in the election of three montagnard representatives in May 1849, was suspended for two months after the insurrection in Paris. Prosecution against an article entitled "La patrie en danger" of June 15 failed.[13]

Auxerre remained a politically turbulent town during the Second Republic: noisy banquets celebrated republican anniversaries, boisterous meetings anticipated elections, rowdy seditious processions escorted socialist soldiers banished to Africa, brawls broke out between workers and loyal soldiers in the garrison, and wild applause greeted a political satire, *Le facteur ou la justice des hommes*, which poked fun at the repressors. Gibras, an umbrella salesman; Férragu, an insurance agent; and Pompier, whose job with the primary schools gave him influence, became familiar faces in the bourgs, hamlets, and villages of the vicinity. Their "lieutenants," men like the shoemaker Michaud in Chablis, and a bookseller in Brienon, often came to Auxerre, which was the source of socialist propaganda and organization in the department.[14]

Joigny, a town of 5,000, was twenty-seven kilometers downstream. Revolutionary Commissioner Arsène Wasse, a faithful republican, was not replaced until August; Dr. Dominique Grenet and his son became the spokesmen of the extreme left. Wasse and Grenet, who had been appointed mayor by Ledru-Rollin, dominated the municipal council. This body illegally registered 250 votes after the law of May 31, 1850, went into effect and brashly refused to pass the 1851 municipal budget, confident that after it had been dissolved the subsequent elections would eliminate the four or five moderates on the council. Because Grenet presided over the commission which selected jury lists, political convictions were rare in Joigny until the prefect ordered the justice of the peace to assume Grenet's duties and to find forty-five men of order for the next list. As president of the Masons, Grenet brought politics into the lodge, and moderates and conservatives stopped coming to the lengthy meetings. Joigny's other ostensibly nonpolitical association, the Cercle industriel, seemed more concerned with montagnard politics than commerce. Its members had stamped the town with an anti-Bonapartist spirit during the 1848 elections, in sharp contrast to the rural arrondissements of Tonnerre, Sens, and Avallon which voted en masse for the emperor's nephew as representative. The hostile reception that greeted the prince-president in Joigny in the summer of 1850 embarrassed the sub-prefect. The National Guard, described by one magistrate as "armed and legally organized demagogy," defiantly shouted "Long live the Republic!" There were even several echoes of the forbidden "sociale."[15] Like Auxerre, Joigny became a center of political radicalism from which the movement's democratic patrons organized the arrondissement.

The Yonne's other important towns, Sens, Tonnerre, and Avallon, were capitals of conservative agricultural arrondissements. Of the three, only Sens, the largest, seemed to show any early signs of radicalizing its district. Sens, the domain of an archbishop who refused a "Te Deum" for the republic, experienced a sweeping administrative purge after the revolution, when the subcommissioner replaced twenty-six mayors and sixteen deputy mayors and dissolved twenty-one municipal councils. A "club des travailleurs" met in the shadow of the cathedral. A shoemaker, Benoît Voisin, gave a speech at the planting of Sens's liberty tree and seemed on the verge of gaining a popular following at the expense of the clergy and the men of order.[16] Like other literate artisans who gained political influence during the Second Republic, Benoît Voisin was

> born in the inferior ranks of society ... he had certain aptitudes, particularly that of editing [he frequently contributed to *L'Union Républicaine*] ... through his position and his abilities, Monsieur Benoît Voisin was responsible for the penetration of the doctrines of the anarchist journals to the very lowest levels of the population.[17]

But the peasants of the Sens region followed the counsel of their traditional superiors. The subprefect explained that "the morals and instincts of the people here are more gentle than those of the populations living in the vicinity of the forests."[18] Socialist influence in the town of Sens declined precipitously after 1848, and two years later, twenty-four men of order were elected to fill positions on the municipal council. The weekly *Républicain du Sens*, for which Benoît Voisin wrote editorials, ceased publication for lack of funds on September 14, 1850 after two different editions had been confiscated. Voisin, who had been defended in court by Michel de Bourges for his participation in Solidarité républicaine, lost most of his influence. The archbishop and eight members of the Légion d'honneur organized an antisocialist group that cooperated with similar organizations in Joigny,

Tonnerre, and Avallon. Sens appeared as avidly Bonapartist as
any district in France.[19]

Montagnard hopes in the towns of Tonnerre and Avallon
depended on two men. In Tonnerre, Dr. Eugène Coeurderoy,
subcommissioner until June, 1848, a few months later organized
the Cercle de l'Union, which had political ties with Auxerre's
Association démocratique. The Tonnerre circle had sixty members, almost all of them artisans or vine-dressers with thirty-five
correspondents in the arrondissement. There were rumors that
the circle had blocked off the chimney of the café where it met
so that conversations in the second-floor meeting room could not
be heard on the ground floor.[20] Prospective members, in the
tradition of bourgeois circles, were introduced to the members,
who then voted to accept them. While most nights only a handful
of members came to play cards and billiards, Sunday meetings
were larger. The subprefect blamed the circle for the dissemination of political brochures and *La Feuille du village, Le Siècle*,
and *La Presse*, which regularly arrived in Tonnerre, while "the
public establishments renounced the journals of order, or left
them on the tables without taking off their wrappers."[21]

Despite Coeurderoy's efforts, however, the subprefect's fears
were groundless. While Louis Napoleon received a hostile
reception in Joigny, he was warmly welcomed by the relatively
prosperous and geographically isolated peasants of Tonnerre and
by delegations from its surrounding area.[22] In November of 1850,
the mayor suggested that an antisocialist association was unnecessary. Only three of the arrondissement's eighty-two mayors
were politically suspect, and, with the dismissal of a justice of the
peace who had applied "socialist doctrines" to the settlement of
labor disputes, all signs of radical political interest disappeared
from his canton. Petitions asking for a constitutional revision to
allow Louis Napoleon to run for another term as president
circulated in fifty-three communes; Coeurderoy faced an impossible task in a region renowned for its Bonapartism.[23]

Another montagnard activist labored almost alone in nearby
Avallon. Eugène Oddoul, an eccentric and shrewd "man of
letters," temporarily "acquired a veritable sovereignty over the

workers" during the first year of the republic.[24] But the towering abbey church on the hill at Vézelay symbolized the clergy's strong influence in this predominantly agricultural arrondissement, which was relatively isolated because of its poor transportation system. There were concentrations of workers only in the cantons of Vézelay and Quarré-les-tombes, and most of the workers in the latter region migrated seasonally. The apparent popularity of the montagnard press among the laboring classes[25] (which reflected a remarkably high percentage of literacy; 80% in three cantons, low only in Quarré-les-tombes[26]) was countered by the propaganda of an antisocialist association.

In 1850, when Oddoul abandoned his political activities, he cited the repression as a factor frustrating his organizational efforts. By 1851, he almost never left his house, claiming to be the most isolated person in Avallon.[27] As his influence waned, a brewer and a bookkeeper developed a popular following. Despite the discovery in November 1851 that a secret society had had some success recruiting "workers and simple peasants," the authorities considered the arrondissement relatively secure at the time of the coup d'état.[28]

The major political problem for the administration remained in the arrondissements of Auxerre and Joigny. The clubs had disappeared during the summer of 1849, but Prefect Haussmann's transfer from the Var in May 1850 intensified what the démocsocs viewed as a "white terror."[29] Haussmann struck quickly at the Auxerre and Joigny montagnards, dissolving Joigny's Cercle industriel and the Masonic lodge, as well as the National Guards of Auxerre, Joigny, St. Florentin, and St. Sauveur, a bourg in the Puisaye showing recent signs of montagnard activism. Regents of the collèges of Auxerre and Joigny were dismissed; Pompier was transferred to Laon, but refused to move.[30]

L'Union républicaine was forced to open a public subscription to pay its fines. Its political stance had not changed since June 1848 when Savatier-Latour prophesied that, with the election of Louis Napoleon as representative, "an Eighteenth Brumaire is at our door . . . the bourgeois republic is not possible." By November 1851, its editors were willing to accept payment in kind for subscriptions.[31]

Dismissals of local officials were commonplace: mayors, like one who "corresponded" with *L'Union républicaine*; schoolteachers ("Isn't it true that you subscribe to Joigneaux?"); and petty functionaries—tax officials, rural mailmen, and particularly employees of the Ponts-et-chausées.[32] When the gardener of a school in St. Sauveur was dismissed, *L'Union républicaine* sarcastically commented that "undoubtedly the man had devoted most his time to the red flowers."[33] In fact, gradually in 1850 it became apparent that the montagnards of Auxerre and Joigny had considerable support in those arrondissements, particularly in the backward Puisaye.

Haussmann expedited the repression, engaging in a notorious "almanac hunt" by rigidly enforcing the laws regulating hawking and peddling and by carrying out thorough household searches. (The mayor, his deputy, the commissioner of police, several gendarmes, the justice of the peace, and apparently even the local police spies invaded the small home of a shoemaker in Vermenton on such a mission.[34]) The arrival of a new police commissioner in Joigny meant more searches in that region, although he initially disgraced himself by sending his poorly disguised assistant to nearby St. Florentin, where the man was hooted out of town. Thereafter, the commissioner proved to be more capable, traveling "200 leagues" in the pursuit of montagnards, and earning the derisive nickname of Badinguet.[35]

Because of the Yonne's proximity to Paris and its location on the well-traveled route to the east and to the Midi surveillance of transients—"vagabond workers," railroad workers, and, after 1850, travelers at the railroad stations—was an important part of the repression. The transportation network helped Parisian press and propaganda reach this relatively literate department.[36] Traveling montagnard representatives, assured of a friendly welcome, often stopped at Auxerre and Joigny. The Paris-Lyon railways, inaugurated in 1849, brought the capital even closer, facilitating trips there by Eude Dugaillon, who wrote a column of "Parisian Correspondence" in *L'Union républicaine*.[37]

Gendarmes monitored the constant stream of "strangers" passing through; workers were "constantly coming and going" along the Yonne River, for example. In 1848, it had seemed to officials that "a notable part of the suspect population of Paris, chased from the capital, came to take refuge in the department."[38] In Coulanges-sur-Yonne, the mayor, whose authority was already being challenged by an unruly group of log-drivers, complained that "bands of people calling themselves workers, coming from Paris, go through the countryside, making the most incendiary remarks."[39] Although various rumors—bands of brigands, the invasion of the department by the railroad workers who had moved into the Côte d'or, and the mysterious presence of Mazzini—proved false, the surveillance of ordinary people became part of the routine of repression.[40]

In 1851, the Yonne presented striking contrasts. The arrondissements of Sens and Tonnerre, politically quiet, were avidly Bonapartist; Avallon displayed both characteristics to a lesser degree. On the other hand, the Joigny and Auxerre regions were montagnard strongholds. Alarmed officials began to report signs of militant republicanism among the rural artisans and proletarians in these regions, particularly in the impoverished Puisaye. With the repression limiting the organizational efforts of the left in Auxerre and Joigny, the procureur général of Paris had hoped that the extreme left would lose all influence, but "exactly the opposite happened." The towns had "been watched and fortified." But when, like Oddoul, members of the radical elite fell silent rather than risk arrest, leaders emerged among the rural artisans and proletarians of the Yonne's poorest region.[41]

Concentrations of underemployed and unemployed rural artisans and proletarians characterized the cantons in which montagnard secret societies successfully organized: in the Puisaye (cantons of St. Sauveur, Bléneau, St. Fargeau, and Toucy), potters, quarrymen, woodchoppers, wheelwrights, day laborers, and rural domestics predominated; in the canton of Coulanges-sur-Yonne, loggers; in Vézelay, woodchoppers, masons, stonecutters, and quarrymen.[42] Margadant suggests that there was probably in the Haute Puisaye (cantons ot St. Sauveur and Toucy) "a substantial movement from agriculture to crafts" during the July Monarchy and that this facilitated "better communications and more active exchange with the exterior." Artisans in this region thus had something to market (pottery, sabots, and some cloth) in Toucy, St. Sauveur, or even Auxerre and Joigny. On the other hand, the Basse Puisaye (cantons of St. Fargeau and Bléneau) became even more isolated during this period with fewer rural artisans and a large concentration of rural proletarians in a desperate situation; the forests and tile works of St. Fargeau, for example, provided only limited work, particularly during an economic crisis.[43]

Of the cantons in which Montagnard secret societies were most active during the last year of the republic, Bléneau was the most backward and wretched. With only one-third of the land cultivated, Bléneau provided a striking contrast with the conservative agricultural regions of the department in which the small property-holders did relatively well. "Les gros" among the 226 proprietors of the canton (compared with 692 proprietors in Toucy canton) had "consolidated their holdings by fortunate speculations, without benefiting the proletarians."[44] Three hundred bargemen in the commune of Rogny were laid off after the revolution of February. In 1849, stories circulated of men who had literally starved to death in the canton, and there were *troubles* involving protest against the free movement of grain. Hatred of the well-off was widespread in a region where "a young and strong man sells himself for fifty centimes a day and food." Only an estimated 3 or 4 percent of the inhabitants could read and write.[45]

The situation within the adjacent canton of St. Fargeau also spawned hatred of the rich. A placard found in July 1848, which purported to represent a mock trial of July 6, reflected social tensions in the tiny (271 inhabitants) commune of Septfonds, which was isolated in the woods:

> List of the names of the twenty-four leading aristocrats of the canton of St. Fargeau, on whom a quadruple contribution will be imposed, in the anticipation of the division of the property owned by the community.

This may have been the work of a tailor named Roux, who was called "the minister of St. Fargeau," or one of his friends, and may have reflected the influence of Étienne Cabet, whose works were discovered in the tailor's house.[46]

Despite some evidence of a relative rise in living standards during the July Monarchy in the cantons of Toucy and St. Sauveur (the Haute Puisaye), the Puisaye as a whole remained poor, and its economic problems were accentuated by the 1846–47 crisis and compounded by the revolution. The "democratic and social republic" had something to offer the poor of these cantons (an end to indirect taxes, education, a campaign against usury, etc.). In the Puisaye, popular hatred of the wealthy, manifested in attacks on property, seemed to have reached its peak in the fall of 1851.[47] In this backward region, officials sadly noted, "destitution contributed to attracting some of these people to secret societies which promised them prosperity."[48] Authorities blamed "outsiders" from Auxerre and Joigny for capitalizing on the "bad passions" of the vulnerable destitute:

> The means of seduction varied according to the localities and the people. In some places, they supported the reduction or even the suppression of taxes, noticeably that on drink; in other places they supported an increase in salaries and the organization of work; elsewhere, they opposed the alleged reestablishment of the feudal *corvées* and of the ecclesiastical dîme.[49]

Nevertheless, local elites and Auxerre and Joigny montagnards played a minor role, if any, in the development of the secret societies of the Yonne. A secret-society "chief" came to Bléneau, either to recruit for the Nouvelle Montagne or to affiliate the Bléneau secret society with it. He approached, so the story went, a wealthy man who seemed to have leftist sympathies and asked him to become a section leader (decurion). The man refused, arguing that "one can fight with ballots; one should not fight with rifles."[50]

To take another example, the mayor of Bléneau (population 1,278) was Alexandre-Réné Dethou, a relatively prosperous property-owner who, in the words of a sabot-maker, "was a worthy man who tried to help the little people." With friends in Joigny, Dethou had been a montagnard political activist; he had once been fined 100 francs for distributing socialist propaganda which he received from Auxerre or Montargis. Maintaining influence in his canton even after the elections, Dethou battled the subprefect's local ally, the justice of the peace, who prevented him from planting a liberty tree in February 1850. Replaced as mayor, Dethou was reelected by his friends on the municipal council, but his political agitation appears to have ended at that point. Probably because of the increasingly high costs of activism, he remained aloof from the secret society, which spread through every commune in the canton.[51]

Several other incidents reveal the decline of democratic patronage in the Yonne. Eude Dugaillon, editor of *L'Union républicaine*, dissociated himself from both the insurrection and the secret societies, claiming that the scarcity of subscribers in the Puisaye, which, as a region, had the lowest rate of literacy in the department,[52] was proof of his innocence. Bourgeois patronage had played an important organizational role in the elections of May 1849, when the arrondissements of Joigny and Auxerre were responsible for the success of the montagnard candidates Robert and Savatier-Latour. A similar organizational effort was anticipated for the 1852 elections. Eugène Germain, a native son who had had the good fortune to become an attorney's clerk in Auxerre, aided Dethou's propaganda efforts. In November 1851, his enthusiasm was such that he "literally ran from house to house spreading propaganda." There is, however, no convincing evidence that he belonged to the Bléneau secret society.[53]

The interrogations of the December 1851 insurgents provide a graphic look at the development of the secret societies in the Yonne.[54] The first affiliations took place in May and June 1850. There is some evidence that similar organizations in the Nièvre influenced the ritual and contributed the model of a conspiratorial organization of decurions and centurions. We know that a former Parisian tanner living in the commune of Druyes became a centurion of the earliest secret society in the department, based in the cantons of Courson and Coulanges-sur-Yonne. An innkeeper-logger from Crain testified that his society's goal was "to obtain the right to work" and that initiations took place in his café. The societies had loosely defined concept of mutual assistance which complemented their attempt to defend "la République en danger." Later secret societies, which were formed in the Puisaye in 1851, pledged to defend the democratic and social republic but apparently had no mutual-aid structures that were not simply fronts. However, some confessed members eventually claimed they had been led to believe that they were joining a mutual-aid society. Mutual assistance was so closely tied to the popular perception of the social republic that it is often difficult to draw the line between a purely conspiratorial organization and a rudimentary mutual-aid group that was, by necessity, conspiratorial.[55]

During November 1850, the secret organizations spread from the bourgs and cantons of St. Sauveur, St. Fargeau, Bléneau, and Toucy into the surrounding areas. Most affiliations took place between July and September 1851; the last one occurred within six days of the coup d'état. Spreading first through the more accessible Haute Puisaye and then into the Basse Puisaye, these organizations seemed to have at first attempted to group by the traditional conspiratorial units of tens (decuries) and hundreds (centuries). The later secret societies of the Basse Puisaye seemed to have been little affected by this classic conspiratorial structure.[56]

The recruitment process in the Toucy vicinity may be reconstructed from the confessions of members. The centurion of this section, called "Vosgian," although it is unlikely that most of the members were aware of the nuances of conspiratorial hierarchy, was Louis Florent Chauvot, thirty-five, member of the departmental general council, a wealthy and educated proprietor (and thus an exception) who had "taken his wife from the working class without having their union blessed by the Church." Four members actively solicited recruits in the surrounding communes of Merry-la-Vallée, Dracy, Villers St. Benoît, Tannerre-en-Puisaye, and Fontaines: among the recruits were Jean Bouillard, a thirty-nine-year-old piano-tuner whose work took him throughout the department; August Ansoult, dyer, described as "an intelligent worker, without morality, without material ease, dangerous"; Théophile Baron, a young musician; and Alexandre Besson, a journeyman locksmith. Camillon Gonneau, a peasant, testified that each Sunday another member of the Toucy group would come to Fontaines, which was five kilometers distant, in search of members. Likely participants would be taken to a café and asked to join. One rural laborer claimed that Alexandre Besson told him he was becoming a member of "an honest society to support the republic," while another later pleaded that he thought he was being asked to join a Masonic ledge. A sabot-maker was at first charmed by Besson's "belles paroles," then terrified by threats of death if he betrayed the society. Most, however, freely admitted attending at least one initiation during which the rites were read from a paper, committed to memory, and then burned. In at least one instance, members gathered to elect a decurion.[57]

Théophile Baron admitted participating in the initiation of the sixty to seventy members in Fontenay, assisted by one centurion, Napoléon Breuiller called Lervet, from nearby Levis. Breuiller had been initiated by the unchallenged montagnard leader of St. Sauveur, Amadée Patasson, a destitute musician of incredible energy. The last commune in the vicinity of Toucy to join the network was Merry-la-Vallée, whose approximately forty members took the oath to defend the democratic and social republic in the fall. At the same time, the society spread in the impoverished canton of Bléneau, enrolling at least 104 men from Rogny, 66 from Bléneau itself, and 30 from Champcevrais.[58]

The initiation rites were almost uniform, although the links to the Nouvelle Montagne and communication with societies in the Loiret, Nièvre, and Paris is not entirely clear.[59] Blindfolded initiates swore on pistols and knives, under pain of death, to defend the "democratic and social republic." The places of initiation were necessarily secluded, as evidenced by the following rich firsthand descriptions by confessed members.

John Baclard, twenty-eight years old, shoemaker of Rogny:

> I present myself voluntarily to tell you that I am a member of the secret society. I was initiated last September 2, in the evening, in the café of Bourillon, by Huyssard, chief, in the presence of Richer, Pierre, Guiblin, Bouillon.

Laurent Boulin, thirty-three years old, locksmith of Bléneau:

> I was won over by Michel Corner, vine-dresser from
> Ouzouer-sur-Trezée. I was initiated in a room in an inn, by
> Paulin, saw-pit worker and carpenter.

Étienne Fiette, twenty-five years old, day laborer, of Rogny:

> Fifteen days before the last harvest, I was initiated in the
> evening in the woods of Javaissière.

Jean Rondet, a twenty-five-year-old mason, joined the secret
society organized by the brewer Pierre Michaud in the cantons of
Avallon and Vézclay.

> M. Michaud, whom we met at the entrance to town, led us
> to a remote house, which I cannot otherwise identify, where
> three bearded men whom I never had seen before, gave me
> the oath, blindfolded, and made me swear on a knife to keep
> the secret under the pain of death. Since then, I have only
> assisted at the initiation of François Poupée of St. Léger.

A thirty-three-year-old mason with the lyric name of Prudent
Saison from Saint-en-Puisaye also recalled his initiation. Here is
a clear instance where "the secret," just referred to by Rondet,
was the rites and symbols of Nouvelle Montagne:

> I admit that I took part in the secret societies. I was initiated
> at the end of last October [1851] in the warren of M. de
> Boutin by Louis Laguin [known as Jolly], animal-trader, and
> Simon Majuean, cultivator, both of Deffant. It was Languin
> who won me over. I was on a bit of a spree. They told me
> that if I should die, they would take care of my wife. It was
> about seven in the evening. They blindfolded me and made
> me swear to defend the democratic and social republic. I
> heard the clatter of weapons, such as rifles and pistols, as
> they moved about. When the blindfold was removed, I was
> alone. They had fled. I believe that they gave me, as a
> password, "the hour," to which one had to respond, "has
> sounded"; and to another question, one had to reply

"Mountain." Aside from this, I have not assisted at any other meeting.[60]

Finally, consider the interrogation of Jean-Clément Poirier called Michelet, twenty-eight years old, a carpenter, living in Champcevrais:

QUESTION: Were you not a member of the secret society of Champcevrais?

RESPONSE: Yes, sir.

Q: You were one of the leaders of this society?

R: No, sir.

Q: At what time were you initiated?

R: I believe that it was in November 1850.

Q: Who brought you into this society?

R: Laplaigné and Plumot called Paulot of Bléneau.

Q: Where were you initiated?

R: In the woods between Bléneau and Champcevrais.

Q: By whom were you initiated?

R: By Plumet and Laplaigné. There were no other.

Q: You took an oath to defend the democratic and social Republic?

R: Yes, sir.

Q: And since your own initiation, you have initiated others?

R: I initiated some others.

Q: You have initiated François Ory, Duidonné Blanchard, François Paquet, Philippe Brouchet, Jacques Libiacier, Pierre Augustin, Bleachot, Jean Sauvart, and Philibert Vildé?

R: I initiated several of those people whom you just named, but I don't remember the others.

Q: You ought to know the people from Champcevrais who are part of this society. Name them.

R: I don't want to name anyone.[61]

In October 1851, Davesiés du Pontes, subprefect of Joigny, toured his troubled district and reported:

The proletarians of St. Sauveur, St. Fargeau, Lavau, Saint-

Privé, Bléneau, Champcevrais, Champignelles, Rogny, Ouzouer, Châtillon-sur-Loing [Loiret], almost all communists, would provide an army of evil, a nucleus which the lure of pillage would quickly have increased if the audacity of these enemies of all order matched their covetousness.[62]

After some investigation, the secret societies were exposed in November. A number of incriminating letters had been seized and a Joigny sabot-maker named Bajolet, probably a police spy, described with some accuracy the spread of the societies from the cantons of Coulanges-sur-Yonne and Courson as far north as part of the cantons of Aillant and Joigny. At the same time, a former soldier of the empire living in Champcevrais notified authorities that his son had been asked to join by a day laborer. The subprefect, and soon Prefect Haussmann himself, arrived on the scene with troops and confronted the accused day laborer with exact details of the initiation rites. The poor man confessed, implicating many of his comrades, including the shoemaker Laplaigné, mentioned above, and the justice of the peace's gardener.[63]

The coup occurred within days. The authorities' preparations in the Yonne were less than perfect, as Haussmann had left to become prefect of the Gironde and the new prefect, Rodolphe d'Ornaud, had not yet arrived in Auxerre. Troops were posted at every entrance to the city and two fresh cavalry units were put on alert in Joigny. Claude Colas and Eude Dugaillon, claiming that that they feared major disturbances if they were arrested at night, turned themselves in to the authorities.[64]

Other montagnards in Auxerre gathered to discuss what seemed a hopeless situation, and they were joined by a number of their colleagues from nearby St. Florentin. The tailor François Levêque left for Toucy to carry the news of Dugaillon's "arrest." Word of the coup spread from the bourgs to the villages and hamlets. Chauvot and the leaders of the Toucy secret society met on the third and allegedly prepared an insurrection for the sixth. In St. Sauveur on the fourth, Amadée Patasson and his brother encouraged resistance. On the sixth and seventh an insurrection began in the Puisaye.

Across the Yonne River from the canton of Coulanges-sur-Yonne lay the arrondissement of Clamecy in the Nièvre, and its capital rose up in defense of the republic. The tocsin sounded in the Yonne communes of Étais, Druyes, Andryes, and Sougères when an emissary from Clamecy arrived to organize a march on that town. The insurgent band moved from Étais to Sougères, Druyes, and then to Clamecy via Andryes. The mayor of Coulonges, backed by the town's bourgeoisie, prevented democrats there from marching toward Auxerre.[65]

The sixth was a market day in St. Sauveur. Amadée Patasson gathered those who had sworn to defend the democratic and social republic. "In the name of the nation, give us the keys," he ordered the curé, seeking to ring the tocsin. Needing guns, his band broke into first the town hall and then into the agricultural school outside of the bourg. After passing through Fontenay, the insurgents numbered approximately five to six hundred. A smaller group headed east to gather the socialist Protestants of Taigny, turned north to Ouanne, and then reached Leugny. They next planned to join the original band outside of Auxerre, where thousands of other insurgents were expected. A still smaller band, arriving in St. Sauveur from Lavau and Treigny to the southwest, followed the first group. Prisoners taken during minor disturbances in cafés in Bléneau, who had been escorted to St. Fargeau by gendarmes, were freed by Bléneau townspeople, who returned home in triumph to take the guns of the National Guard. Demonstrations against the coup and at least one attempt to march followed. Insurgents arrived from Champcevrais, after unsuccessfully trying to take guns from the town hall and to organize resistance among the workers in the woods.

Meanwhile, leaders of the secret society in Toucy left for neighboring communes to recruit members. Octave Touté, tinman, hurried to Villers St. Benoît, and Jean Bouillard, piano-tuner, to Merry-la-Vallée, gathering a force armed with guns from both town halls. This group converged on Toucy via Dracy. In Toucy, the mayor gathered about eighty "good citizens" to turn back the ragged army of montagnards. Troops arrived at about the same time as the band. To the south, Patasson's small army had marched through Saints to Leugny when two démoc-socs from

Toucy told them of the arrival of the troops. Patasson, assuming
the role of a general, moved the best armed of these three groups
of "troops" into the front and led three hundred insurgents the
seven kilometers to Toucy. The troops easily dispersed the first
group, arresting about twenty-five from Villers St. Benoît and
Merry-la-Vallée. The St. Sauveur insurgents arrived almost immediately, and, after Patasson opened fire (or so the government
claimed), the troops fired a volley, killing one.

The remaining montagnards from St. Sauveur were marching
eastward through Lain, Taigny, and Ouanne, gathering both
willing and intimidated ("everyone who does not march will be
shot") followers and National Guard arms. Expecting to join
forces with thousands of montagnard insurgents, they encountered troops at Chevannes, ten kilometers northwest of Leugny.
They then fell back to Escamps, reaching it at about the same
time as the remnants of Patasson's band, which had continued
marching toward Auxerre. There, in the deserted fields near
Escamps, the troops fired, killing several people. One part of the
band reached Villefargeau, only about six kilometers from
Auxerre. After confronting the heavily armed troops, insurgents
fled across the fields and into the forests, leaving behind their
guns and pitchforks.[66] Property-owners joined the soldiers in the
"hunt for the reds" that followed, undoubtedly spurred by false
tales of atrocities committed by the Clamecy insurgents.[67] Toucy,
instead of becoming the first bourg in the Yonne to fall to the
forces of the democratic and social republic, became a bivouac
for troops guarding scores of prisoners and a motley collection
of captured weapons. While resistance in the other cantons had
not materialized despite some organizational efforts, over two
thousand men took arms, many of them fulfilling their secret oath
to defend the democratic and social republic.[68]

What began in the Yonne as the political radicalism of small-
town journalists and lawyers in clubs, political meetings, and
thinly disguised circles in 1848 thus ended in an insurrection of
the rural laboring poor in the backward Puisaye and along the
Yonne River. The confessions of those who appeared before the
military commission of the Yonne during the first months of 1852

Table 8.1   Citizens from St. Sauveur Arrested
for Resisting the Coup

Number	Occupation	Number	Occupation
5	day laborers	1	gunsmith
4	joiners	1	gardener
4	property-owners	1	comb-maker
3	nail-workers	1	journeyman tailor
2	shoemakers	1	baker
1	laborer	1	journeyman shoemaker
1	carpenter	1	journeyman
1	blacksmith	1	harness-maker
1	musician (Patasson)	1	innkeeper
1	farmer	1	no profession
1	house-painter		

SOURCE: AG JM, 225, commune of St. Sauveur

indicate the evolution of radicalization and insurrection in the department. Of 1,167 people, all but about 90 were from the lower ranks of society. Of these 90, 40 *rentiers* may have been small property-holders who had given their land to their children. With the exception of the montagnard elite, most of whom had not been able or were not willing to leave Auxerre and Joigny, the bourgeoisie of the Yonne eagerly supported the coup. The mayors and the bourgeoisie of Coulanges and Toucy blocked the paths of the insurgents, most of whom were workers. Table 8.1 gives the occupations of those arrested from the commune of St. Sauveur, which are illustrative of the social composition of the insurrection. The ten indicted from the commune of Sougères, who had been part of the group who marched on Clamecy, included two domestics, two farmers, one day laborer, one other common laborer, one blacksmith, one property-owner, one bailiff's clerk, and one apprentice saddler.[69] In sum, what the procureur général of Paris aptly called the "obscure soldiers of the socialist army" of the Yonne consisted of impoverished rural day laborers, peasants, and artisans.[70]

Despite the Paris procureur général's expected allegation that the insurrectionaries, because of their "envy of the upper class," were out to murder, rape, pillage, and set fires, the montagnards believed they were defending the democratic and social republic. Economic grievances played an important part in the mobilization of the laboring poor in the Yonne; the social reforms promised by the republic of justice ("la belle," as it was called in the Midi) had a great attraction for those with nothing to lose. This represents a fundamental political awakening among ordinary people.[71] The insurrection in the Yonne was strikingly similar to those in similar regions of the Nièvre (Clamecy region) and the Loiret (Montargis), which were also largely manned by rural artisans and proletarians.[72]

In some ways the Yonne mirrors the experience of the Second Republic. Two arrondissements (Sens and Tonnerre) confirmed the stereotype of peasant Bonapartism once the repression prevented the montagnards from gaining a foothold.[73] With the exception of two cantons, the arrondissement of Avallon was very much under control by December of 1851, and the repression, with difficulty, destroyed the montagnard leadership and organization in Joigny and Auxerre. But as in large areas of the Center and the Midi, the government failed to arrest the spread of the extreme left among the laboring poor of those arrondissements, particularly in the Puisaye. As the repression put the future of the republic in doubt, radical mobilization went underground and, rooted among the rural laboring poor, resisted the coup d'état without the help of the Yonne's democratic patrons.

Epilogue

The coup d'état completed the repression, eliminating all surviving fragments of the montagnard political organization and rooting out the secret societies. Over 26,000 persons faced the mixed commissions, including the démoc-soc activists who had taken no part in the insurrection. The mixed commissions cleared their departments of influential "socialists," "demagogues," and "anarchists," dispensing penalties according to the "danger" represented by each person involved: banishment to Cayenne or Algeria (with or without internment), exile from France or from a particular department, prison, or official police surveillance. Thousands lost positions or suffered in other ways. The Bonapartist purge, generally savage though occasionally merciful, was thorough and effective.[1]

The repression that preceded the coup had been successful despite the fact that a network of secret societies still covered some of the Midi and several departments of the Center. Propaganda and newspapers had not been completely silenced, and during the fall of 1851 there was a marked upswing in socialist propaganda efforts and, it seemed to some procureurs, in montagnard commitment.[2] Only the coup could establish near perfect "order" by placing the entire country in a state of siege. Despite the massive resistance to the coup, accentuated and in some instances provoked by the repression, the repression had achieved its purpose—it had destroyed the bulk of the montagnard organization, rendering impotent those elements most capable of organizing resistance to the regime.[3] Secret societies formed because aboveground political organization became impossible.

The sequence of radicalization and repression bequeathed three legacies to modern France. The first was that of the police state: politics penetrated the community during the Second Republic.

The comings and goings of ordinary people became police business. In our century, bureaucratized political repression would
be even seamier and more brutal. In retrospect, despite the
bitterness of class hatreds and the insensitivity of the repressors
and of the majority of the bourgeoisie, the Second Republic
seems to enjoyed something akin to naiveté. Enemies still rubbed
shoulders at the marketplace, and a consensus seems to have
existed that the sanctions for political dissidence ought to at least
be humane. The police presence was apparent and the repressors
were hated, but prison terms were relatively short for political
crimes and few bourgeois or administrators envisioned systematized brutality as a response to dissidence. The overreaction
of the so-called forces of order in Rouen and Paris in 1848 and in
the capital after the coup did not become an integral part of political and social policing. At the same time, there still existed a
popular feeling that wrongs could be righted and a hope that
justly indignant and enraged citizens could seize power at the
prefecture and bring justice and perhaps the end of a repressive
regime. However, the repression foreshadowed the more powerful regimes of the future, under which protest would be more
forcefully crushed and repression would become more systematic
and even scientific. The sense of hope, "the lyric illusion" of the
revolution of 1848, would change in the twentieth century to a
sense of helplessness and hopelessness in the face of seemingly
immovable conservative coalitions blocking meaningful social
change.

The revolution of 1848 after February was also a social revolution. An awareness of the "social question" spread among
Frenchmen, and not only among workers. In wine-producing
areas people hoped that the social republic would end the drink
tax. Petty proprietors wanted the reimbursement of the forty-five-
centimes tax, credit facilities, and a war on usury. Elsewhere
Frenchmen sought legal hearings without fees, public instruction,
and the abolition of the salt tax, and workers dreamed of "the
right to work," the password of some of the secret societies. The
montagnard movement during the Second Republic grew out of
a revolutionary coalition that was not confined to one social

group or class. As we have seen, the revolution spread from Paris to the provinces, and from cities, towns, and bourgs into their hinterlands. Some bourgeois democratic patrons—principally lawyers and journalists—artisans, urban and rural proletarians, and peasants participated in the struggle for economic and social justice and for political power. Montagnard leaders addressed their appeals to the "travailleurs" of the cities and countryside. The "great social family" included many bourgeois who also worked hard and who sought the resolution of the social question. Although democratic patronage waned as the penalties increased, the active organizational role played by the bourgeois radicals is significant and enables social history to transcend pure class analysis. Not all bourgeois in France cheered on the repression from the safety of their shops. Not all workers voted for democratic socialist candidates when they had the chance, and they would not have done so in 1852. As in the June Days, some workers turned up on what seemed to be the wrong side of the barricades, and one could be "bourgeois" or "aristo" in the sociopolitical parlance of 1848 because of one's attitude toward the social question and the aspirations of the laboring poor, regardless of one's class origin.

Yet Marx was correct when he underlined the importance and ultimate significance of the rapid coalescence of the majority of the French bourgeoisie against the revolution. Their reaction was even more violent than that of the traditional notables whose local power base had been threatened. Marx proved himself a generally astute contemporary observer (although he is often unfairly criticized for his lack of access to firsthand knowledge or to archival materials only available fifty years after the fact) by pointing to the role of the essentially working-class organization during the Second Republic. The 1848 revolution and the Second French Republic *did* mark an important stage (although one hesitates to use the word) in the emergence of working-class consciousness. Many groups of workers began to "go it alone" once deprived of the leadership of the bourgeois ideologues who were in jail or in exile, had lost their commitment, or failed to understand working-class issues.[4] The procureur général of

Limoges reported with some surprise in November 1850, that "in Bellac, the socialist workers are separating themselves from the bourgeois element and declaring that they want to act *for themselves and by themselves.*"[5] This nascent prise de conscience ultimately was most apparent among the workers.

Finally, popular awareness of the social question came to be perceived in political terms. The Second Republic politicized ordinary people who had been excluded from or indifferent to the political process. They saw, for the first time, their own economic and social condition in national political and ideological terms. The revolution gave ordinary people the means to act collectively, the freedom to associate, gather, speak, publish, and vote. Collective violence was "modernized" during the Second Republic as riots to protest taxes and usurpation of forest rights gave way to "ideological disturbances."[6] The politicization of festivity in the Midi was just another indication of the entry of national political considerations into the marketplace. Political tracts reached those who could read and those enjoying literacy transmitted their message to those who could not.

The key to the success of the montagnards and to the politicization of ordinary people was organization. They fell to a more powerful and tested organization, the repressive apparatus. However, the role of written propaganda, the press, voluntary associations, and electoral groups presaged the popular political participation in the Third Republic. Capable organizers utilized the institutional gifts of the republic to reach the "people." Organization more than concentration in urban centers or class origins explains militancy during the Second Republic. The mixed commissions particularly noted the organizational influence of many of the men whose cases they considered during the first months of 1852. Like inquisitors confronting heretics, they sought to cleanse France of what they considered to be an ideological cancer. The following examples show that bourgeois radicals, artisans, and proletarians were considered guilty by virtue of their influence among the laboring poor:

Egel, boatman in Strasbourg: "a much more dangerous

person in that he exercises a great influence on the corporation of boatmen."

Jacquemont, dismissed schoolteacher from Rocroi (Ardennes): "one of those men who really knows the habits of the people of the countryside, over whom he easily exerts influence . . . it would be very dangerous to allow [him] to remain in France."

Dupré, health officer in Strasbourg: "maintains a sort of moral coercion over the people of the countryside."

Charles Schmidt, former schoolteacher and editor of *Volksrepublik* of Mulhouse: "for three years the soul and thought of the socialist party, having perverted opinions and corrupted the consciences with the most anarchic journal which could ever be imagined."

Vitu, shoemaker in Dijon: "has a certain influence on the working class."

Moreau, locksmith of Châtellerault: "very dangerous socialist because of his relations with the working population and because of his intelligence, which places him above the 'vulgar'—occupies himself with incessant propaganda."

Roche, charcoal-burner: "great promoter of socialist propaganda —an educated and dangerous man."

Boulard, woodworker of Périgeux: "intelligent, having received an education above his station . . . lived in Limoges in 1849."

Ancelon, doctor of Dieuze: "his profession provides him with [the opportunity to exert] a most unfortunate influence on the working population."

Crozier, former schoolteacher, member of the general council of Morbihan and a tax expert: "turns the small property-owners against the tax system."

Lavigne, tailor of Nousse (Landes): "enabled by his profession . . . to enter the smallest *chaumières*, he supports the most disturbing doctrines and those which are most likely to seduce those weak in spirit."

Clémenceau, lawyer of Nantes: "is very active as an intermediary between the socialists of Nantes and those of the Vendée."

Peronal, public writer in Vendôme: "maintains the most detestable influence on the people of the countryside and on the illiterate workers."

Mathieu, lawyer of Épinal [called "Wooden leg"]: "has spent his life conspiring against society . . . he has constantly engaged in the greatest activity to propagate the most subversive doctrines among the workers and peasants."

Voivin, no profession listed, department of the Vosges: "It is to him alone that we can attribute the evil doctrines popular in several communes, notably four in the canton of Châtenois."

Louis, Louis: *artiste vétérinaire* of Raon-l'Étape (Vosges): Since the practice of his profession often calls him into the countryside, Monsieur Louis profited from these occasions to spread the most deadly doctrines and to assist the insidious efforts of the red party there.

Bouignier, lawyer of Verdun: "has sacrificed almost all of his fortune to support the [socialist] newspapers and secret societies."

Polellite, vice-president of the club in Rouen in 1848: "he preached disorder to the working classes by preying upon their instincts of hate and vengeance against their bosses."

Boissel, once provisional mayor of Londe (Seine-Inférieure): "Since 1848, Boissel has not ceased to use his influence on the working class to pervert it."[7]

The mixed commissions hoped to crush all organized dissent. The police state of Napoleon Bonaparte continued in that hope. Yet, as we know, cracks began to appear in what the "forces of order" believed was a strong structure that stifled protest and prevented political organization among the laboring poor. Republicans surfaced, and then socialists. The empire became more "liberal," believing that concessions would prevent further protest and organization. The Bonapartist structure (and Louis Napoleon himself) aged badly. Protest grew. Well before the international crisis of the summer of 1870, local officials, such as the procureur général in Limoges, had first hand experience with the militance of the workers. Many were surprised, believing that the "organizational fervor" of the Second Republic had passed and that relative prosperity ensured a docile working class. Underneath the garish Bonapartist trappings, and amid the rebuilding of Paris, however, workers organized. The repression during the Second Republic and the empire had ended neither dissent nor protest. Public works projects and some toleration of nonaggressive unions had failed to satisfy the workers. Louis Napoleon was still Badinguet, with Daumier's Ratapoil lurking behind. The procureur of Limoges, in March of 1870, reported that:

> The upholstery workers of Limoges have just struck, at the instigation of the procelain worker, Monsieur Bergeron, one of the principal delegates of the workers' unions. The pretext for the strike was the refusal of the industrialists to agree to a request for a reduction in the hours of work.

In Limoges, as in other French cities, the workers now seemed more militant and more unified:

> This first evidence of the struggle, which seems to have been growing for several months, in Limoges against the patrons, is not in itself grave ... but [it] takes significance from the organization which brought it about. It is tied to a work of emancipation which is taking place and developing with a remarkable unity in the midst of all of the workers' corporations.

Faced with this organization, the procureur had some fears for the future:

M. Bergeron, the instigator of the strike, is an agitating porcelain worker, involved in the organization of the *chambres
syndicales* and the mutual-aid societies [now] called *caisses
de resistance*. We must presume that through the influence
of the committee of which he is one of the most industrious
agents, the strike will spread to other professions when they
receive the orders. Public opinion seems to be anticipating
his eventuality. As for the industrialists, they do not seem
to be planning any measures to be taken in such an event.[8]

Less than one year later, Paris, and again Limoges, was in
revolution. More workers and more trades were involved. Proletarians were even more prominent among those carrying the red
flag and dreams of social justice to the barricades. Both their
dreams and their improved organization were largely heritages
of the Second Republic. The repression which awaited them was
just as efficient, but far more terrible.

Notes

INTRODUCTION

1. Karl Marx, *The Eighteenth Brumaire of Louis Napoleon Bonaparte*, p. 124.

2. Charles Tilly, "How Protest Modernized in France, 1845–55," p. 235.

3. Ted W. Margadant, "The French Insurrection of 1851," introduction, and chap. 8.

4. Leo A. Loubère, *Radicalism in Mediterranean France*, and Christianne Marcilhacy, "Les Caractères de la crise sociale et politique de 1846 à 1852 dans le département du Loiret," pp. 5–59.

5. Margadant, "The French Insurrection of 1851." Roger D. Price's *The French Second Republic* is the best recent general account of the republic, particularly of its first year.

6. Peter Amann, "The Changing Outlines of 1848," pp. 938–53.

7. Howard C. Payne, "Preparation of a Coup d'État" and *The Police State of Louis Napoleon*.

8. Agulhon, *La République au village*; Philippe Vigier, *La Seconde République*; Jean Dagnan, *Le Gers sous la Seconde République*, vol. 1; Alain Corbin, *Archaïsme et modernité en Limousin au XIXe siècle*; John M. Merriman, "Radicalization and Repression."

9. For example, see Paul Muller, "Le Bas Rhin de 1848 à 1852," pp. 353–66; Robert Schnerb, "La Seconde République dans le département du Puy-de-Dôme"; Marcel Dessal, *La Révolution de 1848 et la Seconde République dans le département d'Eure-et-Loir*.

10. Richard Cobb, *The Police and the People* (Oxford: Oxford University Press, 1965).

11. See, among other works, Charles Tilly, Louise Tilly, and Richard Tilly, *The Rebellious Century* (Cambridge: Harvard University Press, 1975); Tilly, "How Protest Modernized in France"; Charles Tilly, "The Changing Place of Collective Violence"; Tilly, "Food Supply and Public Order in Modern Europe," in *The Formation of National States in Western Europe*, ed. Charles Tilly (Princeton: Princeton University Press, 1975).

12. James Rule and Charles Tilly, "Political Process in Revolutionary

France, 1830–1832," in *1830 in France* ed. John M. Merriman (New York: Franklin Watts, 1975) and Charles Tilly and Lynn Lees, "The People of June, 1848."

13. Agulhon, *La République au village*, and *1848 ou l'apprentissage de la république*.

14. André-Jean Tudesq, *Les grands notables en France, 1840–49*. See also Frederick de Luna, *The French Republic Under Cavaignac, 1848* (Princeton: Princeton University Press, 1969).

15. Peter Amann, *Revolution and Mass Democracy: The Paris Club Movement in 1848*.

CHAPTER ONE

1. Charles Tilly and Lynn Lees, "The People of June, 1848," pp. 173–74.

2. Alfred Cobban, *A History of Modern France* (Hardmondsworth, England: Penguin Books, 1971), 2:131. An earlier version of the material on the Affaire de Limoges appeared in my article, "Social Conflict in Revolutionary France and the Limoges Revolution of April 27, 1848," *Societas—A Review of Social History* 4 (Winter 1974): 21–39.

3. Archives départementales de la Haute Vienne (hereafter cited as ADHV), (former *côte*) M 739, Prefect of Haute Garonne to the Prefect of Haute Vienne (henceforth PHV), July 10, 1833; PHV Report, June 1, 1833; Rivet to Guépin (certainly the Guépin cited in chapter 3), May 20, 1833. Saint Simonian influence in Limoges was noted in 1831, among the workers in 1833; see Antoine Perrier, "Les Saint Simoniens en Limousin," *Bulletin de la Société Archéologique et Historique du Limousin* (hereafter cited as *BSAHL*) 84 (1954): 530–31. Théodore Bac's early career mentioned in AN F[7] 6784, dossier 22 and AN BB[18] 1240, Report of the Procureur Général of Limoges (hereafter cited as PGL), May 11, 1837. Marcel Dussoubs-Gaston's political activities are detailed in ADHV M 789, Reports of PHV, November 28, 1840, February 2, 1841 and November 27, 1841; and Minister of Interior (hereafter cited as Int.) to PHV, February 8, 1841.

4. ADHV, M 740, Report of PHV, July 8, 1847. Leroux moved his journal *L'Éclaireur* from Orléans after being ordered beyond a certain distance from Paris, and then began *Revue Sociale* in October 1845 (Archives Départementales de la Creuse [hereafter cited as ADCr], 4M 72). Reports of socialist meetings in Limoges appear in ADHV M 740, Reports of PHV, March 21, 31 and July 13, 1847, and Report of Police Commissioner, August 1.

5. Limoges had the fourth highest percentage of population increase among major cities in France during the first half of the century (following Toulon, St. Étienne, and Reims); its population in 1801 was 20,550. Noted in Charles Pouthas, *La population française pendant la première moitié du XIXe siècle* (Paris, 1956), p. 99.

6. AN F⁹ 733, Mayor of Limoges to PHV, August 18, 1831.

7. AN C 968, "Enquête sur le travail agricole et industriel, par decret du 25 mai, 1848," Haute Vienne; *Statistique de la France: Industrie*, vol. 4 (Paris, 1852). On artisans, see particularly Christopher H. Johnson, *Utopian Communism in France*.

8. ADHV M 739, Reports of PHV, June 6, 1833 and April 17, 27, and August 8, 1837, PHV to Minister of War (hereafter cited as MG), April 27, 1837, Int. to PHV, May 3, 1833 and Police Report, April 19–20, 1837. The first of the strikes was initiated by the molders and turners, while the second involved the decorators exclusively. The mutual aid societies are listed in ADHV M 777, "Tableau général des sociétés de secours mutuels."

9. ADHV M 1394 (*mercuriales*). There were widespread grain riots in Haute Vienne and Creuse in 1840–41 and 1846–47 (ADHV M 740). See Merriman, "Radicalization and Repression," pp. 22–25.

10. Monique Lachtygier, "Tableau de la vie ouvrière à Limoges de 1800 à 1848" (Thesis, University of Poitiers, 1958), pp. 51, 104.

11. AN BB³⁰ 331, Report of Procureur Général of Poitiers, December 9, 1848, AN BB³⁰ 361, "Cour d'assises de la Vienne: Affaire de Limoges" (hereafter cited as "Affaire"), and "Acte d'accusation" of the Cour d'appel of Poitiers (hereafter cited as "Acte"), December 16, 1848.

12. AN F⁹ 733, Report of PHV, April 10, 1847; the National Guard was performing with "regularity and zeal," having a regular post of twenty-five men commanded by an officer.

13. Ibid. The carton includes the petition. *Annales de la Haute Vienne*, October 1, 1830, noted that the price of a uniform (then) was forty francs, as much as three weeks' wages for most Limoges workers. Corbin, *Archaïsme et modernité en Limousin*, 2:810, indicates that the municipal council was dissolved as a result of the furor.

14. ADHV M 741, Report of PHV, February 20, 1848; "Affaire," p. 71; and Archives of the Ministry of War, Vincennes (hereafter cited as AG), F¹ 1, Report of General St. Amand, February 27 and 28, 1848.

15. "Affaire," p. 71. Corbin, *Archaïsme et modernité en Limousin*, p. 762, describes the crowd invading the prefecture, forcing the prefect out.

16. "Affaire," pp. 29–30, 50, 89; Antoine Perrier, "La Société Popu-

laire de Limoges en 1848," *Actes du Quatre-vingt-dixième congrès des sociétés savantes* 3 (Paris, 1966): 271. Corbin, who located a list of 328 members in the Departmental Archives of Vienne, suggests that the importance of "open" trades like the porcelain industry substantiates the analysis of William H. Sewell, Jr., of closed and open trades in Marseille ("La classe ouvrière de Marseille", pp. 27–63). Corbin, *Archaïsme et modernité en Limousin*, 2:767.

17. AG F¹ 1, Report of Commander of the 3ᵉ chasseurs, March 2; *Affaire*, p. 276. Although Corbin, p. 767, pictures a relatively smooth transition from the provisional committee to the commissioner, it seems certain that the committee continued to exert considerable pressure with regard to such issues as politically motivated dismissals of officials.

18. "Affaire," pp. 73, 276.

19. ADHV M 740 and 741, Decrees of March 3 and February 29.

20. ADHV Annex, R 193, "État des fusils delivrés aux citoyens de la ville de Limoges le 27 février," which gives the name, occupation and address of each citizen receiving a weapon; AN C 940, dossier 3, Report of Citizen Genty, April 19; "Affaire," p. 280.

21. The colonel-elect, Lazare Raybaud, became a strange and controversial figure. Although elected, for all practical purposes, by the workers, he influenced the decision to entrust the Orleanist faction with security in the city. He was later tried as a participant in the Affaire because he did not order the Guard to resist with force.

22. *Le Peuple*, April 6. There were also rumors of the forced disarmament of the National Guard, "Affaire," pp. 58–59, 124.

23. The provisional committee tried to keep the factories open, first calling for business confidence, then asking the banks for a list of businessmen withdrawing their funds (ADHV M 741). The municipal council allocated 30,000 francs to the industrialists; Report of the Committee, March 1; "Affaire," pp. 56, 58.

24. Ernest Vincent, "Les Ateliers nationaux à Limoges en 1848," *BSAHL*, 83 (1951): 336–44; "Affaire," p. 213.

25. ADHV M 741. They complained of wage abuses, particularly of having to pay for porcelain damaged during production, and said that they were forced to accept wage reductions because their employers threatened to hire women at lower wages. See Corbin, *Archaïsme et modernité en Limousin*, pp. 536–39.

26. Pierre Cousteix, "L'Action ouvrière en Haute Vienne sous la Second République," *BSAHL*, 84 (1954): 505–07; and Corbin, *Archaïsme et modernité en Limousin*, pp. 536–39. The other projects included those described in the brochures *Centralisation de l' industrie porcelaini-*

ère, Acte social des ouvriers porcelainiers, and *Projet d'association du capital et du travail*. All of these proposals reflected the influence of the utopian socialists (Corbin, *Archaïsme et modernité en Limousin*, p. 537), particularly the evolution toward "la vie communautaire" envisioned by the Experimental Manufacture of Associated Workers of Limoges.

27. Leroux attended the session of March 25, but soon left for Paris, allegedly because the general commissioner persuaded him that his candidacy would augment social tension; Antoine Perrier, "Une candidature de Pierre Leroux à l'Assemblée Constituante de 1848 dans la Haute Vienne," *Revue d'histoire moderne et contemporaine* 13 (1966): 157–62.

28. "Affaire," pp. 20, 181, 277. The electoral *professions de foi* are virtually complete in ADHV M 163. The most important moderate candidates were Coralli, former liberal opposition deputy and by 1849 a montagnard; Léopold Duras, former editor of *Le National*; Dumas, former National Guard officer; François Allègre, the new procureur général; and Maurat-Ballange, a former opposition leader who was extremely influential in the arrondissement of Bellac north of Limoges. Staunch conservatives included Tixier, an influential Limoges businessman; Brunet, a retired artillery officer; and a number of legitimists, each with his own local power base.

29. See AN C 940, dossier five, for the instructions for the delegates leaving Paris for the provinces.

30. AN 940, dossiers three and five, Reports of Genty, April 15 and 24. His reports, included in the "Affaire," were used against him in the trial. Once his enthusiasm and bias have been weighed, they are a fascinating picture of revolutionary commitment.

31. AN BB³⁰ 361, dossier 2, Letter seized at the Société populaire, dated April 22.

32. "Acte"; "Affaire," pp. 85–87, 107; AN BB³⁰ 361, dossier 2, Testimony (hereafter cited as Testimony) nos. 147, 918.

33. "Acte"; "Affaire", pp. 58, 319; Testimony, no. 374.

34. "Affaire", pp. 171, 319.

35. "Acte."

36. Testimony, no. 132.

37. "Acte"; "Affaire", p. 165. Almost all of the ballots had secretly been removed and only the military ballots remained. Later, witnesses blamed the destruction of the ballots on "young people." The results of the election (AN C 1325 and 1391) were: Dumas, 48,434; Maurat-Ballange, 43,511; Bac, 38,778; Frichon aîné, 36,815; Allègre, 31,841; Tixier, 28,802; Brunet, 27,175; and Coralli, 24,826 (all elected). They

were followed by Dussoubs-Gaston, 24,153; Villegoureix, 21,638; and Duras, 18,923. Corbin, *Archaïsme et modernité en Limousin*, pp. 721–24, sees this as a republican victory, anticipating May 1849, in that Dumas and Maurat-Ballange were staunch republicans, as were Coralli, Frichon, and Bac.

38. "Acte"; "Affaire", pp. 174, 190, 253, 319, etc.; Testimony, no. 760; AN BB[30] 361, dossier 1, report of PGL, April 28. See also the account of Victor Chazelas, "Une épisode de la lutte des classes à Limoges, 1848."

39. Testimony, no. 147. The committee included Bac, Dussoubs-Gaston, Coralli, Bulot, the elder Frichon, Talandier (a socialist lawyer), Vincent, and Briquet (two porcelain workers who played active roles in the Affaire) and a leather-dresser, Bardonnaud, who headed the delegation to the prefecture to demand the commissioner's resignation.

40. "Affaire", p. 166. *Le Peuple* published all of the decrees.

41. "Acte." The incident recalls the notion of the "moral economy" and the popular sense of justice involving local control over food supply. See Louise A. Tilly, "The Food Riot as a Form of Political Conflict in France," *Journal of Interdisciplinary History* 11 (Summer 1972): 23–57, and Charles Tilly, "Food Supply and Public Order in Modern Europe," in *The Formation of National States in Western Europe*, ed. Charles Tilly, (Princeton: Princeton University Press, 1975).

42. "Affaire," pp. 140, 166; ADHV M 741, which contains the committee's correspondence. Of the 200 mayors in the department, 68 were dismissed (34%, compared to 21% in the Corréze and 19% in the Creuse.)

43. AN BB[30] 361, dossier 2, report of PGL, April 30. Corbin, *Archaïsme et modernité en Limousin*, p. 770, notes: "One must say that a great number of terrified *notables* took refuge in the surrounding countryside."

44. "Acte."

45. AG F[1] 7, Report of Commander of 15th Military Division, May 9; *Affaire*, pp. 114, 271.

46, AN BB[30] 361, dossier 2, includes the testimony gathered for the Poitiers trial and related correspondence. Over three hundred fifty witnesses testified and nineteen hundred pieces of procedure were considered. Fifteen of the thirty-nine were found guilty on charges ranging from inciting civil war to invasion of an inhabited house, including Genty, Denis Dussoubs, Lazare Raybaud (see n. 21), Bulot, Villegoureix, the journalist Durin, Briquet and Talandier; most received a sentence of two years in prison plus court costs.

47. André Dubuc, "Les Émeutes de Rouen et d'Elbeuf (27–28 et 29 avril, 1848)," *Études sur la Révolution de 1848* 2 (1948): 246.

48. Ville de Rouen, *Conseil municipal, analyse des procès-verbaux des scéances, 1800—70*, vol. 2 (Rouen: Imprimerie Julien Lecerf, 1892), minutes of February 24; F¹ 1, Report of Commander of the 14th Military Division, February 20.

49. Archives Départementales de la Seine Maritime, U 3129, chambre d'accusations, May 12, 1848; Dubuc, "Les Émeutes de Rouen et d'Elbeuf," pp. 245–46.

50. Account based on BB³⁰ 365, dossier 2, Report of PG Rouen, August 25, 1849, and Report of Sénard, March 26, 1848; AG F¹ 2, Report of Commander of Third Gendarmerie Legion, February 25; F¹ 3, Report of Commander of 14th Military Division, March 27 and 28; F¹ 4, Report of Temporary Commander of 14th Military Division, March 29; and Ville de Rouen, *Conseil municipal*, minutes of February 26 and 28; Dubuc, "Les Émeutes de Rouen et d'Elbeuf," pp. 249–51. Seventy officers and 150 troops were assigned to the Rouen garrison at the time of the revolution (*Situation Générale de l'Armée*, AG, Vincennes, January 1, 1848).

51. Ville de Rouen, *Conseil municipal*, various minutes; AN BB³⁰ 365, dossier 2, Report of the Procureur général of Rennes, May 5; Dubuc, "Les Émeutes de Rouen et d'Elbeuf," p. 249, estimates the new council's composition as one-third members of the former dynastic opposition, one-third members of the former republican opposition, and one-third workers. The higher pay figure applied to workers who provided their own tools; women and children earned forty and thirty centimes per day.

52. AG F¹ 2, Report of Commander of Third Legion of Gendarmerie, February 25; Dubuc, "Les Émeutes de Rouen et d'Elbeuf," p. 247.

53. The provisional government in Paris loaned 300,000 francs to the city (Ville de Rouen, *Conseil municipal*, minutes of May 4).

54. According to *L'Ami du peuple*, March 26; and AN BB³⁰ 365, dossier 2, piece 269. The *Journal de Rouen*, even more conservative, urged on April 23 that the republic be "wise, moderate, tolerant."

55. *L'Ami du peuple*, April 21.

56. Ibid., March 30; Ville de Rouen, *Conseil municipal*, minutes of March 12, 13, 14, 28, etc.

57. AN BB³⁰ 365, dossier 2, Report of the Director of the Prison; Dubuc, "Les Émeutes de Rouen et d'Elbeuf," pp. 252–54; and Archives départementales du Seine Maritime (hereafter cited as ADSM), U 3129,

the decree freeing the prisoner. The ceremony around the liberty tree was planned for April 9.

58. Conservatives were irritated when the municipal council gave the workers night-time use of schools, paper, and lighting facilities to prepare for the elections.

59. AN C 1329, election results; Dubuc, "Les Émeutes de Rouen et d'Elbeuf," pp. 255–57.

60. Account based primarily on AN BB[30] 365, dossier 2, many reports; and Dubuc, "Les Émeutes de Rouen et d'Elbeuf," esp. pp. 260–61. Other accounts include Alexandre Zévaès' polemic, "La lutte des classes à Rouen en avril, 1848," *Revue de la Révolution de 1848* 24 (1927): 204–21, which includes an unsubstantiated account of a murder of a man named Quesnel, who as he was being escorted away by the National Guard, was struck down by a sword "for bravado, to impress the crowd." Zévaès claims that there were fifty killed and hundreds injured. He also relates a story, popular in Rouen in 1848, of a guardsman who states, "We must do away with this *canaille*," while an industrialist forced a worker to make cartridges "to kill off all of these miserable workers." On the other hand, Dubuc is not at all sympathetic to the insurgents, blaming their action on their "distress," particularly in the medieval districts where much of the fighting occurred; he argues that only about one-third of the workers supported the democratic electoral list. Another account is offered by Jacques Toutain, *La Révolution de 1848 à Rouen* (Paris, n.d.).

61. AN BB[30] 365, dossier 2, pièces 264, 266, and 290, all n.d., Reports from PG Rouen and other court officials. ADSM U 3129 lists those arrested.

62. AN BB[30] 365, dossier 2, Report of the Juge d'instruction, May 5.

63. AN BB[18] 1456, Report of PG Rouen, October 9, 1847, who adds that the workers "were subject to the pernicious influence of the communist agitators lurking in the shadow." A gathering of five to six hundred workers took place in October outside a spinning factory.

64. AN BB[30] 365, dossier 2, Report of Juge d'instruction, May 5. *L'Écho d'Elbeuf* exerted a radical influence on the workers.

65. Ibid., and Acte d'accusation (pièce 337); Report of the first Avocat général, pièce 275; pièce 346 lists 47 persons on trial, of which 20 were guilty with extenuating circumstances and 27 not guilty (of 122 originally prosecuted, 521 arrests, and 81 who at least reached the courtroom). Three hundred and twenty-eight witnesses testified (pièce 270).

66. Dubuc, *Les Émeutes de Rouen et d'Elbeuf*, p. 266. Blanqui claimed that two hundred were killed and that two hundred cannon shots were fired by the troops and National Guard.

67. Cited in T. J. Clark, *The Absolute Bourgeois*, p. 143.

68. Tilly and Lees, "The People of June, 1848."

69. Peter Amann, "The Paris Club Movement in 1848," in *Revolution and Reaction*, ed. Price, p. 126.

70. Tilly and Lees, "The People of June, 1848," p. 194.

71. For example, The Association démocratique du département de l'Yonne submitted statutes to the prefect in November, 1848, describing its goal as "the maintenance and development of the democratic Republic based on universal suffrage, the freedom of speech and the press, and the right of assembly and association." Archives Départementales de l'Yonne, III M¹ 132.

72. Agulhon, *La République au village*, esp. pp. 479–80.

73. Merriman, "Radicalization and Repression," p. 77 (ADHV M 741, letter of the mayor of Sauviat, March 5).

74. Tilly and Lees, "The People of June, 1848," p. 173; see particularly Rule and Tilly, "Political Process in Revolutionary France, 1830–32," pp. 55–59.

75. Karl Marx, *The Eighteenth Brumaire of Louis Napoleon Bonaparte* and *Class Struggles in France (1848–1850)*. I am alerted to the dangers of referring loosely to "middle-class resistance" after the revolution and of identifying the bourgeoisie with the July Monarchy, particularly in view of the work of André-Jean Tudesq, *Les grands notables en France, 1840–49*; David H. Pinkney, *The French Revolution of 1830* (Princeton: Princeton University Press, 1973); Patrice L.R. Higonnet and Trevor B. Higonnet, "Class, Corruption, and Politics in the French Chamber of Deputies, 1846–48," pp. 204–23; and others. But in Limoges and Rouen (and, I would argue, in much of the rest of France) the bourgeoisie clearly controlled commerce, justice, government, the National Guard and were closely identified with the Orleanists. See Christopher H. Johnson, "The French Revolution of 1830 in French Economic History," in *1830 in France*, ed. John M. Merriman (New York: Franklin Watts, 1975).

CHAPTER TWO

1. AG Justice Militaire, 1851, 258, dossier Terrain; *Archives Départementales du Cher*, 2M 109, Report of the Prefect of Cher, November 12, 1851.

2. Charles Tilly and Lynn Lees, "The People of June, 1848," p. 179. Irene Collins (*The Government and the Newspaper Press in France, 1814–81*, p. 102) notes 450 papers in Paris during the first months following the revolution; Claude Bellanger, et al. (*Histoire général de la presse française*, 2:208) claim about three hundred new papers began at that time. These two estimates include papers of a single sheet, many of which appeared only once or twice.

3. AN F^{18} 262.

4. The paper first appeared on January 5, 1850.

5. Bellanger et al., *Histoire général de la presse française*, 2:248.

6. AN F^{18} 262.

7. Phillippe Bernard, "La Presse républicaine dans le département du Puy-de-Dôme pendant la Seconde République (1848–51)," p. 123.

8. AN F^{18} 262.

9. AN C 968, Haute Vienne.

10. AN C 969, Yonne, Vosges; C 957, Loiret.

11. Maurice Agulhon, "La Diffusion d'un journal montagnard: *Le Démocrate du Var* sous la Deuxième République," p. 16.

12. Bellanger et al., *Histoire général*, p. 247.

13. M.Agulhon, "La Diffusion d'un journal montagnard," pp. 18, 25.

14. Collins, *Government and the Newspaper Press*, pp. 105, 109.

15. Ted W. Margadant, "The French Insurrection of 1851," chap. 10. Margadant shows that the montagnard conspirators who organized secret societies did not rely upon the press. Numerous press trials took place in such town as Lyon, Paris, Toulouse, Metz, and Dijon, which were outside of the network of secret societies, while towns where the conspiracy thrived such as Avignon, Auch, Toulon, Macon, Valence, and Nîmes had few such proceedings. The growth of the provincial press after the revolution is striking: seven of the Côtes-du-Nord's nine papers in the summer of 1850 had appeared since the revolution, nine of Haute Rhin's ten, eight of Loiret's nine, all five of the Var's, all five of the Haute Marne's, etc. (F^{18} 262).

16. Bellanger et al., *Histoire général*, p. 220. In 1850, papers that did not have to pay caution money included 139 in Paris, 21 in Gironde, 19 in the Nord and Rhône, 11 in Seine Inférieure, 14 in Bouches-du-Rhône, etc., AN F^{18} 262.

17. AN BB^{18} 1470^{c}, Report of the Procureur Général (PG) Riom, February 26, 1849.

18. AN BB^{18} 1470^{c}, Reports of PG Dijon, June 14, 1849, PG Colmar, January 5, 1850.

19. AN BB^{18} 1470^{c}, Reports of PG Douai, December 4, 1849, PG

Toulouse, December 17, 1849; AN BB[18] 1491, Report of PG Aix, October 1, 1851; AN BB[18] 1465, PG Montpellier, November 27, 1849. *L'Émancipation* of Toulouse went so far as to warn that the "democratic party will not hesitate, if it becomes necessary, to once more employ the terror to regenerate France" (AN BB[18] 1488, Minister of the Interior to Minister of Justice [hereafter cited as Int. to MJ] April 27, 1850).

20. For example, AN BB[18] 1487, MJ to PG Paris, September 20, 1850, and MJ to PG Riom, October 11, 1850.

21. AN BB[18] 1470[c], Report of PG Riom, July 15, 1850, Report of PG Dijon, January 21, 1850 and February 5, 1850; Int. to MJ, July 1, 1850 and January 7, 1850.

22. AN BB[18] 1470[c], Report of the PG Douai, February 16, 1850; Report of PG Colmar, March 11, 1849.

23. AN BB[18] 1470[c], Report of PG Toulouse, August 7, 1849; AN BB[18] 1496, report of PG Angers, October 11, 1851.

24. AN BB[18] 1498, Int. to MJ, January 4, 1850; AN BB[18] 1487, Report of the Prefect of Lot after the acquittal of *Le Réformateur du Lot et du Cantal*; AN BB[18] 1470[c], Report of PG Dijon, July 26 and August 23, 1850; BB[18] 1489, PG Dijon, October 9, 1850, June 16, August 1851, etc.

25. AN BB[18] 1470[c], Report of PG Rennes, March 14, 17, 24, June 5, July 24, 1850, October 13, 1849, August 25, 1849, etc.

26. BB[18] 1489, Report of the Prefect of Meurthe, November 22, 1850; Report of PG Nancy, December 6, 1850, April 5, 1851, etc.

27. Bellanger et al., *Histoire général*, p. 235.

28. AN BB[18] 1483. The request of Eugène Benoit of Limoges (AN F[18] 2162[A]) for a printer's license was typical: his politics were checked and the procureur noted that there were already eight printers in Limoges in 1851. The licensing of printers was restricted by the laws of October 21, 1814, and the decree of February 29, 1848.

29. AN BB[18] 1483, Report of the Procureur of Carcassonne, August 24, 1850; AN BB[18] 1487, Report of PG Aix, January 11, 1851.

30. AN BB[18] 1483, Report of PG Besançon, December 10, 1850, etc.; see also AN BB[18] 1500, Report of PG Rennes, October 3, 1851, on the harassment of the printer of *La Sentinelle du peuple*, PG Rennes, October 3, 1851.

31. AN BB[18] 1470[c], Report of the Prefect of Police of Paris, July 22, 1849; AN BB[18] 1494, Int. to MJ, October 12, 1849; Report of PG Aix, June 6, 1850, PG Metz, June 10, 1850.

32. AN BB[18] 1494, Report of PG Lyon, October 21, 1849; MJ to Int.,

November 5, 1849; PG Besançon, March 6, 1850, PG Nancy, May 1, 1851, and especially PG Metz, June 24, 1850.

33. Robert J. Bezucha, *The Lyon Insurrection of 1834* (Cambridge, Mass.: Harvard University Press, 1974), esp. pp. 112–18.

34. AN BB[18] 1470[c], Report of PG Lyon, November 21 and 26, 1849, August 8, and October 20, 1849, March 3, 1849, December 11, 1849, April 29, 1849; and MJ to PG Lyon, May 5, 1849.

35. AN BB[18] 1470[c], PG Lyon, April 30, 1850; AN BB[18] 1488, PG Lyon, September 23, 1850 and November 23, 1850.

36. *L'Égalité*, July 27, 1849. AN F[18] 264 contains a list by department of press convictions from 1830 to 1861. More than half of the reports skipped the Second Republic, but the following totals seem reasonably accurate: Allier, 8; Ardennes, 8; Ardèche, 1; Aveyron, 2; Cantal, 1; Charente, 1; Charente Inférieure, 3; Côte d'or, 27 (1849–51); Doubs, 5; Drôme, 2; Eure, 0; Gard, 2; Haute Garonne, 13 (1849–51); Gers, 5; Gironde, 19; Ille-et-Vilaine, 2; Jura, 3; Loir-et-Cher, 4; Loire, 1; Loire Inférieure, 6; Lot, 1; Manche, 2; Marne, 5; Haute Marne, 4; Mayenne, 1; Meurthe, 9; Morbihan, 1; Moselle, 4; Pas-de-Calais, 9; Basses Pyrénées, 1; Pyrénées Orientales, 1; Bas Rhin, 4; Bouches-du-Rhône, 11; Sarthe, 4; Seine Inférieure, 5; and Deux Sèvres, 3.

37. AN BB[18] 1500, note of MJ, October 19, 1851; AN BB[18] 1487, PG Nancy, September 29, 1850, November 2, 1850; AN BB[18] 1470[c], PG Dijon, March 17, 1850, and October 17, 1850; AN BB[18] 1470[a2], PG Besançon, January 22, 1851.

38. Bellanger et al., *Histoire général*, p. 238.

39. AN F[7] 3450; F[18] 262. Collins, *Government and the Newspaper Press*, p. 114; J. Dagnan, *Le Gers sous la Seconde République*, pp. 398–400.

40. AN BB[18] 1489, MJ to PG Bordeaux, August 14, 1851, and July 16, 1851; MJ note, n.d.

41. Collins, *Government and the Newspaper Press*, p. 114.

42. Expression of PG Limoges, AN BB[30] 378, dossier six, pièce 2, report of December 21, 1848.

43. AN BB[18] 1474[A], Report of PG Aix, April 14, 1849; AN BB[30] 368, dossier 2, Report of PG Bourges, November 1849.

44. AN BB[18] 1470[c], MJ to Procureur of Strasbourg, June 21, 1849. They were printed in Strasbourg.

45. Alexandre Zévaès, "La Propagande socialiste dans les campagnes en 1848," *Révolution de 1848*, 31, (June-July-August 1934), pp. 80–81; AN BB[18] 1501; Prefect of Police of Paris report, August 24, 1851; AN

BB^{18} 1470^c, Report of PG Riom, February 24, 1849; G. Rocal, *1848 en Dordogne* 1:51; AN BB^{30} 368, dossier 2, Report of PG Amiens, February 1850.

46. Zévaès, "La Propagande socialiste," pp. 75, 78–79.

47. Ibid., pp. 82–83.

48. *La Feuille du village*, B.N. Lc^2 2082. Although it cost eight francs per year to subscribe to *La Feuille*, it sometimes was distributed free of charge.

49. P. Joigneaux, with Gilland, Mathieu (de la Drôme), Agricol Perdiguier, Lurnier, Saint-Romme, and Aubry (du Nord), représentants du peuple, *Le Almanach du village pour 1852* (Paris: Librairie de la propagande démocratique et sociale, 1851). The almanac appeared on September 10, 1851.

50. The change is reflected in the instructions of the procureur général to his procureurs, November 27, 1849, AN BB^{30} 385.

51. AN BB^{30} 394, pièce 414 bis, and AG F^1 40. The leaders of Solidarité républicaine, which was founded at the end of October 1848, were pronounced guilty April 12, 1850.

52. AN BB^{30} 392^A Report of Prefect of Police, November 22, 1850 and PG Dijon, April 26, 1851. There were twelve bulletins, a major propaganda undertaking; some were directed to the army.

53. AN BB^{18} 1483, Report of the procureur of Le Mans, February 8, 1850, and MJ to PG Angers, March 16, 1850.

54. AN BB^{18} 1492, Int. to MJ, March 24, 1851 and AN BB^{18} 1483, PG Riom, December 21, 1849; also, AN BB^{30} 393, Int. to MJ, July 23, 1851.

55. AN BB^{18} 1470^c, Report of PG Douai, October 28, 1849, and PG Dijon, April 1, 1849.

56. AN BB^{30} 393, Report of PG Poitiers, July 13, 1851, etc.

57. AN BB^{30} 394, Report of PG Lyon, October 7, 1851 and AG F^1 30–50, various reports. See also, AG F^1 49, Decree of the General commanding the state of siege in the Cher, November 9, 1851. Much of this material was forbidden under the law of August 9, 1849, articles seven and nine.

58. For example, AN BB^{30} 394, Report of PG Paris, August 29, 1851. A secret press was discovered in Lyon, AN BB^{18} 1470^c, Report of the PG Lyon, February 13, 1850.

59. AN F^{18} 568, Int. to MJ, June 19, 1849; under the law of July 27, 1849.

60. AN BB^{18} 1468, Report of PG Lyon, September 19, 1848, Int. to MJ, December 21, 1849; Archives Départementales de la Somme,

107627, report of Subprefect of Abbeville, August 1, 1850. Instructions on hawking and peddling were sent to all mayors in the Somme, AD Somme, Mfs 95275. The same laws also applied to town criers.

61. See for example, Abel Chatelain, "Les Migrations temporaires françaises au XIXe siècle," *Annales de démographie historique* (1967), 9–28; A. Corbin, "Migrations temporaires et société rurale aux XIXe siècle: le cas du Limousin," *Revue historique* 246 (October-December 1971): 293–334.

62. An insurance agent "with the confidence of the people," traveling in the Hérault and Aude, seems typical, AN BB^{30} 393, Report of PG Montpellier, September 29, 1851.

63. AN BB^{30} 378, dossier 6, Report of PG Limoges, October 12, 1848 and AD Creuse, 1M 147, Report of Subprefect of Aubusson, December 1, 1849.

64. Archives Départementales de la Haute Garonne, 4M 69, Prefect of Aude to Prefect of Haute Garonne, May 16, 1851; AD Haute Garonne, 4M 66, Report of Police Commissioner, June 4, 1850.

65. AG F^1 42 bis, Commander of 10th, 11th, and 12th military divisions, n.d.; AN BB^{30} 392^B, Report of PG Rennes, May 16, 1851.

66. AN BB^{30} 394, Int. to MJ, August 28, 1851; Report of PG Pau, September 21, 1849 and October 30, 1851; AN BB^{18} 1470^c, Report of PG Rouen, February 13, 1850; AN BB^{30} 393, Report of PG Dijon, July 7, 1851; AN BB^{18} 1499, Report of PG Grenoble, September 3, 1851.

67. ADHG, 4M 70, Report of the Subprefect of Villefranche, June 1, 1851.

68. ADHG, 4M 69, Note of Commissioner of Police, n.d.; 4M 70, report of the Subprefect of Muret, May 31, 1851.

69. ADHG, 4M 69, Undated reports of the Commissioner of Police, numbered 61, 65, and 72.

70. ADHG, 4M 69, and Report of July 30, 1851.

71. Even in the arrondissement of Loudéac in the Côtes du Nord, the PG Rennes reported an increase in socialist propaganda, AN BB^{30} 383, Report of October, 1851.

72. For example, again to cite a very conservative department, in the Somme, according to the PG Amiens, October, 1851, report, AN BB^{30} 368, dossier 2. See Dagnan, *Le Gers sous la Seconde République*, 1:473.

CHAPTER THREE

1. Rémi Gossez, *Les Ouvriers de Paris*, p. 9. See also Maurice Agulhon, *1848 ou l'apprentissage de la république*, pp. 110–11.

2. Gossez, *Les Ouvriers de Paris*, p. 40.

3. I. Tchernoff, *Associations et sociétés secrètes sous la IIe République, 1848–1851*, pp. 2–3.

4. Bernard Moss, "Parisian Producers' Associations (1830–51): The Socialism of Skilled Workers," in *Revolution and Reaction*, ed. Price, p. 76.

5. Robert J. Bezucha, *The Lyon Insurrection of 1834* (Cambridge, Mass.: Harvard University Press, 1974), pp. 134–48.

6. AN BB³⁰ 1474 A et B.

7. Peter Amann, *Revolution and Mass Democracy*, pp. 326–27.

8. Charles Tilly and Lynn Lees, "The People of June, 1848," p. 194.

9. Amann, *Revolution and Mass Democracy*, pp. 124–28, and John M. Merriman, "Radicalization and Repression," pp. 60–63, 89–90.

10. AN BB¹⁸ 1474 A includes documents relating to the evolution of the decree and its interpretations.

11. See, for example, AN BB¹⁸ 1474 B, Report of the Procureur Général (PG) of Aix, and others.

12. AN BB¹⁸ 1474 A, Report of PG Dijon, March 22, 1849.

13. AN BB¹⁸ 1476, Report of April 14, 1849.

14. AN BB¹⁸ 1474 A, Faucher's speech presenting the law, January 1, 1849.

15. AN BB¹⁸ 1474 A, Extract of circular of the Minister of Justice, June 29, 1849.

16. Police could be present by virtue of the law of August 16–24, 1790; AN BB¹⁸ 1474 A, Report of Procureur général of Orléans, April 14, 1849; Report of Procureur général of the Cour de cassation, April 20, 1849; and Decree of the Minister of Justice, April 20, 1849, officially citing the 1790 law.

17. AN BB¹⁸ 1474 A, Report of Commissioner of Police of St. Quentin to the Mayor, June 13, 1849, and MJ to PG Amiens, n.d.

18. AN BB¹⁸ 1474 A, Report of Commissioner of Police included with Report of PG Dijon, February 2 and 7, and March 6, 1849.

19. AN BB¹⁸ 1474 A Ibid., Faucher speech June 5, 1851; see also BB¹⁸ 1476, Int. to MJ, April 14, 1849, and Report of the Prefect of Aude, April 7, 1849. Some electoral committees in 1849 were actually reincarnations of defunct clubs. The Club démocratique of Narbonne, for example, became the Comité démocratique and then, after it was closed by the commissioner of police, protested against the abridgement of the freedom of assembly. Many more banquets and meetings had been attempted during 1848, particularly in connection with the various legislative elections, but I have found no aggregate figures.

20. Amann, *Revolution and Mass Democracy*, p. xiii. See also Charles Tilly, "The Changing Place of Collective Violence," and "How Protest Modernized in France, 1845–55."

21. Agulhon, *La République au village*, pp. 207–11, 219, 245. He notes that there were 707 chambrées in the Var at that time.

22. AN BB[18] 1474 A, Report of April 28, 1849.

23. Agulhon, *La République au village*, p. 471.

24. AN BB 391, Report of the Procureur général of Montpellier, March 10, 1851. See reports on surprisingly similar societies and *chambrées de lecture* in Finistère, in AD Finistère, 4M 229.

25. AN BB 391, Report of the Procureur général of Montpellier, March 10, 1851.

26. See references in AN BB[30] 393, "Mouvement démagogique antérieur . . . "; AD Haute Garonne, 4M 66, Int. to PHG, April 30, 1850, on the cercle littéraire of Toulouse; AN BB[18] 1474 A, various reports.

27. AN BB[18] 1482, Int. to MJ, November 8, 1851 and MJ to Int., November 22, 1851; AN BB[30] 393, "Mouvement démagogique,"; J. Dagnan, *Le Gers sous la Second République*, 1:428. The grand orient had also been asked to close the lodge in Montargis, but had not done so at the time of the coup d'état.

28. AN BB[30] "Mouvement démagogique"; reports in the respective judicial districts, BB[30] 370–88, etc.

29. Agulhon, *La République au village*, pp. 223, 226. "The mutual-aid society was the licit (even encouraged) form in which the chambrée, which was somewhat suspect [by the authorities] as pure association or a *buveuse* of untaxed wine, could hide."

30. AN BB[30] 391, Report of the Procureur général of Nîmes, February 3, 1851.

31. AN BB[30] 391, report of the Procureur général of Montpellier, March 10, 1851.

32. Ted W. Margadant, "The French Insurrection of 1851," chap. 10.

33. AD Tarn, IV M^2 37, Report of the Subprefect of Castres, April 6, 1849.

34. AN BB[18] 1474 B, Report of the Procureur général of Poitiers, January 18, 1850.

35. Agulhon, *La République au village*, p. 389.

36. In chapter 10 of "The French Insurrection of 1851," Margadant argues that the repression increased popular resentment against the government and actually played a part in swelling the ranks of the insurgents; he is considering the departments in which there was major armed resistance to the coup.

37. *L'Association rémoise*, April 14, 1850; and its statutes AN BB³⁰ 391, pièce 41. The motto of the Société d'assistance mutuelle of the Bas Rhin was, for example, "Union is force; assistance is fraternity."

38. AN F¹² 4813 has information on eighty-four departments. Landes had thirty-four mutual-aid societies in 1850, thirteen of which had been formed since the revolution. Nièvre had seven such societies, four formed since the revolution; Puy-de-Dôme had four, two formed since the revolution. See Rémi Gossez, *Les Ouvriers de Paris*.

39. AN BB³⁰ 391, Report of the Procureur général of Montpellier March 10, 1851.

40. AN F¹² 4813; Dagnan, *Le Gers sous la Seconde République*, p. 424. The Rochefort group had 164 members of various professions who paid a fee of 1,50 francs per month; their funds had aided seventy-six needy workers by the middle of 1850.

41. AG F¹ 41 bis, decree of January 3, 1851; AN BB³⁰ 393, "Mouvement démagogique." See also, for example, the reports on the liquidation of the Société de secours mutuels des imprimeurs sur étoffes of Paris, Int. to MJ, July 11, 1851, in which it is urged that the process be carried out with all possible speed (AN BB³⁰ 393).

42. AN BB¹⁸ 1474 B, Report of the Prefect of the Rhône, August 22, 1849.

43. Moss, "Parisian Producers' Associations," p. 75.

44. Ibid., p. 76.

45. See Bernard Schnapper, "Les Sociétés ouvrières de production pendant la second république," pp. 162–91, who argues convincingly that the movement towards association was spontaneous, before the allocation of funds. Requests for money, etc., are found in AN F¹² 4618.

46. Moss, "Parisian Producers' Associations," p. 80; AN BB¹⁸ 1474 B, Preamble of the statutes of the Association fraternelle, with Report of PG Lyon, January 23, 1850.

47. AN F¹² 4618.

48. Schnapper, "Les Sociétés ouvrières de production."

49. Moss, "Parisian Producers' Associations," p. 81.

50. Ibid., p. 82; F¹² 4618 provides sketchy information on the surveillance of the associations awarded funds; many failed rather quickly, although there were several notable exceptions, such as the association for "fabric designs" of Paris. Schnapper, "Les Sociétés ouvrières de production," suggests some of the same reasons for failure. The government "revoked" the loans in twenty-one of the fifty-five cases for which there is information.

51. AN BB¹⁸ 1474 B, Report of the PG of Lyon, January 23, 1850.

52. Ibid. See also Bezucha, *The Lyon Insurrection of 1834*, and Fernand Rude, *Le Mouvement ouvrier à Lyon de 1827 à 1832* (Paris: Les Éditions sociales, 1969).

53. AN BB[18] 1474 B, Report of the PG Lyon. January 23, 1850.

54. Ibid., report and statutes.

55. Ibid., which includes a numerical breakdown of suspected members for each organization and a brief history of their activities since 1830. The café "Des Industries réunis" and the meeting place of the Société des travailleurs réunis were both compromised because participants had allegedly organized the insurrection there.

56. The centenary of the revolution of 1848 was the occasion for an article by Gustave Laurent, "Les Événements de l'année 1848," in Comité départemental marnais de célébration du centenaire de la Révolution de 1848, *Le Département de la Marne et la Révolution de 1848*, (Châlons-sur-Marne: Archives de la Marne, 1948).

57. Ibid., p. 73. Bressy was described in the *acte d'accusation* of September 21, 1849, as "blessed with great intelligence and an extraordinary force of persuasion. Bressy exercises a remarkable power over the mass of workers and over himself."

58. Christopher H. Johnson, *Utopian Communism in France*, pp. 192–95.

59. Marc Vincent, "La Situation économique et le condition des travailleurs dans le département de la Marne," in *Le Département de la Marne et la Révolution de 1848*, ed. Comité départemental marnais, pp. 92–93.

60. AN BB[18] 1487, Report of PG Paris, September 6, 1850; statutes of L'Association rémoise, printed in the newspaper of the same name, January 25, 1849; Laurent, "Les Événements de l'année 1848," p. 75. The affiliated corporations included: chamois-workers, carpenters, drivers, shoemakers, roofers, retailers, spinners (by cards), spinners (with combs), metalworkers, masons, joiners, combers, painters, stonecutters, tailors, dyers, ditchdiggers, sorters, weavers, shearers, and barrel-makers.

61. AN BB[18] 1487, Report of PG Paris, September 6, 1850, *L'Association rémoise*, printed prospectus; Laurent, "Les Événements de l'année 1848," p. 74. A. Bressy, ed., *Almanach démocratique de 1850* (Reims, 1850), p. 103; G. Laurent and G. Boussinesq, *Histoire de la ville de Reims depuis les origins jusqu'à nos jours*, 2:645–46.

62. *L'Association rémoise*, January 25, 1849.

63. Laurent, "Les Événements de l'année 1848," p. 75. *L'Industriel Républicain*, published at the same time, was acquitted of at least one

press offense in January 1850 (AN BB³⁰ 383, Report of PG Paris, January 15, 1850).

64. *L'Association rémoise*, January 10, 1850.

65. *L'Association rémoise*, prospectus.

66. *L'Association rémoise*, January 11, 1849 and following.

67. *L'Association rémoise*, prospectus, esp. January 28, 1849 (salt tax) and April 29, 1849 (taxes).

68. *L'Association rémoise*, February 18, 1849; AN BB¹⁸ 1487, Report of September 6, 1850.

69. Laurent and Boussinesq, *Histoire de la ville de Reims*, pp. 647–50.

70. Ibid., pp. 650, 654.

71. Ibid., pp. 655–61.

72. AN BB¹⁸ 1487, Report of PG Paris, June 1, 1850.

73. AN BB¹⁸ 1487, Minister of Agriculture to MJ, September 21, 1850, report of PG Paris, June 1, 1850 and September 3, 1850 (also cited by Tchernoff, *Associations et sociétés secrètes*, pp. 241–46). The role of the chambre du travail in a strike in Reims is noted in AN BB³⁰ 383, report of PG Paris, November 23, 1850 and January 15, 1850; during the strike, the workers met in a cabaret owned by an active member of the Association.

74. Bressy, *Almanach démocratique de 1850*.

75. AN BB¹⁸ 1474 B, Report of PG Metz, February 6, 1850; like the Reims group, this association paid members for performing jury duty.

76. AN BB¹⁸ 1474 B, report of PG Metz, May 5, 1850.

77. AN BB¹⁸ 1474 B, report of May 14.

78. AN BB¹⁸ 1474 B, Report of May 14, 1850. The same procureur cited the influence of the Society of the Rights of Man in Vouziers (AN BB³⁰ 383).

79. AN BB¹⁸ 1474 B, Report of May 14, 1850.

80. *L'Association rémoise*, June 6, 1850; the associations in Rethel and Metz were deprived of meeting places.

81. Laurent and Boussinesq, *Histoire de la ville de Reims*, p. 662; AN BB³⁰ 383, Report of the PG Paris, November 29, 1851, which notes that the leaders of the corporations were meeting to draw up plans to raise the necessary 1,800 francs caution money; AN BB³⁰ 396, report of PG Paris, January 26, 1852, which states others arrested included a grocer, a pork-butcher, a stonecutter, a wigmaker, two tailors, and one man with no listed profession.

82. Guépin arrived in Limoges in 1833 in search of adherents for the Saint Simonian "school," mentioned in John Merriman, "Radicalization and Repression," p. 37.

83. See Yannick Guin, *Le Mouvement ouvrier nantais*, esp. pp. 143–81. Guin is generally quite critical of Guépin and the other bourgeois radicals in Nantes: "His politics were nothing more than an objective betrayal of the working class, but at the time this was passed off as timidity, because of the antecedents of the doctor, his philanthropy, his propaganda in favor of socialism which allowed the workers to believe that he was one of them" (p. 152).

84. AN BB[18] 1474 B, reports of the Procureur général of Rennes, June 12, 1849 and November 22, 1850; AN BB[18] 1473, Report of the PG Rennes, November 22, 1850; Guépin, *Philosophie du socialisme ou étude sur les transformations dans l'humanité (1850)*, p. 729.

85. AN BB[18] 1474 B, Reports of the PG Rennes, June 12, 1849 and November 22, 1850 Minister of Marine to MJ, December 10, 1850, relative to the workers of Indret; and Reports of PG Rennes, November 28 and 29, 1850; Guin, *Le Mouvement ouvrier nantais*, pp. 173–74. Guin tells a slightly different story, indicating that the critical moment arrived when the mayor asked the cooperative bakery to legally "regularize" its position by applying for a master baker's license. According to Guin, this caused a serious split between the Société fraternelle universelle and the cooperative bakery. The workers who were members of the mutual-aid society did not want to comply, because they viewed their organization as "means for the establishment of socialism." Thus, during a noisy general assembly, they evicted the bourgeois faction who, with the bakery directors, had wanted to follow the mayor's suggestion. On same day, the prefect pronounced the society dissolved and began an investigation which culminated in a trial in April 1851, in which nine of ten accused were acquitted. Guin cites the workers' attempts during the republic to reconstitute both the cooperative bakery and the mutual-aid society.

86. See Tchernoff, truly worth rediscovering, *Associations et sociétés secrètes* esp. p. 5; Agulhon, *La République au village*, p. 346; and Margadant, "The French Insurrection of 1851," chap. 10.

87. Agulhon, *La République au village*, p. 346.

88. Agulhon, *La République au village*, p. 339. See also Tchernoff, *Associations et sociétés secrètes*, p. 22.

89. A. Guépin, *Le Socialisme expliqué aux enfans du peuple* (Paris, 1851), p. 9.

90. Agulhon, *La République au village*, p. 338.

91. AN BB[18] 1474 B, report of PG Lyon, January 23, 1850. The reference to the "new barbarians" is attributed to Deputy St. Marc Girardin at the beginning of the July Monarchy.

92. AN BB[18] 1473, Int. to MJ, cited by Tchernoff, *Associations et sociétés secrètes*, pp. 30–31; the PG Paris (report of November, 1850, BB[30] 368, dossier 2) noted of a mutual-aid society in Précy-sous-Thil: "Its almost exclusively democratic composition makes one suspect its real goal."

93. Agulhon, *La République au village*, p. 340.

94. See André-Jean Tudesq, *Les grands notables en France, 1840–49*. Agulhon points out that authorities in the Var were quick to exclude bourgeois cercles from the postcoup ban.

95. Agulhon, *La République au village*, pp. 332–33; the procureur général of Aix reported on April 7, 1851 (BB[30] 392 A) that the cork-workers produced better corks than their former bosses' enterprises.

96. Tchernoff, *Associations et sociétés secrètes*, p. 19.

CHAPTER FOUR

1. Robert J. Bezucha, *The Lyon Insurrection of 1834* (Cambridge, Mass.: Harvard University Press), p. 76. John Baughman, "The French Banquet Campaign of 1847–48," pp. 1–15.

2. AN BB[18] 1469, Reports of PG Amiens, May 8, 1849, PG Aix, December 7, 1848, PG Limoges, May 9, 1849, Int. to MJ, Jan. 24, 1849, etc. See Roger H. Shattuck, *The Banquet Years: The Origin of the Avant-garde in France, 1885 to World War I* (New York: Vintage Books, 1968).

3. AN BB[18] 1469, Report of PG Colmar, May 22, 1849; on demonstrations against the Jews, AN BB[30] 360, dossier 1.

4. AN BB[18] 1469, Report of PG Paris, May 6, 1850; PG Rouen, January 15, 1850, PG Orléans, May 5, 1850; Circular of Prefect of Haute Garonne of April 30, 1851, warning mayors not to tolerate banquets, AD Haute Garonne, 4M70.

5. AN BB[18] 1469, Report of PG Grenoble, February 1, 1850. An example of trouble resulting from breaking up a banquet is the "Affaire du banquet à cocardes rouges," Report of PG Montpellier, February 6, 1850.

6. AN BB[18] 1469, Report of PG Orléans, September 3, 1850.

7. AG F[1] 38, Report of Gendarmerie of Haute Saône, October 22, 1850.

8. Robert J. Bezucha, "Masks of Revolution: A Study of Popular Culture during the Second French Republic," in *Revolution and Reaction*, ed. Roger D. Price (London: Croom Helm, 1975), quotes on p. 250.

9. AN BB[30] 392 A, pièce 73, Report of PG Montpellier, March 24,

1851. See the correspondence about a banquet planned for February 24, 1851, in Toulouse, Archives Municipales de Toulouse, 2I 63, Prefect of Haute Garonne to Mayor of Toulouse, February 11, 1851.

10. AN BB³⁰ 394, Report of PG Aix, September 9 and 24, 1851, on the feast day of St. Roch in the Var; Maurice Agulhon, *La République au village*, pp. 265–66, 416–417, etc.

11. AN BB¹⁸ 1482, Report of PG Besançon, June 14, 1850; AN BB³⁰ 393, pièce 353, Reports of the PG Lyon.

12. Bezucha, "Masks of Revolution," p. 247.

13. AN BB³⁰ 364, Report of PG Poitiers, February 15, 1850, also cited by Bezucha, "Masks of Revolution," p. 247.

14. AN BB³⁰ 366, dossier 2, report of PG Toulouse, March 28, 1851, also cited by Bezucha, "Masks of Revolution," pp. 249–50.

15. AD Tarn IV M² 38, June 14, 1850.

16. Maurice Agulhon, *1848 ou l'apprentissage de la République*, p. 108.

17. See Natalie Zemon Davis, "The Reasons of Misrule: Youth Groups and *Charivaris* in Sixteenth-Century France," *Past and Present* 50 (February 1971): 45, 65.

18. AD Cher 25M 89, Report of the mayor of Vierzon, July 6, 1844.

19. "Since the February revolution, there has been much singing in Gers." Jean Dagnan, *Le Gers sous la Seconde République*, p. 508.

20. Maurice Agulhon, *La République au village*, p. 161.

21. Cf. the general correspondence of the Minister of War, AG., which frequently calls attention to such receptions.

22. Agulhon, *1848 ou l'apprentissage de la République*.

23. J. Dagnan, *Le Gers sous la Seconde République*, p. 511.

24. Ibid., pp. 527–29.

25. AN BB³⁰ 393, pièce 205, Report of PG Dijon, June 12, 1851.

26. AD Haute Garonne, 4M 69, Gendarmerie Report of May 2, 1851; AN BB³⁰ 393, Report of PG Metz, June 10, 1851; other strikes of note during the Second Republic, including some with political overtones, are reported in BB¹⁸ 1479 (Colmar, Roubaix, Ribeauville, Toulouse, Sedan, Crespin, Chalot, Sablé, La Ferté-Bernard, Angoulême, and Pacy, among others).

27. Margadant, "The French Insurrection of 1851," Chap. 10.

28. AN BB³⁰ 392ᴬ, Report of PG Aix, March 25, 1851; PG Montpellier, September 5, 1851; report of MJ, August 21, 1851; Report of Military Commander of 5th and 6th Divisions, February 13, 1851, etc.

29. Maurice Agulhon, *Les quarante-huitards* (Paris: Éditions Gallimard/Julliard, 1975), pp. 58–59; Albert Soboul, "La Question paysanne

en 1848," and "Documents. Les Troubles agraires de 1848"; and especially Charles Tilly, "The Changing Place of Collective Violence," and "How Protest Modernized in France, 1845–1855."

30. Margadant, "The French Insurrection of 1851," chap. 10.

31. Tilly, "The Changing Place of Collective Violence." See also John M. Merriman, "The 'Demoiselles' of the Ariège, 1829–31," in *1830 in France*, ed. John Merriman (New York: Franklin Watts, 1975).

32. AG F¹ 31, Report of Commander of First Military Division, February 5, 1850; AN BB¹⁸ 1491, Report of PG Aix, January 6, 1851; AN BB¹⁸ 1487, Reports on Louis Napoleon's trip, especially Int. to MJ, September 22, 1850, PG Besançon, September 2, PG Metz, November 9.

33. AN BB¹⁸ 1468, Report of PG Riom, January 22, 1849. Subsequent (and certainly related) carnival troubles cited by Bezucha, "Masks of Revolution," pp. 243–44, from AN BB³⁰ 365, report of March 1, 1849. Other tax disturbances of importance occurred in Draguignan, Vallerange (Moselle), Turriers (Basses Alpes), Grasse, Beaune, Auxerre, and Bar-sur-Aube.

34. Margadant, "The French Insurrection of 1851," chap. 10; AN BB³⁰ 368, dossier 2, PG Lyon, February and March 1850.

35. Margadant, "The French Insurrection of 1851," chap. 10. For example, in the arrondissement of Béziers (Hérault), the following events took place during April and May 1851: (1) rebellion in Villeneuve; rebellion in Florensac; (2) beating of a man who denounced a secret society in Béziers; (3) appearance of a red flag at Guinguete de Gandauge, on a mountain top; (4) the alleged secret manufacture of gunpowder in Béziers; (5) incendiary placards; (6) the destruction of trees belonging to an unsympathetic witness to an unspecified montagnard protest; (7) placards in Montblanc; (8) propaganda, attacks against property, seditious cries, and warnings of more attacks when the true republic arrived; (9) seditious songs in Magalas; (10) devastations of property in Magalas; (11) rebellion and the singing of the "Marseillaise"; (12) workers attack a boss and a man called "Blanc le Républicain," in Bessan; (13) rebellion, leading to the injuring of the mayor in Villeneve; (14) judicial proceedings opened against a secret society in eight communes, especially Bédarieux. AN BB³⁰ 392ᴮ, pièce "statistique des procedures pour faits politiques dans l'arrondissement de Béziers, avril-mai, 1851."

36. AN BB¹⁸ 1482, Int. to MJ, March 10, 1849, and March 18, 1849; MJ to Int., March 16, 1849; and PG Caen report, April 14, 1849.

37. Numerous examples are found in AN BB³⁰ 393 and 394 and AG General Correspondence.

38. AN BB³⁰ 394, September 4, 1851, report of PG Grenoble, Sep-

tember 4, 1851 and AN BB³⁰ 393, report of PG Dijon, June 12, 1851.

39. Peter McPhee, "The Seed-time of the Republic: Society and Politics in the Pyrénées-Orientales, 1848–1851," *Australian Journal of Politics and History* 22 (1976): 211.

40. AN BB¹⁸ 1476, Int. to MJ, March 22, 1849, and Report of the Procureur of Niort, March 13; AN BB¹⁸ 1491 A², Report of PG Poitiers, January 4, 1851; and AN BB¹⁸ 1486, MJ to PG Grenoble, June 25, 1851.

41. Merriman, "The '*Demoiselles*' of the Ariège, 1829–31," Tilly, "How Protest Modernized in France, 1845–55," and Eric Hobsbawm and George Rudé, *Captain Swing: A Social History of the Great English Agricultural Uprisings of 1830* (New York: Pantheon Books, 1968).

42. For example, AN BB¹⁸ 1498, Report of the Procureur of Wassy, July 8, 1851, MJ Report of July 15, 1851; AN BB³⁰ 394, Report of PG Paris, August 12, 1851, and PG Grenoble, August 25, 1851; and AG F¹ 50, Report of Commander of Tenth Military Division on placards related to the "Second Bulletin to the People."

43. AG F¹ 40, Report of Gendarmerie of Mortain, December 10, 1850.

44. AN BB¹⁸ 1482, Report of PG Besançon, September 11, 1850.

45. AD Tarn, IV M² 37, March 30, 1849; AN BB¹⁸ 1481, Int. to MJ, November 28, 1849 (citing article 6 of the law of August 11, 1848); AN BB¹⁸ 1482, Report of PG Bordeaux, August 2, 1848 and MG to PG Bordeaux, August 24, 1848.

46. AN BB¹⁸ 1492, Report of PC Paris, July 13, 1850; AN BB³⁰ 393, Report of PG Montpellier, July 2, 1851.

47. AN BB³⁰ 393, MJ to PG Poitiers, July 11, 1851; AN BB³⁰ 392ᴬ, Report of the Procureur of Lille, March 12, 1851, on a little play performed at carnival time in that city. Examples are endless. Cf. mocking references to Badinguet in Zola's *L'Assommoir*. Badinguet was the common workman in whose clothes Louis Napoleon escaped from the fortress of Ham in 1846.

48. AN BB¹⁸ 1481, 344, 464 in 1848 and 350, 640 for 1850; AN BB³⁰ 368, dossier 2, monthly report of August, 1851, PG Besançon.

49. *La Ruche*, May 11, 1849, cited in G. Rocal, *1848 en Dordogne*, 2:17.

50. AN BB³⁰* 424, Register.

51. AN BB¹⁸ 1481, Compilation of PG reports, January 1850.

52. AG F¹ 38, October 26, 1850.

53. AD Haute Garonne, 4M 40, Report of the Police Commissioner of Toulouse, October 23, 1851.

54. Eugène Ténot, *La Province en décembre 1851*, p. 52. Likewise, a report from the gendarmerie in Apt (AG F[1] 49, October 27, 1851) speaks of "the *habitués* of the café Beaudoin [who] are longtime republicans."

55. AG F[1].

56. AG F[1]; F[1] 48, Report of the Paris Prefect of Police, October 20, 1851, for example.

57. AD Haute Garonne 4M 70, Report of the Commissioner of Police for Toulouse, October 23, 1851 and Monthly Report for January, 1850.

58. AG F[1] 49, Report of the Gendarmerie of Morbihan, April 6, 1851. This cat-and-mouse game is described by J. Dagnan, *Le Gers sous la Seconde République*, pp. 404–19.

59. AD Haute Garonne, Report of January 6–7, 1851. See also Dagnan, *Le Gers sous la Seconde République*, 418–19.

60. Margadant, "The French Insurrection of 1851," chap. 7, describes the process of "building underground." Dagnan, *Le Gers sous la Seconde République*, p. 404.

61. See Jean Bossu, "Un Républicain d'autrefois: Mathieu d'Épinal et son temps," *1848 et les révolutions du XIXᵉ siècle* 37 (Autumn and Winter 1946): 35–59, 27–64, for a bibliographic account of this shadowy figure. He was born in Épinal in 1800, later became a member of the carbonari, was jailed in 1834, was involved in the 1839 conspiracy, and "participated modestly" in the changeover in Rouen in February 1848. During the Second Republic, he ran unsuccessfully for the National Assembly in 1849 and was active in the Société populaire in Épinal.

62. AN BB[30] 396, Report of January 28, 1852.

63. AN BB[30] 394, pièce 349, Report of PG Dijon, September 23, 1851; AN BB[18] 1477, Report of PG Orléans, July 2, 1849; AG F[1] 37, Report of Gendarmerie of Mamers, September 15, 1850, etc. Reading the daily correspondence in AG F[1] is the best way of following the activities of the montagnard leadership.

64. AN BB[30] 394, pièce 341, Report of PG Toulouse, September 15, 1851; AN BB[30] 394[A] pièce 114, Report of the PG Nîmes, May 5, 1851; AN BB[30] 392[B] pièce 166, Report of PG Orléans, May 18, 1851, etc.

65. AN BB[18] 1483, Report of PG Colmar, March 7, 1850, complaining that Cassal's accusation was "completely inexact." The matter was discussed in the National Assembly.

66. AD Haute Garonne 4M 69, Report of September 20, 1850.

67. Ibid., Prefect of Haute Garonne to Prefect of Police in Paris, November 21, 1851; AD Haute Garonne, 4M 66, Telegram of Prefect of Gironde, n.d. and Report of Commissioner of Police, August 3, 1851. The list of activists is found in AD Haute Garonne 4M 67.

68. AG F¹ 34, Report of the Prefect of Police, May 3, 1850; AN BB³⁰ 392ᴮ pièce 159, Report of the Prefect of Police, May 30, 1851 and pièce 173, Note of the Minister of Interior, May 7, 1851 and Report of PG Pau, June 7, 1851.

69. AD Tarn IV M² 38, Int. to Prefect of Tarn, August 2, 1850; AN BB¹⁸ 1487, Report of PG Nancy, August 18, 1850, Report of Prefect of Police, September 3, 1850 and Cour d'appel de Nancy, August 17, 1850, Avis et signalement. See also Abel Châtelain, "Les migrations temporaires et la propagation des idées révolutionnaires en France au XIXᵉ siècle," pp. 6–18.

70. AD Tarn IV M² 38, June 3, 1850.

71. Margadant, "The French Insurrection of 1851," chap. 10.

72. For example, there were searches in the Blois vincinity in August 1851, at six in the morning, in the homes of a gardener, a locksmith, a bonnet-maker, a mechanic, a café-owner, a turner, a joiner, an ex-professor, and two farmers. The object of the search was weapons and vases marked "Long live the democratic and social republic!" (AN BB³⁰ 394, Report of PG Orleans, August 20). Typical of the political booty to be found were pamphlets and books seized at a miller's house in St. Germain-en-Laye in October 1850 (AG F¹ 38, Gendarmerie Report, October 20). The use of secret police was common, although hard to document in many cases; it was difficult to infiltrate most tightly knit communities within a town, impossible in the countryside. Reports of police spies do appear, for example of "serviteur 51" in March 1851, in Toulouse ("on the rue de Canard, there is a butcher's shop where troublemakers gather," Archives municipales de Toulouse, 2i 63).

73. Margadant, "The French Insurrection of 1851," chaps. 7, 10.

CHAPTER FIVE

1. David Appelbaum, "Justice is Politics: Counter Revolution and the Cantonal Magistrates, 1848–1851," unpublished manuscript.

2. See Howard Machin, "The Prefects and Political Repression: February 1848 to December 1851," in Roger D. Price, *Revolution and Reaction*, ed. Roger D. Price (London: Croom Helm, 1975).

3. ADHV M 741. In Eure-et-Loir, there were sixteen dismissals and eleven resignations (AD Eure-et-Loir M 192).

4. AN C 977, "Tableau comparatif de nombre des maires et adjoints en fonctions au févier, 1848 et du nombre de ces fonctionnaires qui ont été réélus par les conseils municipales." The 178 politically motivated dismissals in the Saône-et-Loire appear to be the highest total.

5. AN C 977, Minister of Interior to the President of the Commission Charged with Examining the Proposed Law on the Nomination of Mayors, March 20, 1850.

6. Ibid.

7. AN C 977, "Analysis des rapports des préfets sur les résultats de l'application du decret du 3 juillet, 1848."

8. Examples drawn from reports in AG F^1 32, 36, 38, 42, AN BB^{18} 1480, and J. Dagnan, *Le Gers sous la Seconde République* pp. 330–31.

9. Ted W. Margadant, "The French Insurrection of 1851," chap. 10, p. 14.

10. Robert J. Bezucha, "Masks of Revolution," in *Revolution and Reaction*, ed. Price.

11. AN BB^{18} 1496, report of PG Montpellier, May 5, 1851.

12. AN C 977. The subprefect of Castres complained in February 1850, about the mayors and their assistants who had been "named in a time when political passions had upset all ideas . . . the moral authority of the administration had been profoundly shaken by the new method of nominating mayors and deputy mayors" (AD Tarn IV M^2 38, February 19, 1850).

13. AD Haute Garonne 4M 69, April 4, 1851.

14. AN C 977, Extract of a report from the Prefect of Bouches-du-Rhône, May 10, 1850.

15. AN C 977, "Table des révocations de maires et adjoints du 1 janvier 1837 au 31 décembre, 1841 et pendant l'année 1849."

16. Maurice Agulhon, *1848 ou l'apprentissage de la république.*

17. AN C 977, "Table des révocations," note, and "Tableau comparatif des dissolutions prononcées par ordonnance Royale en 1845 et en 1846 et celles prononcées de l'avis du conseil d'état en 1849 et 1850."

18. AN BB^{30} 392^A, report of PG Grenoble, March 24, 1851.

19. AN C 977, "Tableau des révocations."

20. Ibid., and "Résumer des décisions rendues par le conseil d'état. . . ."

21. AD Tarn IV M^2 38, n.d., note.

22. AN C 977, "*Analysis des rapports des préfets.*"

23. Margadant, "The French Insurrection of 1851," chap. 10, states "Until the *coup d'état* shattered republican hopes for victory in 1852, municipal officials would only make life unpleasant for themselves if they functioned as policemen for the state." Margadant also describes the hesitation of some prefects to compose a municipal council by decree because they feared the commune's hostile reaction. Indeed, there seem to have been more politically motivated dismissals in depart-

ments in which there was armed resistance to the coup than in departments in which the montagnards enjoyed electoral success in 1849, but in which there was no major resistance in 1851. This supports the general argument that in some areas the repression increased the possibility of insurrection by turning communities against the government.

24. AN C 977, "Résumer des décisions."

25. Ibid.

26. J. Dagnan, *Le Gers sous la Seconde République*, p. 332.

27. AN BB^{30} 393, pièce 289, Int. to MJ, August 20, 1851; MJ note of August 12, 1851 and Report of PG Angers, August 18, 1851.

28. AD Tarn IV M^2 38, Report of April 2, 1850.

29. Account of Ardèche troubles in Margadant, "The French Insurrection of 1851," chap. 10, pp. 30–35; AN BB^{30} 392^A, pièce 14, PG Nancy, April 3, 1851; AN BB^{18} 1478, PG Orléans, July 12, 1849. The correspondence of the Ministry of War offers a dependable source for studying the révocation of minor officials; they usually came to the attention of the relevant ministry through the minister of war, to whom gendarmerie and army reports were sent.

30. Georges Duveau, *Les Instituteurs* (Paris: Seuil, 1957), pp. 71–72.

31. Ibid., p. 83.

32. Alfred Cobban, "The Influence of the Clergy and the '*Instituteurs Primaires*' in the Election of the French Constituent Assembly, April 1848," pp. 339–61. See also H. Dubeiq, "Arsène Meunier, instituteur et militant républicain," in Bibliothèque de la Révolution de 1848, *Études* 15 (Nancy, 1954): 17–42.

33. Cobban, "Influence of the Clergy," p. 344.

34. AN F^{17} 12746, dossier Morer.

35. Félix Ponteil, *Histoire de l'enseignement en France* (Paris: Sirey, 1966), p. 239; Cobban, "Influence of the Clergy," p. 340.

36. G. Rocal, *1848 en Dordogne*, p. 117.

37. AN F^{17} 12528, including Reports of the Prefect of Police, October 25 and 30 and November 6, 1849 and January 9 and February 4, 1850.

38. AN BB^{30} 358, dossier 1, PG Aix Report of December 12, 1849.

39. AN F^{17} 9313.

40. AN F^{17} 9313, Prefects' Reports.

41. Duveau, *Les Instituteurs*, pp. 89–90. By virtue of the "petite loi" (January 2, 1850), the prefect named schoolteachers, who could be either laymen or religious. The Falloux Law nominally returned the selection of schoolteachers to the municipal councils, but as Duveau notes, "this article remained a dead letter."

42. Max Ferre, *Histoire du mouvement syndicaliste révolutionnaire*

chez les instituteurs (Paris: Société universitaire d'éditions et de librairie, 1954), p. 19 (citing E. Meyer, *L'Enseignement primaire de 1815 à 1850* [Elbeuf, 1932]).

43. AN BB[18] 1484, Report of the Rector of the Academy of Bourges; AG F[1] 42 bis, Report of the Gendarmerie Commander of Pontaudemer (Eure), March 7, 1850.

44. Dagnan, *Le Gers sous la Seconde République*, pp. 168, 294, 299.

45. Ibid., pp. 303–06.

46. AG F[1] 40, Commander of Calvados Gendarmerie, December 12, 1850, who described trouble in Falaise when a banquet was planned for a recently dismissed schoolteacher.

47. AN BB[18] 1484, Int. to MJ, July 14, 1850 and Reports of PG Nancy, March 3, 1850, PG Poitiers, July 2, 1850; and PG Aix, April 9, 1850; AN BB[18] 1496, Int. to MJ, June 27, 1850. Contributions were as modest as ten centimes and were listed in several papers. A brochure printed in Troyes was sold to benefit dismissed teachers. Unlike subscriptions for political prisoners, such charity solicitations were legal.

48. AN F[17] 9313, Report of the Prefect of Cantal.

49. AN BB[30]* 424, Register.

50. Paul Gerbod, *La Condition universitaire en France au XIXe siècle*, pp. 257–63.

51. Ibid. Likewise, the dean of the Faculty of Letters in Bordeaux was dismissed because he used his history course "to increase the workers' hatred for the rich"—the workers' corporations were attending his lectures and applauding (AN BB[30] 391, Report of PG Bordeaux, January 27, 1851).

52. AN F[17] 12746, dossier Michelet, Various reports, particularly February 7 and 28, 1850.

53. AN F[17] 12746, dossier Michelet, Report of February 27.

54. AN F[17] 12746, dossier Michelet, especially Reports of the Administration of the Collège de France, April 14, 1851 and Decree of suspension, March 12. Michelet was not officially dismissed until after the coup.

55. S. Coquerelle, "L'Armée et la répression dans les campagnes (1848)," in *L'Armée et la Seconde République*, ed. J. Bouillion et al., p. 151.

56. P. Chalmin, "La Crise morale de l'armée française," in *L'Armée et la Seconde République*, ed. J. Bouillion et al., pp. 50, 72; R. Girardet, "Autour de quelques problems," in *L'Armée et la Seconde République*, ed. J. Bouillion et al., p. 15.

57. Chalmin, "La Crise morale," p. 60; and R. Gossez, "Notes sur la

composition et l'attitude politique de la troupe," in *L'Armée et la Seconde République*, ed. J. Bouillion et al., p. 86.

58. Girardet, "Autour de quelques problems," p. 11; Chalmin, "La Crise morale," p. 65; and AG F¹, General Correspondence. Girardet notes that the military voters seem to have reflected the politics of their home region.

59. J. Bouillion, "Les Démocrates et l'armée aux élections de 1849," in *L'Armée et la Seconde République*, ed. J. Bouillion et al., p. 112.

60. Nicole Villa, "L'Iconographie militaire de la Seconde République au cabinet des estampes," in *L'Armée et la Seconde République*, ed. J. Bouillion et al., p. 26.

61. Bouillion, "Les Démocrates," p. 113; Villa, "L'Iconographie militaire," p. 26.

62. For example, AG F¹ 49, Gendarmerie report, November 8, 1850.

63. AG F¹ 34, Report of Commander of Fourteenth Military Division, May 13, 1850.

64. AG F¹ 36, Int. to MG, July 18, 1850.

65. AG F¹ 49, Report of November 8, 1851, and Report of Commander of Seventh Military Division, November 12, 1851. The Commander of the First Military Division noted (F¹ 33, April 11, 1849) that the montagnards had the most influence with the military classes of 1848 and 1849.

66. AG F¹ 35, MG to Commander of Seventh Military Division, June 8, 1850; F¹ 33, Report of the Minister of Interior, April 4, 1850; F¹ 32, Commander of Fifth and Sixth Military Divisions, February 21, 1850; Fourteenth Division Commander, Report of February 20, 1850, etc. Other measures included demoting junior officers and even eliminating the pensions of retired officers known for their montagnard activism.

67. AN BB³⁰ 392ᴮ, pièce 156, Report PG Besançon, May 19, June 12, 19, 21 and August 14, 1851; AN BB¹⁸ 1484, Report of PG Poitiers, April 4, 16, 1850 and PG Rennes, April 2, 8, 13.

68. Gossez, "Notes," p. 90.

69. AG F¹ 35, 36, 39 and 46 bis, various reports.

70. AG, Unclassfied register of the Gendarmerie; I have used Creuse, I, 1823–57, Haute Vienne, I, 1823–57, and Corrèze, II, 1844–47. These registers give the name, birthplace, home, original occupation, and military experience of all gendarmes. In this region, the repressive zeal of Gendarmerie Commander Dalché d'Esplanels in the Corrèze was often noted (reported for example, in AG F¹ 31, Prefect of Corrèze, February 14, 1850); d'Esplanels drew up a list of voting patterns in each commune.

71. Margadant, "The French Insurrection of 1851," chap. 10.

72. Troop movements and allocations may be followed in the AG F^1 correspondence, particularly AG F^1 43, which contains reports on the Yonne, Gard, and Gers. The "Situation Général de l'Armée" in the AG contains the reports on troop strengths that were issued four times per year.

73. AN BB^{18} 1480, particularly report of General Castellane, November 9, 1850, Telegram of December 23, 1850, Report of February 13, 1851. Castellane's tendency to exaggerate must be taken into consideration. AN BB^{30} 368, dossier 2, PG Lyon, June 1851.

74. AN BB^{18} 1480, Report of PG Lyon, December 23, 1850, and MG to Int., January 6, 1851; AN BB^{30} 391, pièce 52, Report of Prefect of Police of Paris, November 7, 1850; AN BB^{18} 1477, report of PG Besançon, September 13, 1850; AG F^1 36, Director of Administration of Customs to Minister of Finance, August 19, 1850.

75. Quoted in George Rudé, *Robespierre: Portrait of a Revolutionary Democrat* (New York: Viking, 1975), p. 101.

76. ADHV M 193, Letters of mayor of Vayres, July 12, mayor of Pierrebuffière, March 9, and mayor of Oradour-sur-Glane, April 5.

77. Louis Girard, *La Garde Nationale, 1814–1871*, which is almost exclusively concerned with the National Guard in Paris.

78. Information on dissolutions is summarized in the lengthy "Gardes nationales, dissolutions, suspensions, et révocations d'officiers," in AN F^9 423; further information in AG F^1, General Correspondence, the BB^{30} and BB^{18} series (especially AN BB^{30} 392^B), and Report of PG Aix, May 15, 1851.

79. Girard, *La Garde Nationale*, 329–31, and Reports in AN F^9 423.

80. AN F^9 423, Reports of Prefect of Meurthe, May 12, 1851, Prefect of Charente, June 5, 1851, Prefect of Oise, April 20, 1851, Prefect of Côtes-du-Nord, April 12, 1851; AN BB^{30} 392^B, Report of PG Grenoble, May 8, 1851, and Telegram of Castellane, May 8, 1851.

81. AN F^9 423, precise report date misplaced.

82. ADHV Annex R 196, Report of PHV, March 18 and 25, 1851, and September 1, 1851.

83. AN F^9 432, Note on Hérault; AG F^1 43, Report of Prefect of the Drôme, April 12, 1851, stating that 96 communes of 362 were armed, with 5,668 guns. In the Isère, the number of guns per commune ranged from one in Bonnefamille to 2,687 in Vienne; J. Dagnan, *Le Gers sous la Seconde République*, p. 429. Of 467 communes in the Gers, 130 had had National Guard units during the republic and 54 of these were disarmed in 1851. AG F^1 correspondence describes the disarmament of the National Guard units and the situation in each department.

84. AN F⁹ 422, "Gardes nationales, dissolutions."

85. AN F⁹ 422, "Gardes nationales, dissolutions." The carton also includes a register of dissolutions enacted after the coup. One "friend of order" urged the formation of elite battalions "composed of citizens interested in maintaining order and property." The prefect of Corrèze suggested that the firemen (*sapeurs-pompiers*) might offer such a natural unit. See ADHV Annex R 196, for Circular of the Minister of Interior to Prefects considering the usefulness of maintaining an armed elite, as opposed to arming everyone, or no one.

86. AN BB¹⁸ 1468, Extract of PG Rouen, June 13, 1850.

87. AN BB¹⁸ 1468, April 8, 1850.

88. AN BB¹⁸ 1485ᴬ, note. Letters in this dossier indicate that officials were very much aware of the contrast between urban and rural voters eliminated by the law.

89. Agulhon, *1848 ou l'apprentissage de la république*, pp. 150–51; Gossez, "Notes," pp. 358–59; AN F¹⁰ III Meurthe 16.

90. AN BB¹⁸ 1485ᴮ, "Rapport sur les poursuites auxquelles ont donné lieu les pétitions contre le projet de loi électorale, voté le 31 mai, 1851." A total of 527,000 signatures were collected in all departments except Ille-et-Vilaine, Hautes Alpes, Corse, Loir-et-Cher, Lozère, Deux-Sèvres, Vendée. See R. Huard, "La DeFénse du suffrage universel sous la Seconde République," pp. 315–36.

91. AN BB¹⁸ 1485ᴮ, Report of the PG Riom, November 6 and December 26, 1850. Gendarmes used a standard, printed interrogation form when attempting to verify signatures.

92. Ibid., Two assistant justices of the peace in the Manche signed (AN BB¹⁸ 1485ᴮ, Report of PG Caen, June 25, 1850).

93. AN BB 1468, Report of PG Limoges, April 8, 1850. The petition campaign thus fell into the "plot" category, AN BB³⁰ 366, "Renseignements transmis . . . sur le complôt formé dans plusieurs départements à l'occasion de la réforme électorale."

CHAPTER SIX

1. Ted W. Margadant, "The French Insurrection of 1851."

2. William L. Langer, "The Patterns of Urban Revolution in 1848."

3. Alain Corbin, *Archaïsme et modernité en Limousin au XIXᵉ siècle*, pp. 758–80.

4. *Le Peuple*, May 31, 1848.

5. Jacques Bouillon, "Les Élections législatives du 13 mai, 1849 en Limousin," *Bulletin de la Société Archéologique et Historique du Limousin* (hereafter cited as *BSAHL*) 84 (1954): 467–96; Corbin *Archaïsme et*

modernité, pp. 751–54; AN C 1335. The other radical candidates were Daniel-Lamazière, who became mayor of St. Léonard after the revolution and founded a club; Coralli, who began as a moderate republican, became a radical and remained one until his death in 1851; and Laclaudure and Frichon the elder, who defended the accused at Poitiers before the election in 1849.

6. Corbin, *Archaïsme et modernité*, pp. 790–820, 824–31.

7. *Le Peuple*, May 27, 1848.

8. AN BB³⁰ 361, dossier 1, pièce 63, Report of PGL, April 29, 1849.

9. Municipal Council Minutes, Hôtel de ville de Limoges; *Le peuple*, May 9, 1848; and Ernest Vincent, "Les Ateliers nationaux à Limoges," *BSAHL* 83 (1951): 336–44. The municipal council minutes for December 8, 1848, show that the workshops had cost the city 268,189.55 francs to that point.

10. *L'Ordre*, August 1, 1848.

11. AN BB³⁰ 333, Report of PGL, September 24, 1848, cited in Corbin, *Archaïsme et modernité*, p. 775; see also *Le Peuple*, November 2 and December 3, 1848. Louis Napoleon received 53,522 votes in Haute Vienne; Cavaignac, 3,566; Ledru-Rollin, 1,737; Raspail, 882; and Lamartine, 114. The cantons of Limoges gave 692 votes to Raspail, 594 to Ledru-Rollin, and 43 to Lamartine.

12. *La Province*, May 18, 1849.

13. AN F¹ᵇ I, Titot report, August 19, 1848; and ADHV M 2, Letter of December 30, 1848. The legitimist paper *L'Avenir National* attacked Titot in its last issue, August 26, 1848.

14. ADHV M 2. De Mentque's "fortune" was estimated at 11,500 francs.

15. AN ADXIXⁱ Haute Vienne 7, Proclamation of January 23, 1849.

16. AN BB³⁰ 361, dossier 2, pièce 152; Antoine Perrier, "Une journal Limogeois pendant la Révolution de 1848," *BSAHL* 96 (1969): 177–87. *Le Peuple* published its last 1848 issue in late June.

17. ADHV M 926, Int. to PHV, October 20, 1849. Corbin, *Archaïsme et modernité*, p. 802.

18. AN BB¹⁸ 1470ᶜ, Report of PGL, November 27, 1849, and March 21, 1850; *Le Carillon Républicain*, November 15, 1849; and AN BB²⁰ 150, 2nd trimester, Cour d'assises de la Haute Vienne. One of the other editors was a defrocked priest from St. Léonard, an unsuccessful candidate in the 1849 elections.

19. AN BB¹⁸ 1470ᶜ, by virtue of the law of August 11, 1848, as described in Report of PGL, January 7, 1850; AN F¹⁸ 263, PHV report on the press, September 15, 1850.

20. AN BB[18] 1470[c], Report of PGL, February 2 and 7, 1850. Ducoux, the candidate of the Democratic Committee of Haute Vienne, won by 29,615 to 26,651 (AN C 1335); de Mentque allegedly threatened to cut off funds for a public works project if the workers failed to vote for Bataille.

21. AN BB[30] 372, pièce 178, Report of PGL, November 21, 1851; *Le Travailleur*, November 14, 22, and 28, 1851.

22. AN BB[30] 378, dossier 6, pièce 2, Report of PGL, December 31, 1848; BB[18] 1449, Report of PGL, May 13, 1850; and AG F[1] 40, Report on *Solidarité Républicaine*, November 1848.

23. AN BB[18] 1449, Report of PGL, May 26, 1850; AN BB[18] 1470, Report of PGL, January 9, 1850.

24. AN BB[18] 1481, MJ to Int., November 21, 1851.

25. AN ADXIX[i] Haute Vienne 7, Prefect's proclamation of July 15, 1849.

26. AN BB[18] 1474[A], Circular of June 29, 1849.

27. AN BB[18] 1481, MJ to Int., November 21, 1851.

28. *Le Peuple*, April 9, 1849.

29. AN BB[18] 1470, Report of PGL, January 9, 1850; AN BB[30] 372[B], pièce 178, Report of PGL, May 21, 1850; and Pierre Cousteix, "L'Action ouvrière en Haute Vienne sous la Second République," *BSAHL* 84 (1954): 510; Corbin, *Archaïsme et modernité*, p. 537–38; and John M. Merriman, "Radicalization and Repression," pp. 250–51. A letter from a shoemaker to a soldier in the Limoges garrison reflects the bravado of at least one man:—"I tell you that everything is in the state of agitation . . . the people await any coup d'état. Oh! That he finally shows himself! We have waited impatiently long enough . . . Poor Republic, you have been beaten long enough." There is, however, no indication of any secret society, nor of any plan for an uprising.

30. The pamphlet *La Franc Maçonnerie Limousine* by the lodge Les Artistes réunis (Limoges, 1949) indicates that Pierre Leroux was initiated on April 4, 1848, and that several candidates presented their professions de foi at the lodge before the election. See Corbin, *Archaïsme et modernité*, pp. 791, 313–17. A producers' cooperative was established in June 1850, and it survived until 1869; see Corbin, *Archaïsme et modernité*, p. 538 and Gaston Boisserie, *Les Coopératives ouvrières de production dans l'industrie de la porcelaine à Limoges de 1848 à nos jours* (Paris, 1912).

31. AN BB[18] 1449, Letter dated February 8, 1850.

32. The popular appeal of the Napoleonic heritage was kept alive by newspaper serials, veterans of Napoleonic campaigns (for example,

in the gendarmerie), and Napoleonic bric-a-brac hawked in the markets.

33. ADHV M 163, *Speech of Léon Faucher, made at the reception given him by the Central Committee of Haute Vienne, October 20, 1849.* This speech was printed and distributed in the city.

34. ADHV M 163, dated May 30, 1851.

35. For example, *La Province*, January 20, 1850.

36. AG F¹ 45, Commander of the Thirteenth Military Division, Report of June 1, 1850.

37. For example, AG F¹ 38, Report of the Subdivision Commander, October 20, 1851.

38. *La Province*, February 19, 1849.

39. AG F¹ 41 bis, Report of the Commander of the 11th Gendarmerie, February 25, 1851.

40. Maurice Agulhon, *La République au village*, pp. 479–80; see Corbin, *Archaïsme et modernité*, pp. 796–99, for example, p. 798, citing a report on the workers of the Bellac region who "tend to want to succeed for and by themselves ... they now suspect the bourgeois leaders of demagogy."

41. AG F¹ 46 bis, Report of Commander of Eleventh Gendarmerie, August 25, 1851; AG F¹ 48, Reports of October 3, 4, and 7, 1851, and Report of Commander of 13th Military Division, October 6, 1851; AN BB³⁰ 378, dossier 7, October 4, 1851.

42. AN BB¹⁸ 1468, Report of PGL, April 8, 1850.

43. AG F¹ 7, Report of Commander of Fifteenth Military Division, May 25, 1848; AG F¹ 33, Commander of Thirteenth Military Division, reports of April 4, and 21, 1850; AG F¹ 34, letter of May 24, 1850; AG F¹ 37, MG to PHV, September 14, 1850; AN BB²³ 66, register number 6166, Report of PG Riom, February 1, 1851; AN BB³⁰ 361, dossier 1, pièce 123, Report of PGL April 4, 1850; AN BB³⁰ 378, dossier 6, pièce 9, Report of PGL, May 8, 1850. The soldiers were condemned May 31, 1850, and the sentences were confirmed on June 4, 1850, although at least one of the death sentences was commuted. A montagnard lawyer and five workers were also tried and convicted.

44. AN F⁹ 423, "Gardes nationales, dissolutions, suspensions, et révocation d'officiers."

45. ADHV Annex, R. 196, Report of Mayor of Limoges, July 22, 1851, and AN F⁹ 733, Report of PHV, June 3, 1849.

46. *Le Peuple*, February 11, 1849; *L'Ordre*, July 9, 1848; ADHV Annex R. 196, Int. to PHV, June 7, 1849; AN BB¹⁸ 1470ᶜ, Report of PGL February 16, 1849; AN BB¹⁸ 1474ᴬ, Report of PGL, February 4, 1849; and AN BB²⁰ 147, 2nd trimester, Haute Vienne.

47. AN F¹ᶜ Haute Vienne 4, pièce 68, Report of PHV, May 10, 1850.
48. Merriman, "Radicalization and Repression," pp. 190–200, 212.
49. Ibid., pp. 202–11.
50. F. P. Codaccioni, "Le Textile lillois durant la crise, 1846–51," pp. 29, 37; A. Jardin and A. J. Tudesq, *La France des notables* (Paris: Éditions du Seuil, 1973), 2:159–61.
51. Leon Machu, "La Crise de l'industrie textile à Roubaix," p. 65; A. Chanut, "La Crise économique à Tourcoing (1846–1850)," *Revue du Nord* 33,149 (January-March 1956): 88; and Jardin et Tudesq, *La France des notables*, pp. 153–55.
52. F. Lentacker, "Les Ouvriers belges dans le département du Nord au milieu du XIXᵉ siècle," p. 5.
53. Ibid., pp. 12–14; and, for example, AD Nord, M 139/4, Report of Subprefect of Valenciennes, September 23, 1850.
54. Chanut, "La Crise économique à Tourcoing," p. 89; Machu, "La Crise de l'industrie textile," p. 71; and A. M. Gossez, *Le Département du Nord sous la Deuxième République*, p. 405; Gossez also offers a good general analysis of the industrial situation and the workers' quality of life in the department during the republic (pp. 224–91).
55. M. Gillet, "Aspects de la crise de 1846 à 1851 dans le bassin houiller du Nord," p. 25; and Gossez, *Le Département du Nord*, pp. 124–28.
56. Codaccioni, "Le Textile lillois," p. 45. The general commissioner was Delescluze, who met with three delegates from the spinners and three representatives of the industrialists.
57. AN F¹² 4813, Report of August 19, 1852; AN F¹⁸ 263 Nord.
58. Gossez, *Le Département du Nord*, pp. 107–09. The textile industrialists broke with the July Monarchy when it refused to impose high tariffs.
59. AN F¹⁸ 263, "État des journaux ou écrits periodiques cautionnées..." Other "ardently democratic" papers appearing in 1850 and 1851 included *La Verité* (Hazebrouck), *L'Ami du peuple* (Hazebrouck, linked to *Le Messager du Nord*), *Le Démocrate du Nord* (Douai), *L'Écho du Cambrai*, and *L'Indépendent du Nord* (Maubeuge). There were about thirty political papers (ten montagnard, four moderate republican, five legitimist, and nineteen noncautioned announcement papers).
60. AN BB³⁰ 377, Report of PG Douai, December 16, 1849.
61. Ibid.
62. Gossez, *Le Département du Nord*, pp. 25–26, 120–24; and Marcel Dessal, *Charles Delescluze, 1809–1871* (Paris: Librairie Marcel Rivière, 1952).

63. AN BB³⁰ 377, Report of PG Douai, August 16, 1850.

64. ADN M 139/4, Int. to PN, January 5, 1850; and Report of the Commissioner of Police, October 21, 1850.

65. ADN M 139/4, Int. to PN October 1, 1851; Report of SP Hazebrouck, August 3, 1851; Minister of Justice in Brussels to PN, June 19, 1850.

66. ADN M 139/24, individual dossiers, various reports (for example, Verger, Report of the Subprefect of Douai, January 17, 1850; Ponte, Interior to PN, May 16, 1851). Reports of the three police spies may be found in ADN, M 139/16; AN BB³⁰ 368, dossier 2, Report of February, 1851; ADN 139/22, Report of Police Commissioner of Tourcoing, June 19, 1849.

67. ADN M 139/22, Report of the Police Commissioner of Tourcoing, June 19, 1849, which mentions Leloir. Delatombe is mentioned in M 139/16, Reports of the Subprefect of Valenciennes, September 1, 1851. Leloir is also mentioned in Machu, "La Crise de l'industrie textile," p. 71; Debuchy's dossier is in ADN M 139/24.

68. Gossez, Le Département du Nord, p. 351; AN BB³⁰ 377, Report of PG Douai, February 2, April 11, 1851; AN BB³⁰ 368, dossier 2, monthly reports, especially December 1849 to March 1850.

69. Gossez, Le Département du Nord, pp. 306–12.

70. ADN M 39/22, Report of the Subprefect of Dunkerque, February 5, 1849; Report of Subprefect of Douai, March 8, 1849; Int. to PN, April 19, 1850; and M 139/19, Report of PN, April 18, 1851; and Gossez, Le Département du Nord, p. 366.

71. Jardin and Tudesq, La France des notables, p. 162; ADN, M 139/4, n.d. list.

72. Gossez, Le Département du Nord, pp. 358–59.

73. ADN M 139/6, Int. to PN, July 29, 1851, and Report of the Justice of the Peace of Lysoing to the Procureur of Lille, June 6, 1851; Various reports in ADN M 139/7, including Director General of the Post Office to PN, February 18, 1850; and M 139/6, Report of PN, April 30, 1851.

74. Gossez, Le Département du Nord, pp. 367–68; ADN M 139/5, Report of Commissioner of Police of Lille, February 23, 1849. The National Guard and municipal council of Avesnes had previously been dissolved.

75. ADN M 139/4, Report of the Police Commissioner of Douai, July 29, 1851; Report of the Subprefect of Douai, March 16, 1850; and AG F¹ 46 bis. Report of the Gendarmerie of Avesnes, August 24, 1851.

76. ADN M 139/22, lists of démoc-socs by commune; ADN M 139/6, Report of the Subprefect of Valenciennes, November 24, 1851.

77. Gossez, *Le Département du Nord*, pp. 386–87; and interesting reports in ADN M 139/16. The use of horses to do some tasks previously done by miners was another grievance at Anzin. There was a banquet one week before the coup in Escaupont, with one hundred participants.

78. Codaccioni, "Le Textile lillois," pp. 56–63; Chanut, "La Crise économique à Tourcoing," p. 91; and Machu, "La Crise de l'industrie textile," p. 75. The latter suggests that there was a marked increase of the textile crisis in 1850 and 1851 in Roubaix.

79. Machu, "La Crise de l'industrie textile," p. 74.

80. AN BB[30] 377, Report PG Douai, of May 9, 1851.

81. Gossez, *Le Département du Nord*, pp. 387–88; AN BB[30] 377, Report of the PG Douai, November 12, 1851, which reported that, in general, the "situation has ceased to be reassuring." AN BB[18] 1489, Report of PG Douai, October 9, 1850; Int. to MJ, May 10, 1851, Reports of PG Douai, June 16, August 1, August 25, 1851.

82. AN BB[30] 377, Report of PG Douai, November 15, 1850.

83. Gossez, *Le Département du Nord*, pp. 287–88.

CHAPTER SEVEN

1. See Maurice Agulhon, *La République au village*, particularly pp. 42–125.

2. Albert Démangeon, "La Montagne dans le Limousin," *Annales de Géographie*, 20 (1911): 316–37; Abel Châtelain, "Les migrations temporaires françaises au XIXe siècle," *Annales de démographie historique* (1967), 9–28; A. Corbin, "Migrations temporaires et société rurale aux XIXe siècle: le cas du Limousin," *Revue historique* 246 (October–December 1971): 293–334; and Corbin's *Archaïsme et modernité en Limousin au XIXe siècle*, esp. 1: 177–225. Statistics on property unit size are from *Statistique de la France*, second series, (Strasbourg, 1870), 12:6.

3. Archives Départementales de la Creuse (hereafter cited as ADCr), 6M 250 and 6M 7.

4. Martin Nadaud, *Mémoires de Léonard, ancien garçon maçon*.

5. *Le Peuple* (Limoges), March 18, 1848.

6. Martin Nadaud, *Mémoires de Léonard*, p. 194; ADCr, 3M 123, Nadaud's electoral proclamation. Nadaud added, as "candidate and worker," that "this title which, hardly a month ago, would have brought a smile of contempt to the lips of privileged electors, far from being a motive for exclusion today, should bring success."

7. AN C 938, dossier 1, pièce 260, Nadaud's reports to Citizen Longepied, April 10 and 14, 1848.

8. AN C 938, dossier 3, Report of Citizen Ratier, n.d.; Jacques Levron, *Une révolte de contribuables* (*1848*) (Paris, 1936); AN BB³⁰ 361, dossier 1, pièces 29–49.

9. Nadaud finished eleventh (AN C 1325). Corbin, *Archaïsme et modernité*, suggests that intense rivalries between the "Brulas" and "Bigaros" factions of the migrants in Paris and the fact that Nadaud was virtually unknown among the migrants to Lyon (pp. 724–28) may have contributed to his defeat.

10. See Corbin, *Archaïsme et modernité*, pp. 748–49, 817–820.

11. ADCr 4M 72, Report of the Prefect of Creuse (hereafter cited as PCr), May 6, 1847, March 3, and June 16, 1845, and letter of Int. to PCr, March 28, 1845; Pierre Félix Thomas, *Pierre Leroux: sa vie, son oeuvre, sa doctrine* (Paris: Alcan, 1904), p.84.

12. B.N. Le⁷⁰ 348.

13. Ibid., and ADCr 3M 124. Corbin, *Archaïsme et modernité*, p. 828 makes an important point when noting that the professions de foi of the montagnards offered rather precise suggestions for reforms, while those of the conservatives tended toward "the affirmation of values and principles [which were] flexible."

14. AN F¹² 4618, "General State of the Workers' Associations"; ADCr 4M 72, Minister of Agriculture and Commerce to PCr, April 9, 1849 and March 5, 1850.

15. AG F¹ 17, Five Days Report, July 1–5, 1849; AN BB²⁰ 147, Creuse, second and fourth trimesters; AN BB³⁰ 378, dossier 6, Report of PGL to MJ, February 8, 1850; and ADCr 4M 72, Pierre Leroux to PCr, August 31, 1849 and PCr to Minister of Agriculture and Commerce, March 5, 1850.

16. AG F¹ 38, Report of Gendarmerie Commander in Boussac, October 8, 1850.

17. B.N. Le⁷⁰ 278, Nadaud's electoral proclamation.

18. ADCr 1M 157, Report of Subprefect of Aubusson, December 1, 1849; AG F¹ 46 bis, Report of Gendarmerie Commander of the Creuse, August 29, 1851; AG F¹ 49, Commander of the Eleventh Gendarmerie's report of October 26, 1851; AG F¹ 41 bis, Report of Commander of Bourganeuf Gendarmerie, February 28, 1851.

19. *Le Conciliateur*, October 23, 1851. This issue also announced the formation of a committee of "order" like that of Limoges.

20. Corbin, *Archaïsme et modernité*, esp. p. 753.

21. Compiled from ADCr 6M 250 and Jacques Bouillon, "Les

Élections législatives du 13 mai, 1849, en Limousin," *Bulletin de la Société Archéologique et Historique du Limousin*, 84 (1954):467–96, and A. Corbin, *Archaïsme et Modernité*, p. 746, on evidence of the propaganda role of the migrants.

22. AN ADXIX[i] Creuse 7, February 1849.

23. AG F[1] 44, Report of Gendarmerie of Guéret, May 5, 1851. In addition, as Corbin suggests, the future emperor's lavish public works projects may have already begun to win him support.

24. Compiled from ADCr 6M 250 and Jacques Bouillon, "Les Elections legislatives."

25. Corbin, *Archaïsme et Modernité*, p. 753.

26. ADHV Annex 3U 50 trois.

27. See J. Dagnan, *Le Gers sous la Second République*, 1: 299–306; and AN F[17] 9313, "Rapport sur la situation de l'instruction primaire en 1849."

28. ADCr 1M 147 and 3M 184.

29. ADCr 3M 184 and AN F[1c] III Creuse 5, Report of PCr, October 31, 1850.

30. ADCr 6M 250 and 6M 7 (census), 3M 215 to 258 (Sardent, 255), Report of PCr, July 17, 1849; AG F[1] 8, Report of the Commander of the Departmental Gendarmerie, June 14, 1848; AG F[1] 46 bis, Report of Commander of Eleventh Gendarmerie, August 26, 1851; AG F[1] 49, Report of the Commander of Eleventh Gendarmerie, September 1, 1851; AG F[1] 39, Report of Gendarmerie Commander of Bourganeuf, November 3, 1850 and Int. to MG, November 18, 1850.

31. ADCr 1M 165 and 3M 185; AG F[1] 9, MG to Int., June 30, 1849.

32. AN BB[8], dossier of Parrot, Justice of the Peace of Boussac.

33. AN ADXIX[i] 7 Creuse, September 10, 1849.

34. AN BB[20] 150, Creuse, second trimester, 1850; AG F[1] 41 bis, Report of the Bourganeuf Gendarmerie Commander, February 28, 1851, and August 4, 1851; and BB[30] 361 dossier 1, MG to MJ, December 14, 1849.

35. John Merriman, "Radicalization and Repression," pp. 198–99 (drawn from AN BB[30] 396 and 401).

36. Archives of the Prefecture of Police of Paris, A[a] 433, pièce 6, *Enquête sur le 2 décembre—les faits qui le suivent* (n.n., Bruxelles); Nadaud, *Mémoires de Léonard*, pp. 218–24; AG B 361, dossier Nadaud. Nadaud went first to Belgium and then to England, where he studied factory conditions. In 1871, following the end of the war, he was named prefect of the Creuse by his friend Gambetta. After one unsuccessful

campaign to become a deputy, he was elected in 1876 and served almost without interruption until his death on December 29, 1889.

37. Merriman, "Radicalization and Repression," pp. 208–10; seventy-three people from the Creuse appeared before the departmental mixed commission.

38. Charles Tilly, "The Changing Place of Collective Violence," and "How Protest Modernized in France, 1845–55."

39. John M. Merriman, "The 'Demoiselles' of the Ariège, 1829–31," in *1830 in France*, ed. Merriman (New York: Franklin Watts, 1975), pp. 87–118.

40. Name given to this conflict by François Baby, *La Guerre des Demoiselles en Ariège, 1829–72* (Montbel, Ariège, 1973).

41. Merriman, *1830 in France*, esp. pp. 91–92; Louis Clarenc, "Le Code de 1827 et les troubles forestiers dans les Pyrénées centrales au milieu du XIXe siècle," *Annales du Midi* 77, 3 (1965): 293–317.

42. André Armengaud, *Les Population de l'Est-Acquitain au début de l'époque contemporaine*, pp. 71, 196. The population of the Ariège was 196,450 in 1801; 250,535 in 1846; 267,435 in 1851; and 251,318 in 1856.

43. An C 945, Ariège; Philippe Morère, "L'Ariège avant le régime démocratique," *La Révolution de 1848*, 10, 56 (May–June 1913): 91–116 [113]; 11, 63 (July–August 1915): 213–37.

44. AN C 945, Ariège.

45. Clarenc, "Le Code de 1827," p. 312.

46. AN C 945, Ariège, response from the canton of Tarasçon.

47. Ibid. For example, approximately 10 percent of males could read and write in the canton of Oust, and "no" women; canton Pamiers, 20% men, 4% women; St. Girons, 10% of men and women; Ax, 20% above the age of thirty, etc.

48. Philippe Morère, "La Révolution de 1848 dans un pays forestier," 12 (1916): 206–30; 13 (1917): 27–51 (account of visit of the bishop of Pamiers from p. 228); Suzanne Coquerelle, "Les Droits collectifs et les troubles agraires dans les Pyrénées en 1848," pp. 345–63. (Woods and common lands occupied about 17% of the department's territory in 1863). The areas troubled by unrest after the revolution of 1848 had been virtually immune from disturbances during the revolution of 1830 and the appearances by the "demoiselles."

49. Morère, "La Révolution de 1848," and Clarenc, "Le Code de 1827," p. 316. Because of the "King of the Mountains," 900 cows and 7,300 sheep had lost much of their pasturage during the July Monarchy.

50. Philippe Morère, "Le Recouvrement des 45 centimes dans l'Ariège," *Révolution de 1848* 22 (1945): 226.

51. Armengaud, *Les Populations*, pp. 349–54. Four moderate republicans, two conservative republicans, and one former Orleanist deputy were elected.

52. Ibid.; and Archives Départementales de l'Ariège (hereafter cited as ADA), 5M 2, Report of the Subprefect of St. Girons, January 13, 1848.

53. Armengaud, *Les Populations*, pp. 370–71; Louis Clarenc, "Riches et pauvres dans le conflit forestier des Pyrénées centrales, vers le milieu du XIXᵉ siècle," p. 314.

54. Armengaud, *Les Populations*, p. 364, from *L'Émancipation* (Toulouse), December 13–14. Armengaud cites other factors: the low voting turnout (57.7%), the assistance the subprefect of Pamiers may have given the montagnards, and, above all, the unpopularity of the candidates of order, identified with the ownership of the forests (p. 377).

55. ADA 5M 2, Report of the Subprefect of St. Girons, October 1849.

56. Baby, *La Guerre des Demoiselles*, p. 19. The minister of finance wrote the minister of war that there had been only a few appearance of "these local people armed with rifles, their faces covered with soot, wearing a shirt above their clothes," AG F¹ 30, November 23, 1849.

57. AG F¹ 32, Int. to MG, February 27, 1850; number of troops cited in AG F¹ 34, Report of the Commander of the Ninth Military Division, May 24, 1850.

58. Description that of Armengaud, *Les Populations*, p. 386, comparing Piétri to Maupas, prefect of Haute Garonne.

59. ADA 5M 2, Report of the Subprefect of Pamiers, September 15, 1849. Totals for the other arrondissements would necessarily be much less, because of the lower literacy rate. During the July Monarchy, two-thirds of the electors were from the Pamiers district. The procureur général of Toulouse did blame *Le Républicain de l'Ariège* for corrupting the cantons of Foix and Tarascon (report of February 1850, AN BB³⁰ 363, dossier 2).

60. ADA 5M 2, Report of the Prefect, October 18, 1848.

61. ADA 5M 2, especially the Report of the Subprefect of St. Girons, July 5, 1849, ADA 2M 69⁸.

62. Clarenc, "Riches et pauvres," p. 309; see also Merriman, "The '*Demoiselles*' of the Ariège," for a discussion of the role of the mayors during the time of the "demoiselles," p. 98.

63. ADA 2M 69⁸, register of mayors from 1848 to 1855. I thank Anne Locksley for helping me gather this information.

64. ADA 5M 2, especially the Report of the Subprefect of St. Girons, July 5, 1849.

65. AN F⁹ 423, summary of National Guard dissolutions and suspensions and révocations of officers; on Massat, see Merriman, "The 'Demoiselles' of the Ariège," pp. 93–95.

66. Armengaud, Les Populations, p. 385.

67. AN BB³⁰ 368, dossier 2, Report of PG Toulouse, June 1851. There was an upswing of Napoleonic support in 1851 in the Ariège; a moderate also won the election to replace Pilhes, condemned after the June 13, 1849, insurrection; personal rivalries among the democratic candidates helped the victor.

68. Armengaud, Les Populations, p. 391.

69. There were at least eight appearances by "demoiselles" between 1848 and 1872, according to Baby, La Guerre des Demoiselles, p. 93.

70. Yves Le Gallo, Brest et sa bourgeoisie sous la monarchie de juillet, 2 vols. (Paris: P.U.F., 1968); André Jardin and A. J. Tudesq, La France des notables (Paris: Éditions du Seuil, 1973), 2: 15–16. In 1850, there were only four mutual-aid societies in the department, two created since the revolution.

71. Archives Départementales du Finistère (hereafter cited as ADF), 2M, dossiers Brissot-Thiran and Bruno-Davès.

72. ADF 4M 263, especially the letter of a member of the club La Fraternité, April 4, 1848; ADF 4M 280, Prefect of Finistère to the Mayor of Quimper, March 19, 1848; AN BB³⁰ 364, dossier 3, Reports of the Procureur général of Rennes, March 23, July 7 and 14, 1848.

73. AN BB³⁰ 368, dossier 2, Report of PG Rennes, November 1849.

74. ADF 4M 269, various subprefect reports; ADF 2M, dossier of Dezille, Subprefect of Quimperlé.

75. AG F¹ 39, MJ to MG, December 2, 1850, and Report of the Prefect of Finistère, November 13, 1851; AN BB¹⁸ 1491 on disorders involving the fishermen of Douarnenez in December, 1850.

76. Jardin and Tudesq, La France des notables, p. 14.

77. AN BB³⁰ 368, dossier 2, Report of PG Rennes, October 31, 1851. Robinet was hawking subscriptions to Théophile Blin's Le Républicain Breton.

78. AN BB³⁰ 368, dossier 2, Report of May 1, 1851.

79. See, for example, AG F¹ 33, Report of General Castellane, April 29, 1850; ADF 4M 268, Report of Subprefect of Châteaulin, February 22, 1849.

80. ADF 4M 270, Report of the Subprefect of Quimperlé, January 1, 1849.

81. ADF 4M 283, circulars and correspondence.

82. ADF 4M 283, verse of "Les nouveaux Brutus."

83. ADF 4M 283, especially Report of Subprefect of Morlaix, August 10, 1850; Int. to Prefect, October 9, 1851; Prefect's circular to Subprefect, etc. There were four political papers in the department, two Orleanist (450 subscriptions), one legitimist (600), and one without preference (201). Songs in Breton noted in AN BB^{30} 392 B, pièce 164, Report of PG Rennes May 16, 1851, and AN BB^{30} 368, dossier 2, Report of PG Rennes, October 31, 1851, both dealing with seizure of copies of the song "Au Dru Rollin."

84. ADF 4M 275, List of Socialists in Brest and Landernau and Report of the Subprefect of Brest, January 22, 1852. During the summer of 1850, a small socialist banquet took place in Brest (AN BB^{30} 368, dossier 2, Report of PG Rennes, June 1, 1850). The Prefect of the Finistère resigned in protest after the coup.

CHAPTER EIGHT

1. Ted W. Margadant's "The French Insurrection of 1851" is the definitive study of the montagnard secret societies and the insurrection.

2. This brief description owes much to an unpublished paper of Timothy E. Clifford, "*Démagogie* in the *Campagnes*: The Rural Radicalization of the *département* of the Yonne during the Second Republic" (senior essay, Yale University, 1976), pp. 3–12. In the Yonne, medium-sized holdings accounted for 38.4% of the cultivated land. Small holdings accounted for 31.7%; large holdings for 29.9%. The small units were increasing in proportion. "Morcelé à l'infini" was the description of Haussmann in his initial proclamation to the people of the Yonne upon becoming prefect in May 1850.

3. AN C 969 Yonne.

4. AN BB^{30} 383, Report of the procureur général of Paris (hereafter cited as PGP), June 19, 1850.

5. AG Justice militaire (hereafter cited as JM), 1851, 259, dossier Colas; M. Quantin, "Memorandum de ce qui s'est passé à Auxerre et dans le département de l'Yonne en 1848," in *Le livre du centenaire*, ed. Société des sciences historiques et naturelles de l'Yonne (Auxerre, 1956).

6. Archives départementales de l'Yonne (hereafter cited as ADY) III M^1 140, Decree of Commissioner and Letter of Minister of Finance to Commissioner, March 3. Quantin, "Memorandum," pp. 46–59.

7. Société des sciences historiques et naturelles de l'Yonne, ed., *Le livre du centenaire* (Auxerre, 1956) (hereafter cited as *Centenaire*), p. 64.

The prefect noted 2,160 cases of cholera, including Representative Robert, who died in Paris on September 2, 1849 (ADY III M¹ 126, Report of Prefect, November 19).

8. Letters related to the clubs are found in ADY III M¹ 130. See particularly ADY III M¹ 125, Report of Prefect (hereafter cited as PY), August 26, 1848; *Centenaire*, p. 11; Quantin, "Memorandum," p. 49; and relevant dossiers in JM, 259.

9. Quantin, "Memorandum," p. 59; ADY III M¹ 131, Report of PY, July 7, 1849, mentions a search of the home of a shoemaker: "These unfortunate people live in the state of nothing . . . no bed, no linen, no shirts, indeed nothing, absolutely nothing!" Municipal council members mentioned in *L'Union républicaine*, August 8, 1848, were assessed by the prefect as "almost entirely . . . illiterate men, and known for the intensity of their opinions."

10. *Centenaire*, p. 43. Several songs and poems were, for example, published in *Les Républicains auxerrois* in 1850. They were the work of two journeymen carpenters, a house painter, etc. Savinien Lapointe (1812–93), the "voice of the working class," spoke at the planting of the liberty tree in Auxerre after the revolution; he is mentioned by Edgar Leon Newman in "Sounds in the Desert: The Socialist Worker Poets of the Bourgeois Monarchy," in *Proceedings of the Third Annual Meeting of the Western Society for the Study of French History*, ed. Brison Gooch (1975), pp. 269–70.

11. ADY III M¹ 131 includes a dossier on the Association démocratique; see particularly Int. to PY, November 6, 1848, and PY to Procureur of Auxerre, October 22. Pompier is mentioned in ADY III M¹ 142, PY to Minister of Public Information, October 18, etc. ADY III M¹ 130 includes an undated list of 103 members of the circle.

12. ADY III M¹ 131, Members to PG, November 9, 1848; Club President to PGP, April 18, 1849; procès verbaux of April 27, 1849, etc.; JM 1851, 251, dossier Paulevé. ADY III M¹ 133, Report of PY, January 7, 1849 mentions that Uzanne wrote the PGP that "under the republican government, political meetings are indispensable." Paulevé edited a newspaper, *La Voix du peuple*, which became a victim of the repression.

13. ADY III M¹ 139, Int. to PY, June 20, 1849; JM, 1851 dossiers Dugaillon and Colas. *L'Union républicaine* appeared three times weekly after the revolution, then once again became a biweekly in April, exchanging increasingly bitter barbs with *La Fraternité*, a moderate paper which began March 21 and admitted its legitimist sympathies in the fall of 1850.

14. ADY III M¹ 144, Report of PY, April 13, 1850; Decree of PY banning the play, December 10, 1850; AN BB³⁰ 363, dossier 3, PGP report of May 7, 1850; etc.

15. JM, 259, dossier Grenet; ADY III M¹ 130, Report of the Subprefect of Joigny (hereafter cited as SPJ), June 22, 1849; AN BB³⁰ 383, Reports of PGP, June 19, 1850, September 8, 1850, and November 29, 1851. The procureur général of Paris reported on January 16, 1851 that "the demagogues are still agitating in Joigny" (AN BB¹⁸ 1491).

16. ADY III M¹ 134, Report of the Mayor of Sens, November 25, 1848, and Report of the Subprefect of Sens, May 2, 1849; a list of dismissals may be found in ADY III M¹ 141. The population of Sens in 1853 was 9,279 according to *Dictionnaire général des villes et bourgs de la France* (Paris, 1853).

17. ADY III M¹ 184, Report of Subprefect of Sens, April 18, 1856, cited in H. Forestier, *L'Yonne au XIXᵉ siècle*. Forestier has listed relevant documents, by carton. Voisin finished a distant twenty-fourth (4,121 votes) in the April voting.

18. AN BB³⁰ 396, January 26, 1852.

19. ADY III M¹ 135, Report of Subprefect of Sens, October 24, 1849; AN BB³⁰ 383, PGP Report, January 24 and November 23, 1850; AN BB³⁰ 363, dossier 3, MJ to Int.; AG F¹ 38, Gendarmerie Report, November 2, 1850. *Le Républicain du Sens* had begun August 25, 1849; its main theme was opposition to the drink tax. The municipal council, during the brief "socialist" phase when it was preoccupied with this tax, reduced the salary of the police commissioner, which brought strong official protest.

20. ADY III M¹ 132, Report of the Commissioner of Police of Tonnerre, November 30, 1850, cited in Forestier, *L'Yonne au XIXᵉ siècle*. Tonnerre was a town of a little more than 4,000.

21. ADY III M¹ 132, various reports, particularly that of the Subprefect, November 23, 1850; ADY III M¹ 127, Report of the Subprefect, May 25, 1851. He was still writing of the "disastrous effects produced by the revolutionary papers distributed in the countryside" on October 27, 1851.

22. AN BB³⁰ 383, Report of PGP, September 28, 1850.

23. ADY III M¹ 126, Report of Subprefect of Tonnerre, July 20, 1849; ADY III M¹ 144, November 4, 1850. The subprefect believed that the relatively good harvests helped the cause of "order" (ADY III M¹ 127, June 24, 1851). The Cercle de l'union was dissolved in 1850, and Coeurderoy was saved from dismissal at the *hospice* only because the men of order recognized his "extraordinary zeal" during the cholera

epidemic. In 1851 he was convicted after writing an article for *L'Union républicaine* and entered jail in November.

24. JM, 251, dossier Oddoul; a police commissioner's report of January 1, 1850, noted that Oddoul knew how to avoid the police because he "hung around" with police spies when he was twenty, that is, in about 1832.

25. ADY III M¹ 127, Report of the Subprefect of Avallon, May 24, 1851, mentions 165 subscriptions, notably to *L'Union républicaine* and *La Feuille du village*.

26. AN 969, Yonne.

27. ADY III M¹ 127, Report of Subprefect of Avallon, June 24; JM, 251, dossier Oddoul.

28. ADY III M¹ 145, Report of Subprefect of Avallon, January 20, 1851; JM, 251, dossiers Michaud and Durelle. It was written that "[Michaud] takes advantage of his connections with café-owners and innkeepers to recruit [secret-society] members in the countryside among the workers and simple peasants." He allegedly "corresponded" with Joigneaux, which may mean that he simply subscribed to the paper.

29. *L'Union républicaine*, January 25, 1851.

30. AN BB³⁰ 383, Report of PGP, November 23, 1850; AN BB³⁰ 366, Report of PGP, September 1850.

31. *L'Union républicaine*, February 24, 1849, April 18, 1849, June 10, 1848, October 15, 1851, etc.; AN BB³⁰ 393, Int. to MJ, July 23, 1851; AN BB³⁰ 383, Report of PGP, November 29, 1851. *L'Union Republicaine* also attempted to sell shares at seven francs each, in October 1851. *Le Républicain* began on August 12, 1851, "to aid this courageous paper . . . struggling alone." Interesting documents on Louis Napoleon's election as representative from the Yonne may be found in AN F¹ᶜ III Yonne 4; he was elected twice in 1848 (June 4 and September 17), after apparently being disqualified because he had accepted Swiss citizenship. The minister of interior clearly opposed his election in September, on the grounds of disputed citizenship and dubious republican sympathies (Int. to PY, August 31, 1848). The PY mentioned the noticeable rise in Bonapartism in the agricultural cantons (Report of August 26).

32. AN BB³⁰ 363, dossier 3, Report of PGP, September 18, 1849, etc. ADY III M¹ 145, Report of Subprefect of Tonnerre, February 27, 1850; ADY I M¹² 124, Report of Subprefect of Avallon, July 12, 1851; various reports in ADY III M¹ 143 and 144.

33. *L'Union républicaine*, March 27, 1850.

34. *L'Union républicaine*, January 30, 1850, January 29, 1851; ADY III M¹ 145, Report of the Police Commissioner, June 5, 1850. Dugaillon's

home was searched. See also Haussmann's *Mémoires*, vol. 1 (Paris, 1890), esp. pp. 411–17. The future baron noted that, as in the Var, he was "constantly occupied with assuring or reestablishing some sort of public order" (p. 415).

35. AN BB[18] 1491, Int. to MJ, April 5, 1851 and PGP, January 1, 1851. The Former police commissioner had been accused of "relations with the demagogic party." Margadant, "The French Insurrection of 1851," chap. 10, notes the increasing authority of police commissioners during the Second Republic, particularly in 1851. The police commissioner's assistant was dubbed "Ratapoil" after Daumier's famous caricature.

36. AN C 969, Yonne. For example, an 80% literacy rate was estimated for St. Florentin and Cauzy cantons; 80–90%, for canton of Avallon; 90–95%, for canton of Flogny. Most of the railroad workers, including some who raised the red flag in Tanlay, had left the department after the Yonne section was completed in 1849.

37. ADY III M[1] 144, Report of PY, January 2, 1851; Reports on Dugaillon in ADY III M[1] 145 mention a visit to Greppo in Paris.

38. AN BB[30] 383, Report of PGP, August 24, 1850; Haussmann notes in his *Mémoires*, p. 413, that he could really only count on the gendarmerie for assistance.

39. *Centenaire*, p. 26, citing report of June 29, 1848.

40. ADY III M[1] 143, Report of Subprefect of Tonnerre, June 5, 1849; AN BB[30] 383, dossier 3, Report of PGP, June 15, 1849 and January 15, 1851. Between four and five hundred pardoned workers, who had previously been employed in the national workshops, were sent to the department to work on the railroads (ADY III M[1] 126, Report of Subprefect of Tonnerre, July 20, 1849). Like employees of the Ponts-et-Chausées, railroad employees frequently posed political problems in the Yonne (for example, ADY III M[1] 145, PY to Subprefect of Tonnerre, February 27, 1850).

41. AN BB[30] 383, Report of PGP, August 21 and October 21, 1851.

42. AN C 969 Yonne. These loggers were the source of frequent administrative complaints, particularly after a public works decision to cut back their number by one-third in November 1850 sparked fears of clashes with loggers living in the Nièvre (AG F[1] 39, Report of Commander of First Military Division, November 25, 1849).

43. Margadant, "The French Insurrection of 1851," chap. 3.

44. AN C 969, Yonne; ADY M[1] 145, Report of SPJ, November 28, 1851. This report is extremely sympathetic to the plight of the poor, asking if emigration to Algeria might not have offered a solution.

45. ADY III M¹ 145, Report of SPJ, November 28, 1851; ADY III M¹ 141, Reports of PY, May 2, 1848, Letter of Wasse, May 31, 1848, and Anonymous letter to "M. the Captain," June 15, 1851, all cited in Forestier, *L'Yonne au XIXᵉ Siècle*. The Inquiry of 1848 gives estimates of literacy which are very different from those noted by Clifford, "*Démagogie* in the *Campagnes*," citing Emile Duché, "L'Instruction primaire dans le département de l'Yonne," *Annuaire de l'Yonne* (1866), p. 332 ff. According to Duché, 27.7 % of the people in the canton of Bléneau could read in the 1831–40 period; 38.5 %, during the 1841–50 period. These rates seem quite exaggerated in view of contemporary impressions, although the figures provided by the Inquiry are almost certainly too low. Both sources, however, agree that Bléneau was the least literate of the Yonne's cantons and that the Puisaye had the lowest literacy rate among the department's regions.

46. ADY III M¹ 145, Report of SPJ, November 28, 1851; ADY III M¹ 141, Report of SPJ (Wasse), July 16, 1848; and Report of Gendarmerie, July 23, 1848. JM, 259, dossier Portier (of St. Fargeau) provides other evidence of Cabet's influence in the region.

47. AG F¹ 49, Int. to MG, November 5, relaying the PY's urgent request for more troops: "the security of the principal land-owners seems threatened, the woods are being devastated, in disrespect for the law and the injunctions of the local police; the evildoers demonstrate more and more audacity each day"; also ADY III M¹ 145, Report of SPJ, November 25, 1851; and AN BB³⁰ 383, Report of PGP, May 31, 1850, noting cries of "Down with the rich" during the feast day of Bléneau. One barrel-maker's hatred of the rich and the bourgeoisie had reportedly become a "state of monomania."

48. ADY III M¹ 145, Report of SPJ, November 28, 1851. Not all purely political protests vanished. There was trouble in St. Sauveur in March 1851, when gendarmes cut down a recently planted liberty tree to cries of "Long live the Republic!" Five arrests followed (AG, F¹ 44, Gendarmerie Report of March 21). A story published in *L'Union républicaine* on April 17, 1850, made the rounds: the wife of one notable had allegedly said, at a reception, "Frankly, ladies, I would rather as much find myself face to face with cholera than with a red."

49. AN BB³⁰ 396, Report of PGP, January 26, 1852.

50. In fact, the recruiter was allegedly a Bordeaux wine merchant.

51. JM, 257, dossier F. Guenu, sabot-maker; AN BB³⁰ 383, PGP Report of October 25, 1850.

52. JM, 259, dossier Dugaillon; AN C 969 Yonne. Yet there were several documented cases of people being read to in cafés.

53. JM, 251, dossier Germain (born, 1828 in Bléneau). Certain witnesses accused Germain of joining the secret society in October 1851; on December 6, he rode out to Chevannes, though he claimed that he made the trip only to see if fifteen hundred insurgents would really arrive. One witness said Germain repeatedly asked "The hour?" as if to anticipate "has sounded," the passwords of Nouvelle Montagne. Germain's political zeal was such that he refused a pardon in 1852. Although Bajolet accused him of having organized the Bléneau society, there is insufficient evidence to accept this allegation. Bajolet also claimed that Dugaillon and Colas were members (AN BB³⁰ 394, Report of PGP, September 12, 1851), but it is quite clear that they were not. It is more likely that another bourgeois radical, Férrégu fils of Joigny, helped initiate secret organizations in the cantons of Aillant and Joigny.

54. JM, 251–59. There is no inventory of this series; I thank Ted Margadant for saving me much haggling by providing the relevant numbers for the Yonne. Most of those accused, including many who freely came forward and admitted their participation in secret societies, were interrogated two and three times. They were often most helpful the second or third time around because the interrogators were able to confront them with the results of other sessions. Most of those interrogated were cooperative, though M. Danville, a hawker from Sens, was not: "Q: You were continually occupied . . . with socialist propaganda. R: That's a lie. Q: I ask you, in your own interest, to explain yourself in a more appropriate manner. R: You can do whatever you want with me" (JM, 252).

55. See, for example, JM, 252, dossier Vincent; JM, 251, dossier Pautot; JM, 258, dossiers Fouchares and Biotot.

56. JM, 1851, 251–59. See Margadant, "The French Insurrection of 1851," chap. 8.

57. JM, 251, 252, 253, 259, esp. 251, dossier Gonneau, peasant, who implicated Théophile Barron and Alexandre Besson of Toucy (population in 1853, 2,682). Bouillard's workbook, filed in his dossier in JM, 253, is absolutely fascinating.

58. JM, 252 (especially dossier Charpy), 255 (Patasson), 253 (Napoleon Breuiller), 257 and 258 (Baron).

59. See, for example, JM, 252, dossier Louis Delapierre, wheelwright, of Merry-la-Vallée, who was initiated early in 1851 in Saintsen-Puisaye by a man from the Nièvre. On the Nouvelle Montagne, see Margadant, "The French Insurrection of 1851," Chap. 8. Ties with the Loiret would seem natural, because of geographic proximity. Indeed, many of those implicated were born in the Loiret.

60. JM, 256, dossiers Baclard, Boulin, and Fiette; 251, dossier Rondet, and 258, dossier Saison.

61. JM, 257, dossier Poirier dit Michelet.

62. ADY III M¹ 127, Report of SPY, October 1851.

63. AN BB³⁰ 394, Report of PGP, September 12, 1851; AN BB³⁰ 383, Report of PGP, September 11; ADY III M¹ 145, Gendarmerie reports, November 1851 and Report of SPJ, November 25 and 28, plus a note of SPJ dated September 30, speaking with some accuracy of the secret societies in Toucy and Saint Sauveur. A policy spy sent a detailed report on the same day (ADY III M¹ 145, cited by Forestier), noting links with Clamecy and Loing region (Loiret). Bajolet was mentioned as a policy spy in the letter of September 12, 1851; he named members in eleven communes, including fifteen in Joigny (never substantiated), claiming that Ledru-Rollin, Louis Blanc, Michel de Bourges, Greppo, and others were behind the conspiracy, which was closely linked to the Nièvre. He swore he had attended meetings in Joigny and complained that the other sabot-makers blackballed him, preventing him from finding work. ADY III M¹ 144, Prefect of Police to PY, September 24, 1850, notes a 200–franc payment for secret police in the Yonne. Haussmann, *Mémoires* p. 416, notes that secret police had been hired during the administration of his predecessor, and that, contrasting his experience in the Yonne with that in the Var: "Without chambrées to watch, I had to occupy myself with the secret societies" (p. 411).

64. AN BB³⁰ 396, Report of PGP, January 26, 1852; JM, 259, dossiers Colas and Dugaillon. Grenet's dossier and Colas's letter to Louis Napoleon in February 1852, are examples of pathetic political squirming, in sharp contrast to Eugène Germain's refusal to accept a pardon.

65. AN BB³⁰ 396, Report of PGP, January 26, 1852; JM, 258, dossiers from Coulanges-sur-Yonne; ADY III M¹ 149, Report of PY, November 16, 1868 (almost certainly requested in the hope of disproving Eugène Ténot's account of the resistance in *La Province en décembre, 1851*, first published in 1865). A crowd was dispersed by force, and there were seven arrests at the Avallon post office.

66. This account of the insurrectionary movements is derived from JM, 257–58; JM, 255, dossier Patasson; AN BB³⁰ 396, Report of PGP, January 26, 1852; ADY III M¹ 149, Report of PY, November 16, 1868; etc.

67. Ténot, *La Province en décembre, 1851*, pp. 74, 85; the story of a child whose throat was slit while being held in the arms of his mother

was invented by a journalist. See Ténot, *La Province en décembre, 1851*, pp. 47–73, and Margadant, "The French Insurrection of 1851."

68. Margadant, "The French Insurrection of 1851," chap. 1, p. 25; AN BB[30] 396, Report of PG Paris, January 26, 1852, mentions four hundred arrests at the time of the resistance.

69. JM, 253, commune of Sougères.

70. AN BB[30]* 424; AN BB[30] 396, Report of PGP, January 26, 1852, duplicated in ADY III M[1] 164–84. Because the following totals of arrests include many montagnard organizers (Colas, Dugaillon, Grenet, etc.) who had not resisted, they exaggerate bourgeois participation in the insurrection:

263	day laborers	25	wheelwrights	7	plasterers
152	peasants	21	tailors	7	bakers
44	joiners	20	clerks	7	turners
41	masons	19	makers of barrel staves	7	tile-workers
39	rentiers	16	locksmiths	7	tinsmiths
37	shoemakers	16	saw-pit workers	6	cabinetmakers
32	sabot-makers	15	stonecutters	6	millers
31	barrelmakers	15	domestics	5	pottery-makers
31	innkeepers	13	doctors	5	merchants
30	carpenters	13	harness-makers	5	house painters
29	weavers	12	lawyers	5	hatmakers
28	ironworkers	10	gardeners		
28	river-workers	9	roofers		

71. Maurice Agulhon, *La République au village*, pp. 259–84. Pierre Michault of Chablis was a "child of the people" who developed political influence among the laboring poor. He used this influence to ensure the election of a municipal council which "humiliates the bourgeoisie," that is, the wine merchants (ADY III M[1] 178, Report of PY, November 15, 1851, cited by Forestier, *L'Yonne au XIXe siècle*).

72. Christianne Marcilhacy, "Les Caractères de la crise sociale et politique de 1846 à 1852 dans le département du Loiret," pp. 5–59.

73. The Yonne voted 92,049 "oui" and 7,839 "non" (3,030 in the arrondissement of Joigny). There were 373 invalid votes. The procureur général realized that this was deceptive (AN BB[30] 396, January 26, 1852): "The number of socialists is considerable in the arrondissement of Auxerre, much greater than the results of the December vote of the 20th and 21st would have us think ... some voted 'oui' ... and would not be the least reticent, if the circumstances permitted, to throw the country into the disorder and convulsions of anarchy once more." After the coup, 120 communes (34 in the arrondissement of Auxerre,

20 in that of Joigny, 21 in the district of Sens and 16 in that of Tonnerre) either had mayors replaced or municipal councils dissolved (ADY I M¹² 125–29).

EPILOGUE

1. See Vincent Wright, "The *Coup d'État* of December, 1851: Repression and the Limits to Repression," in Roger D. Price, *Revolution and Reaction.*

2. For example, note the reports of the procureurs of Metz and Riom in November 1851, which express alarm at the spread of socialism into previously unaffected areas, AN BB³⁰ 368, dossier 2.

3. Howard C. Payne, "Preparation of a coup d'état."

4. Maurice Agulhon, *La République au village*, esp. pp. 479–80.

5. Alain Corbin, *Archaïsme et modernité* p. 798, Procureur général of Limoges, December 10, 1850.

6. Charles Tilly, "The Changing Place of Collective Violence."

7. Drawn from AN BB³⁰ 396–402, Reports of the Mixed Commissions, by department, within each judicial district.

8. AN F¹ᶜ III Haute Vienne 11, March 25, 1870.

Selective Bibliography

Agulhon, Maurice. "La Diffusion d'un journal montagnard: *Le Démocrate du Var* sous la Deuxième République." *Province historique* 10, 39 (January–March 1960).

———. *1848 ou l'apprentissage de la république*. Paris: Seuil, 1973.

———. *La République au village*. Paris: Plon, 1970.

———. "La Résistance au coup d'état en province: esquisse d'historiographie." *Revue d'histoire moderne et contemporaine* 21 (January–March 1974): 18–26.

———. *Une Ville ouvrière au temps du socialisme utopique, Toulon de 1815–51*. Paris: Mouton, 1971.

Amann, Peter. "The Changing Outlines of 1848." *American Historical Review* 68, 4 (July 1962): 938–53.

———. *Revolution and Mass Democracy: The Paris Club Movement in 1848*. Princeton N.J.: Princeton University Press, 1975.

Armengaud, André. *Les Populations de l'Est acquitain au début de l'époque contemporaine*. Paris: Mouton, 1961.

Bastide, Paul. *Doctrines et institutions politiques de la Second République*. 2 vols. Paris: Hachette, 1945.

Baughman, John. "The French Banquet Campaign of 1847–48." *Journal of Modern History* 31 (1959): 1–15.

Bellanger, Claude; Godechot, Jacques; Guiral, Pierre; and Terrou, Fernand. *Histoire général de la presse française*, vol. 2. Paris: Presses Universitaires de France, 1969.

Bercé, Yves-Marie. *Croquants et nu-pieds*. Paris: Collections archives, 1975.

Bernard, Philippe. "La Presse républicaine dans le département du Puy-de-Dôme pendant la Seconde République." *Revue d'Auvergne* 81, 2 (1957): 107–24.

Bouillion, J. "Les Démocrates-socialistes aux élections de 1849." *Revue française de science politique* 6 (1956): 70–95.

277

Bouillion, J.; Chalmin, P; Coquerelle, S; Girardet, R; Gossez, R.; and Villa, N. La Roche-sur-Yon: Imprimerie centrale de l'ouest, 1953.

Charles, Albert. *La Révolution de 1848 et le Deuxième République à Bordeaux et dans le département de la Gironde.* Bordeaux: Éditions Delmas, 1945.

Chatelain, Abel. "Les Migrations temporaires et la propagation des idées révolutionnaires en France au XIXᵉ siècle." *1848, Revue des révolutions contemporaines* 188 (May 1951): 6–18.

Chazelas, Victor. "Une Épisode de la lutte des classes à Limoges, 1848." *Revue d'histoire de la révolution de 1848* 7 (November–December 1910): 161–80, 240–56, 326–49, 389–412; 8 (January–February 1911): 41–66.

Chevalier, Louis. *Laboring Classes and Dangerous Classes in Paris.* New York: Howard Fertig, 1973.

————. *Les Fondements économiques et sociaux de la vie politique dans la région parisienne.* Paris: Bibliothèque universitaire de la Sorbonne, 1951.

Clarenc, Louis. "Riches et pauvres dans le conflit forestier des Pyrénées centrales, vers le milieu du XIXᵉ siècle." *Annales du Midi* 79, 3 (1967): 307–15.

Clark, T. J. *The Absolute Bourgeois: Artists and Politics in France, 1848–1851.* London: Thames and Hudson, 1973.

Cobban, Alfred. "The Influence of the Clergy and the '*Instituteurs Primaires*' in the Election of the French Constituent Assembly, April 1848." *English Historical Review* 57, 227 (July 1942): 339–61.

Codaccioni, F. P. "Le Textile lillois devant la crise, 1846–51." *Revue du Nord* 38, 149 (1956): 29–63.

Collins, Irene. *The Government and the Newspaper Press in France, 1814–81.* Oxford: The University Press, 1959.

Comité départemental marnais de célébration du centenaire de la Révolution de 1848. *Le Département de la Marne et la Révolution de 1848.* Châlons-sur-Marne: Archives de la Marne, 1948.

Coquerelle, Suzanne. "Les Droits collectifs et les troubles agraires dans les Pyrénées en 1848." *Actes du 78ᵉ Congrès*

National des Sociétés Savantes. (Toulouse, 1953): 345–63.

Corbin, Alain. *Archaïsme et modernité en Limousin au XIXe siècle.* 2 vols. Paris: Éditions Marcel Rivière et Cie, 1975.

Dagnan, Jean. *Le Gers sous la Seconde République.* 2 vols. Auch: Imprimerie Brevetée, 1928–29.

Dansette, A. *Louis Napoléon Bonaparte à la conquête du pouvoir.* Paris: Hachette, 1961.

Daumard, Adeline. *Les Bourgeois de Paris au XIXe.* Paris: Flammarion, 1970.

Dautry, J. *1848 et la Seconde République.* Paris: Éditions sociales, 1957.

De Luna, Frederick. *The French Republic under Cavaignac, 1848.* Princeton; N.J.: Princeton University Press, 1969.

Dessal, Marcel. *La Révolution de 1848 et la Seconde République dans le département d'Eure et Loir.* Chartres: Imprimerie Lainé et Tantet, 1948.

Dupeux, Georges. *Aspects de l'histoire sociale et politique du Loir-et-Cher, 1848–1914.* Paris: Mouton, 1962.

Duveau, Georges. *1848: The Making of a Revolution.* New York: Vintage Books, 1969.

Fasel, George W. "The French Elections of April 23, 1848: Suggestions for a Revision." *French Historical Studies* 5 (1968): 285–98.

Forestier, H. *L'Yonne au XIXe siècle.* 4 vols. Auxerre, 1957–65.

Gerbod, Paul. *La Condition universitaire en France au XIXe siècle.* Paris: Presses Universitaires de France, 1965.

Gillet, M. "Aspects de la crise de 1846 à 1851 dans le bassin houiller du Nord." *Revue du Nord* 38, 149 (1956): 15–27.

Girard, Louis. *La IIe République.* Paris: Calmann-Lévy, 1968.

———. *Étude comparée des mouvements révolutionnaires en France en 1830, 1848 et 1870–71.* Paris, 1960.

———. *La Garde nationale, 1814–1871.* Paris: Plon, 1964.

Godechot, J., ed. *La Révolution de 1848 à Toulouse et dans la Haute Garonne.* Toulouse: Prefecture, 1948.

Gossez, A.-M. *Le Département du Nord sous la Deuxième République.* Lille: Gustave Leleu, 1904.

Gossez, Rémi. *Les Ouvriers de Paris.* Paris: Bibliothèque de la

Révolution de 1848, 1971.

———. "Diversité des antagonismes sociaux vers le milieu du XIXe siècle." *Revue économique* 1 (July 1956): 436–57.

Guillemin, H. *Le Coup du 2 décembre.* Paris: Gallimard, 1951.

Guin, Yannick. *Le Mouvement ouvrier nantais.* Paris: François Maspero, 1976.

Higonnet, Patrice L. R., and Higonnet, Trevor B. "Class, Corruption, and Politics in the French Chamber of Deputies, 1846–48." *French Historical Studies* 5, 2 (Fall 1967): 204–23.

Huard, R. "La Défense du suffrage universel sous la Seconde République: la réaction de l'opinion gardoise et le pétitionnement contre la loi du 31 mai, 1850 (1850–51)." *Annales du Midi* 83, 3 (October–December 1971): 315–36.

Jennings, Lawrence C. *France and Europe in 1848.* Oxford: The University Press, 1973.

Johnson, Christopher. *Utopian Communism in France: Cabet and the Icarians, 1839–1851.* Ithaca; N.Y.: Cornell University Press, 1974.

Labrousse, Ernest, ed. *Aspects de la crise et la dépression de l'économie française au milieu du XIXe siècle, 1846–1851.* Paris: Bibliothèque de la Révolution de 1848, 1956.

———. "1848, 1830, 1789: Comment naissent les révolutions." In *Acts du congrès historique du centenaire de la révolution de 1848.* Paris, 1948.

Langer, William L. "The Patterns of Urban Revolution in 1848." In *French Society and Culture since the Old Régime*, ed. Evelyn M. Acomb and Marvin L. Brown, Jr. New York: Holt, Rinehart and Winston, 1966.

Lentacker, F. "Les Ouvriers belges dans le département du Nord au milieu du XIXe siècle." *Revue du Nord* 38, 149 (1956): 5–14.

Laurent, G., and Bossinesq, G. *Histoire de la ville de Reims depuis les origins jusqu'à nos jours.* 2 vols. Reims: Matot-Braine, 1933.

Loubère, Leo. *Radicalism in Mediterranean France: Its Rise and Decline.* Albany: State University of New York Press, 1974.

Machu, Léon. "La Crise de l'industrie textile à Roubaix." *Revue du Nord* 38, 149 (January–March 1956): 65–75.

McKay, Donald C. *The National Workshops.* Cambridge, Mass.:

Harvard University Press, 1933.

Marcilhacy, Christianne. "Les Caractères de la crise sociale et politique de 1846 à 1852 dans le département du Loiret." *Revue d'histoire moderne et contemporaine* 6 (January–March 1959): 5–59.

Margadant, Ted W. *"The French Insurrection of 1851."* Forthcoming manuscript.

Marx, Karl. *The Eighteenth Brumaire of Louis Napoleon Bonaparte.* New York: International Publishers, 1969.

———. *Les Luttes de classes en France (1848–1850).* Paris: Éditions sociales, 1946.

Merriman, John. "Radicalization and Repression: The Experience of the Limousin, 1848–1851." Ph.D. dissertation, University of Michigan, 1972.

———. "Social Conflict in France and the Limoges Revolution of April 27, 1848." *Societas—A Review of Social History* 4, 1 (Winter 1974): 21–38.

Morère, Philippe. "La Révolution de 1848 dans un pays forestier." *Révolution de 1848* 12 (1916–17): 206–30.

Muller, Paul. "Le Bas Rhin de 1848 à 1852." *Révolution de 1848* 6, 36 (January–February 1910): 353–66.

Nadaud, Martin. *Mémoires de Léonard, ancien garçon maçon.* Paris: Egloff, 1947.

Payne, Howard C. *The Police State of Louis Napoleon Bonaparte.* Seattle: University of Washington Press, 1966.

———. "Preparation of a Coup d'Etat." In *Studies in European History in Honor of F. C. Palm,* ed. F. J. Cox, Richard M. Bruce, Bernard C. Weber, and John Fransey. New York: Bookman Associates, 1966.

Ponteil, Félex. *Les Institutions de la France de 1814 à 1870.* Paris: Presses Universitaires de France, 1966.

Price, Roger D. *The French Second Republic: A Social History.* London: Batsford, 1972.

———, ed. *Revolution and Reaction: 1848 and the Second French Republic.* London: Croom Helm, 1975.

Renard, Georges. *La République de 1848. Histoire socialiste,* edited by Jean Jaurès, vol. 9. Paris: Rouff, n.d.

Rocal, G. *1848 en Dordogne*. 2 vols. Paris: Occitania, 1934.

Rougeron, G.; Monceau, Y.; et al. *La Révolution de 1848 à Moulins et dans le département d'Allier*. Moulins: Imprimerie A. Pottier et Cie, 1950.

Schmidt, Charles. *Des Ateliers nationaux aux barricades de Juin*. Paris: Presses Universitaires de France, 1948.

Schnapper, Bernard. "Les Sociétés ouvrières de production pendant la Seconde République: l'exemple girondin." *Revue d'histoire économique et sociale* 48 (1965): 162–91.

Schnerb, Robert. "La Seconde République dans le département du Puy-de-Dôme." *Révolution de 1848*, vols. 22–24, nos. 113, 114, 120, 121, 122 (1926–27).

Seignobos, Charles. *La Révolution de 1848 et le Second Empire (1848–1859)*. Histoire de la France contemporaine, edited by E. Lavisse, vol. 6. Paris: Hachette, 1926.

Sewell, William H., Jr. "La Classe ouvrière de Marseille sous la Seconde République: structure sociale et comportement politique." *Mouvement social* 76 (July 1971): 27–63.

Soboul, Albert. "Documents. Les troubles agraires de 1848." *1848 et les révolutions du XIXe siècle* 39, 180 (June 1948): 1–20.

———. "La Question paysanne en 1848." *La Pensée* 18 (1948): 55–66; 19 (1848): 25–37; 20 (1848): 48–56.

Société des sciences historiques et naturelles l'Yonne. *Le livre du centenaire*. Auxerre, 1956.

Tchernoff, I. *Associations et sociétés secrètes sous la IIe République, 1848–1851*. Paris: Alcan, 1905.

Ténot, Eugène. *Paris en décembre 1851*. Paris: Le Siècle, 1876.

———. *La Province en décembre 1851*. Paris: Le Siècle, 1876.

Tilly, Charles. "The Changing Place of Collective Violence." In *Essays in Theory and History*, edited by Melvin Richter. Cambridge, Mass.: Harvard University Press, 1970.

———. "How Protest Modernized in France, 1845–55." In *The Dimensions of Quantitative Research in History*, edited by William O. Aydelotte, Allan G. Bogue, and Robert William Fogel. Princeton, N. J.: Princeton University Press, 1972.

Tilly, Charles, and Lees, Lynn. "The People of June, 1848." In *Revolution and Reaction: 1848 and the Second French Republic*, edited by Roger Price. London: Croom Helm, 1975.

Tilly, Charles; Tilly, Louise; and Tilly, Richard. *The Rebellious Century*. Cambridge, Mass.: Harvard University Press, 1975.

Tudesq, André-Jean. *L'Élection présidentielle de Louis Napoléon Bonaparte, 10 décembre 1848*. Paris: A. Colin, 1965.

———. *Les Grands Notables en France, 1840–49. Étude historique d'une psychologic sociale*. 2 vols. Paris: Presses Universitaires de France, 1964.

———. "La Légende napoleonienne en France en 1848." *Revue historique* 81 (1957): 65–85.

Vigier, Philippe. *La Seconde République dans la région alpine*. 2 vols. Paris: Presses Universitaires de France, 1963.

Weill, Georges. *Histoire du parti républicain en France (1814–1870)*. Paris: Alcan, 1928.

Zévaès, Alexandre. "La Propagande socialiste dans les campagnes en 1848." *Révolution de 1848* 31 (1934): 204–21.

Principal Archival Sources

Series BB^{18}, General Correspondence of the Criminal Division of the Ministry of Justice: 1456, 1465–69, 1470^c, 1474^A–96, 1498–1501. Of particular importance are: BB^{18} 1469, banquets; 1474^{A-B}, clubs and associations; 1481, cabarets; and 1482, seditious emblems, and symbols.

Series BB^{30}, Office of the Ministry of Justice: 323, 358–65, 368, 370–88, 391–94, 396, 398–402, 423, *424. I have relied heavily upon 361, Affaire de Limoges; 365, Insurrection in Rouen; 368, Summaries of the monthly reports of the procureurs généraux, which began in November 1849; 423 is an interesting series of reports by local magistrates on the resistance to the coup, which were gathered in an attempt to counter the allegations of Eugène Ténot's book; *424 is a register of the more than 26,000 people who appeared before the mixed commissions after the coup.

Series C, National Assembly: 931, 945, 957, 967, 969, 1325, 1485. 977 is crucial, containing reports on the administrative purge.

Series F^1, General Administration:

I^c III various departments, III Meurthe 16, Haute Vienne 11, etc.

9 Military Affaires, 422–23 (National Guard)

12 Commerce and Industry, 4613, 4618 (Associations)

17 Public Instruction, 9313, 12528, 12746

18 Printing and Bookselling, 262–64 (press), 568 (printing)

ARCHIVES OF THE MINISTRY OF WAR VINCENNES

Justice Militaire (not inventoried), 251–259, Yonne

F^1, General Correspondence of the Ministry of War, 1–50. These invaluable reports are organized chronologically, by

day. I have gone through them systematically for the first four
months of the republic, and from November 1, 1849, through
the coup d'état.

NATIONAL LIBRARY OF FRANCE

Bressy, A. *Almanach démocratique de 1850.*
Guépin, A. *Le Socialisme expliqué aux enfans du peuple*, 1851.
————. *Philosophie du socialisme ou étude sur les transformations
dans l'humanité*, 1850.
Joigneaux, P., et al. *Almanach du village pour 1852.*
Nadaud, Martin. "Profession de foi" (Le[70] 278), and others.

Newspapers:

L'Ami du peuple (Montargis)
L'Ami du peuple (Rouen)
L'Association rémoise
Le Conciliateur (Creuse)
Le Carillon républicain (Limoges)
La Feuille du village
Le Messager du Nord
Le National de l'Ouest
L'Ordre (Limoges)
Le Peuple (Limoges)
Le Prolétaire elbeuvin
La Province (Limoges)
Le Républicain de l'Yonne
Le Républicain de Rhin (Colmar)
La Sentinelle des travailleurs (Rouen)
Le Travailleur (Haute Garonne, Ariège, et du Midi)
Le Travailleur (Limoges)
L'Union républicaine (Auxerre)

DEPARTMENTAL ARCHIVES

Series M groups a wide range of topics dealing with the general
administration of the department, including the correspondence

of the prefect and other reports related to general policing.
Ariège (Foix)
  5M 2
  2M 68[8]
Cher (Bourges)
  25M 80, 89, 109, 265
  16M 4
Corrèze (Tulle)
  M 11, 39–40, 54, 58, 73, 282–284, 286, 385, 582, 649, 782–783, 795, 797, 1064
  2R 9–10, 79R 2, 93R 3–5 (Military Affaires)
Creuse (Guéret)
  1M 146–149, 155, 157–158, 164–165, 167–168
  2M 1, 7, 8, 9
  3M 123–124, 184, 215–258
  4M 72–74, 76, 79–80, 82
  6M 7, 250, 332, 378, 397, 410
  7M 84
  9M 3–4, 21
Eure-et-Loir (Chartres)
  M 192–193
Finistère (Quimper)
  4M 213, 232, 268–270, 276, 283–284
Haute Garonne (Toulouse)
  4M 66, 69–70
Nord (Lille)
  139/4–9, 16, 21–24
Pas-de-Calais (Arras)
  M 51, 954
Seine Maritime (Rouen)
  U 3129 (Justice)
Somme (Amiens)
  Mf 95412, 80793, 80849, 107027
  Mfd 80896
  Mfs 95275
Tarn (Albi)
  IV M^2 37–39

Haute Vienne (Limoges)
M 2, 6–8, 131, 163, 171, 249, 397–409, 490, 492, 581, 622, 736–37, 739–741, 743, 777, 926, 929, 1116–1117, 1128–30, 1289, 1394–95, 1467, 1777–1778, 3198
R 169, 188–197 (Military, including National Guard)
U 432–433, 435, 438, 440–441, 447 (Justice)
Yonne (Auxerre)
III M¹ 125, 127, 131–132, 134–135, 140–146
I M¹ 4

MUNICIPAL ARCHIVES

Limoges
Conseil municipal de Limoges. Register of deliberations.
Dossiers "D" and "I"
Toulouse
2Q 7
2i 63

Index